NATIONAL DEFENSE

JAMES FALLOWS

NATIONAL DEFENSE

VINTAGE BOOKS
A Division of Random House
New York

Grateful acknowledgment is made to the following for permission to reprint previously published material.

The *Bulletin of the Atomic Scientists:* Excerpt reprinted by permission of the *Bulletin of the Atomic Scientists,* a magazine of science and public affairs, from the October 16, 1980, issue. Copyright © 1980 by the Educational Foundation for Nuclear Science, Chicago, Illinois 60637.

Business Week: Excerpt reprinted from the August 11, 1980 issue of *Business Week* by special permission, © 1980 by McGraw-Hill, Inc., New York, N.Y. 10020. All rights reserved.

Encyclopaedia Britannica: Excerpt from "Krupp Family" in *Encylopaedia Britannica,* 15th ed. (1974), 10:540. Reprinted by permission.

Foreign Affairs: Excerpt by McGeorge Bundy from the *Foreign Affairs* October 1969 issue. Reprinted by permission of *Foreign Affairs.* Copyright 1969 by Council on Foreign Relations, Inc.

McGraw-Hill Publishers: Excerpts from *MiG Pilot,* by John Barron Copyright © 1980 by Reader's Digest Association, Inc. Reprinted by permission of McGraw-Hill Publishers.

The *New York Review of Books:* Material from "The Myth of Missile Accuracy," by Alexander and Andrew Cockburn. Reprinted from the *New York Review of Books* (November 20, 1980) Copyright © 1980 Nyrev, Inc.

W. W. Norton & Company, Inc.: Excerpts reprinted from *Self Destruction: The Disintegration and Decay of the United States Army During the Vietnam Era,* by Cincinnatus, by permission of W.W. Norton & Company, Inc. Copyright © 1981 by Cincinnatus.

The *Public Interest:* Excerpts from "How to Save the All-Volunteer Force," by Charles C. Moskos, reprinted with permission of the author from the *Public Interest* (Fall 1980), pages 76, 80, 82 and 88, © 1980 by National Affairs, Inc.

Routledge & Kegan Paul Ltd.: Excerpts from *On War,* by General Karl von Clausewitz, translated by Colonel J. J. Graham. Reprinted by permission of Routledge & Kegan Paul Ltd., London.

Sage Publications, Inc.: Excerpt from "The Will to Fight," by William Hauser, is reprinted from *Combat Effectiveness* (SAGE RESEARCH PROGRESS SERIES ON WAR, REVOLUTION, AND PEACE-KEEPING, Vol. 9), Sam Sarkesian, Editor, Copyright 1980, pages 193, 194, 196, by permission of the Publisher, Sage Publications (Beverly Hills/London).

The University Press of Virginia: Excerpt from *The All Volunteer Force and American Society,* John B. Keeley, ed., 1978. Reprinted by permission of University Press of Virginia.

The *Washingtonian Magazine.* Excerpt from "Women Can't Fight" by James Webb. Reprinted by permission of The Washingtonian Magazine.

The Washington *Post:* Excerpt from the Washington *Post* (January 25, 1981), by George Wilson Copyright © 1981 by The Washington Post. Reprinted by permission.

The Washington *Star:* Excerpt from the Washington *Star* (December 17, 1980). Reprinted by permission © The Washington Star 1980.

Library of Congress Cataloging in Publication Data
Fallows, James M.
National defense.
Originally published: New York: Random House, © 1981.
Includes bibliographical references and index.
1. United States—Military policy.
2. United States—Defenses. I. Title.
[UA23.F343 1982]   355'.033073   81-52873
ISBN: 0-394-75306-2   AACR2

For My Sons

Acknowledgments

MY GOOD FORTUNE in journalism has been to work for a series of gifted magazine editors who have also been teachers and friends. The first was Charles Peters of the *Washington Monthly*, who originally suggested the idea for this project five years ago. For his counsel and friendship over the years, I am deeply grateful. William Broyles of *Texas Monthly* has taught me many things about writing and life. Robert Manning of the *Atlantic*, among other favors, helped shaped an earlier article on this subject, and the *Atlantic*'s Richard Todd and William Whitworth gave valuable advice on this work. I am grateful to them and to Mortimer Zuckerman for giving me time off from the magazine to finish this book. I have profited from the acute insights that Jason Epstein of Random House has brought to this as well as many other subjects. I also give sincere thanks to my agent, Wendy Weil.

Among the many people who have been generous with their time and advice, I would especially like to thank Thomas Amlie, Bowman Cutter, Philip Gallery, Richard Garwin, Fred Kaplan, Tom Kelly, Edward Luttwak, Colonel Dandridge Malone, John Morse, Charles Moskos, Robert Pranger, Everest Riccioni, Charles Stevenson, James Webb, James Woolsey, plus the public affairs officers at the Pentagon and at bases around the country. There are others whose current positions would make it imprudent to thank them publicly. They know who they are.

Much of this book concerns the blessings and curses of modern technology. I have glimpsed this balance first-hand, because of my experience with the computerized word-processing system I have used since 1979. Without it, it would have taken me at least twice as long to complete this book, so I am grateful to Frank Zerad for convincing me that such a system would be feasible, and to Bill Kavage, Bill Jones, and Marv Miller of the Optek corporation for getting me started. My real hero is Leland Mull of Vienna, Virginia, a craftsman of the old school who was always willing to repair my machines or even lend me a new computer when mine broke down at particularly awkward times.

I owe a special mention to those who have spent hours and hours helping me understand the subject or attempting to improve my presentation. They are Nicholas Lemann, Larry Smith, John Boyd, and Pierre Sprey. As with the others I have mentioned here, they won't agree with everything I have said, nor I with all their views, but I will always be grateful to them as friends.

This project has created a number of practical problems for my parents, my children, and most of all my wife. No family could have borne up with greater support and good humor than they have shown. No wife could have been more loving or loved than mine.

J. F.
Washington, D.C.
January 1981

Contents

INTRODUCTION xiii

ONE · Realities 3

TWO · Managers 19

THREE · Magicians 35

FOUR · Two Weapons 76

FIVE · Employees 107

SIX · Theologians 139

SEVEN · Changes 171

Reference Notes 185

Index 195

Introduction

THIS BOOK is designed to give the general reader better ways of thinking about defense. In the first few years of the 1980s, the United States will have to make choices of enormous consequence about the size, purpose, and composition of its military force. These include whether to restore the draft, build new nuclear missiles and bombers, enlarge the Navy, equip a "rapid deployment force" for intervention overseas. They also include, at a level less visible to the public, several persistent and sometimes bitter controversies within the defense establishment: defining the right and wrong role for high technology in the military; examining the ways officers are chosen, motivated, and promoted; revising the relationship between the military and the private companies whose weapons it buys.

Each of these decisions holds serious, long-run implications for the nation's security, both military and economic. This book is aimed at readers who are concerned about such consequences but have not been steeped in the details of military policy. My hope is that, after finishing the book, they will be able to approach these decisions with a much clearer sense of what is at stake, and what arguments, interests, and outlooks lie on each side.

Three themes run through this book. The first and most important is that our national defense is in constant danger of being so borne away by theory that it loses touch with facts, historical experience, and simple common sense. In the third part of *Gulliver's Travels*, Captain Gulliver visits the kingdom of Laputa. There he finds a nation given over to philosophical speculations and "pure reason," rather than common sense. Its citizens are ill-clad, since their tailors design clothes with compass and quadrant rather than fitting them to the wearer. Its houses are always tumbling down, because everyone is more interested in drawing clever plans on paper than in seeing that the angles are square and the roof sound. I will suggest in this book that there is much of the Laputan in our plans for and public arguments about defense.

To give perhaps the clearest example, if there is any compelling "lesson" from the history of combat, it is its fundamental unpredictability. For all of the military planning that went into the preparations for World War II, as of 1939 none of the major powers had decided to pursue the weapon that would ultimately prove decisive, the atomic bomb.[1] How, then, can we hope to foretell the exact nature of military conflict in the 1990s? Yet the constant temptation in defense planning is to try to predict the future with minute precision, and then make plans based on those predictions. Defense intellectuals will argue about the number of aircraft carriers needed to assault the Kola peninsula in the Soviet Union, or just what forces will be needed for war on the Arabian desert in the 1990s. Then they will clamor for weapons designed to operate in those special circumstances. The only thing resembling a certainty about future military contingencies is that we are likely to face threats that we do not now foresee. Through the rest of this book, there will be discussions of the traits that make airplanes, missiles, soldiers effective or ineffective in combat. Through these discussions, it may be hard to envision just where the tanks and soldiers might be used. The proper response to that uncertainty is not to conclude that because we need no tanks today we will never need them, nor to concoct battle scenarios of spurious precision. Instead, the common-sense approach to defense is to recognize that the future is uncertain, and to develop forces and strategies that give us the greatest possible capacity to adapt to whatever the future brings.

In political arguments about defense, there is a Laputan tendency to stick to the plane of generalization, rather than concentrating on detailed, case-by-case assessments of the facts. When public discussions about defense move away from the specifics, their real subject usually becomes something other than defense itself. They may be displays of right- and left-wing ideologies; they may be tests of "hard" and "soft" philosophies of international relations. They may even be proxies for whether one was raised as a child to consider the world hostile or benign. Most often, they collapse into the familiar choice between "more" and "less" defense, measured solely by money spent and programs begun. For partisans of "strength" and "restraint" alike, the unspoken assumption has been that what finally matters in defense is the overall budget figure. To those who favor "more defense," a dollar spent on one weapon is about as good as a dollar spent on another. Those who call for "reordering national priorities" or an end to the arms race are rarely heard supporting any weapon at all. Both sides suffer from the ancient fallacy of measuring input, rather than output—judging how hard you try, rather than what you accomplish. Neither goes far toward ensuring that items that would come first, second, third, on any rational list of what the nation needs for defense are the ones we end up having.

A second theme is that the conduct of war, and the preparations to avoid it, are basically different from other things that human beings do, and that the only way to think about them seriously is to understand them on their own terms. An army is not just another part of the labor force doing its job; its weapons must meet different standards than those for factory tools. Solutions that make sense in other walks of life may lead to disaster when applied wholesale to defense.

The third theme is that the truly urgent military questions have little to do with how much money we spend. Indeed, more money for defense, without a change in the underlying patterns of spending, will not make us more secure, and may even leave the United States in a more vulnerable position than before.

My purpose is to be suggestive, rather than encyclopedic or definitive; I hope to illustrate the patterns in which things go right or wrong in American defense policy, rather than detail their application in each specific case. Much of the story is told through anecdotage and case history, but these particulars are meant to suggest certain casts of mind, certain rules of organizational life, certain economic and political interests that will apply to next year's decisions as they did to those of the past.

This is a book about defense, not about foreign policy. Obviously, there are connections between the two. The only reason a nation raises armies is to defend the interests its policy defines. The only way to judge whether a military establishment is adequate is to ask whether it can sustain the commitments the nation has made. During the fifties and early sixties, the United States based its defense planning on a "two and a half wars" policy, which assumed that American troops might have to fight the Soviet Union, China, and some smaller nation (the "half" war), all at the same time. Men were drafted and deployed, equipment was purchased, taxes were levied, all in the name of that foreign policy rationale. By the end of the sixties, when American foreign policy had changed to recognize the fact that the Soviet Union and China were more likely to fight each other than to join to fight the United States, American military doctrine changed to "one and a half wars." To give a current example, decisions about the size of the Rapid Deployment Force, or about its very existence, depend on one's definitions of American interests overseas and the proper way to defend them.

At certain points, this book addresses foreign policy choices, but I have deliberately avoided them wherever possible. The reason is not that I consider them unimportant, but rather my strong feeling that foreign policy discussions usually aggravate the worst tendencies in thinking about defense. Foreign policy, by its nature, tends to drift up into the thin air of grand abstraction; as it rises, it draws discussion of defense up with it. At this time in American history, foreign policy discussions often degenerate within milliseconds into ideological slogan-fests, in which minds close rather than open and reflex replaces discrimination. The most important choices in defense have nothing to do with slogans. No matter what one's reading of Soviet intentions, the drawbacks of "managerial" and "technological" defense must be faced. Whether one believes in fortress America or forward-deployed forces around the globe, the weapons we buy should work; no matter how many soldiers are in the army, they will be subject to the social and psychological constants that, through history, have distinguished effective from ineffective troops. At this late stage in the twentieth century, we should also have learned that the givens of foreign policy can change much more quickly than the fundamentals of our military establishment. Some things in international relations are constant—the geography of oceans and nations, the fragmentation of international politics—but specific policies and alliances can change with disturbing speed. One year we have a client and staunch ally in the Shah; the next year, the rulers of Iran identify America as Great Satan. It is impossible to transform our weapons or our grand strategy at quite that pace, and it is dangerous to develop systems whose effectiveness depends on a specific set of circumstances. Most of the themes raised in this book will apply through the rest of this decade, no matter what twists our foreign policy is forced to undergo.

I have never served in the military, nor have I worked as a professional military "analyst" of any sort. This makes me humble in my assertions, especially about the nature of combat. The more I have talked with people about combat and read first-hand accounts, the more I have become convinced that it is not something that can be truly understood through talking and reading. This also increases my concern about the pattern I discuss in chapter 5: the increasing social striation of military service. Beginning in Vietnam, and continuing at a much faster pace with the volunteer army, military service has become the province of poor, uneducated whites, plus blacks and Hispanics. Unless the pattern changes, we will very soon reach the point at which almost no educated white people—who, for the foreseeable future, will make up the class with the greatest influence in politics, business, education, and communications—will have had any first-hand exposure to the military. This cannot be a help in the effort to make better choices about defense.

My own background has also forced me to wrestle with, and disclose, another tangled aspect of the same question. I came of military age during the war in Vietnam. As I have described at length elsewhere,[2] I deliberately avoided service in that war. The rights and wrongs of those years are a subject for another day; their residual effect on one's view of defense is what concerns me here. As I suggest in the final chapter of this book, raw, confused, unexpressed emotional forces can distort our decisions about defense. The military has always been the instrument of the most hateful and brutal of man's activities, but at the same time it has always represented the pinnacle of a certain kind of manly valor. The tensions between these forces, when not faced, can take views of the military down dark alleys far from the realm of reason. One example I discuss in the last chapter is that many of those who have been most strident in their calls for "more" defense never themselves wore the uniform. In undertaking this work, I have tried to be aware of the directions in which the pressures of my own background might drive me, whether toward excessive hostility to the military to validate previous views, or toward undue embrace of martial virtues in an attempt to assume, at a late date, the warrior's aura. None of us is free of bias, and I alert the reader to the possible direction of mine, even though I have done my best to avoid it in pursuing this work.

NATIONAL DEFENSE

ONE

REALITIES

To THINK about American defense is really to think about the time-less characteristics of war, as they are altered by the technical, economic, and political circumstances of the late twentieth century. The purpose of this chapter is to suggest three realities that grow out of this combination of forces, against which all our military plans should be tested.

The first reality is that the American economy does not permit easy, substantial increases in defense spending, even if "more" defense, by itself, would solve our military's problems or make the nation more secure.

The second is that the world offers a rich, rapidly changing, and unpredictable variety of threats to American interests, the diversity and volatility of which our defense plans must accommodate.

The third is that there are certain intangible qualities that often turn out to be more important in warfare than the cut-and-dried features, and that plans for defense are imperiled by the common, rational tendency to devalue anything that cannot be reduced to facts and figures.

MONEY

THE MOST confining of these realities is the economic constraint. It is a basic article of the politician's creed that no one can ever "put a price on national defense," but the truths of economic life have sharply raised the difficulty of adding to the budget. It is not widely known that, ever since the end of the Korean War, the United States has spent essentially the same amount of money on defense , in real terms, every single year. Through the Eisenhower era, the "missile gap" of the early sixties, the Vietnam war, and the supposed decline of defense budgets after Vietnam, the United States has spent about $125 billion (measured in 1980 dollars), plus or minus $10 billion, each year. That represents a smaller share of the gross national product in the eighties than it did in the early sixties (about 5 percent of the gross national product, compared to 8 1/2 percent during the Administration of John Kennedy). Even so, it may be much harder to increase the defense budget now than it was then.

The outlines of the problem appear when the American economy is divided into its three essential spheres: consumption, investment, and government. Consumption is food, travel, everything that people buy and use; investment is expansion of productive capacity, financed by money that someone has saved rather than consumed; government is the cost of the state, federal, and local bureaucracies. Fifty years ago, when the teachings of John Maynard Keynes were finally applied—not so much during the Great Depression as in World War II—an increase in the government share led, miraculously, to expansions in the other two sectors. Twenty or thirty years ago, in the days of Eisenhower and Kennedy, the strong, steady growth of the private economy enabled all three shares to expand at once. Since the early seventies the three shares have been competing for the fruits of an economy whose growth is fitful and slow. For as much of the future as can be foreseen without reliance on the promises of the "Laffer Curve,"* an increase in the size

---

*An economist from the University of Southern California named Arthur Laffer contends that in certain cases the government can bring in more tax revenue by cutting the tax rates. The political implication of this theory is to permit a "free lunch," since the government would theoretically be able to let businesses and consumers keep more of their income, while still taking in more tax money for programs like defense. The only part of the theory that Laffer can demonstrate is that if the tax rates are 100 percent, the government will take in no taxes, since there will be no business activity, so if it cuts its rates below 100 percent, its revenues will rise.

of any one share—especially the government's—will mean an immediate decrease in the other two. If the share that rises is the government's, the ultimate sacrifice asked of the other two is even greater. An increase in investment, which can be used to build more modern factories or devise more efficient techniques, will, in the end, mean more income for consumers and more taxes for the government, even though it must be paid for, in the short run, by reductions in the shares claimed by the consumer or the government. Increases in government spending also require reductions in the other two, without (in most cases) adding to productive capacity in the long run. This is not to say that government spending serves no purpose; only that all government efforts, including those for defense, come at a price.

How much slack is there in the consumption or investment shares, which might be taken up to pay for "more" defense? During the late seventies the government was rudely reminded that it had reached some sort of limit to its encroachments on each of the other two shares. The consumer's share is mainly reduced by inflation, which makes income worth less even when it seems to rise. The government cannot be blamed for all inflation, except by those who favor overly simple schemes, but few politicians have read the trends of the eighties as an invitation to increase taxes, and thereby reduce the consumer's share further still.

As for the pressure that government places on investment, a dramatic moment of enlightenment occurred in the first few months of 1980 when President Carter announced his proposed budget for fiscal year 1981, which would begin in October 1980. The budget's projected deficit—the difference between the revenue it expected and the spending it planned—was about $40 billion. Many people in the Administration believed that the worst harm caused by the deficit would be another small increase in the inflation rate. Better this, they reasoned, than to risk the disappointment and wrath they would provoke with cuts in federal spending. Other Administrations had made that choice before, and in general they had gotten away with it.

But as soon as the budget was announced, the Administration learned that this time the calculation was wrong. As reports of the $40 billion deficit spread, the nation's bond markets underwent a crash that was worse, in absolute terms of dollars lost and in relative terms of decline in value, than the stock-market catastrophe of 1929. The reason for the crash was the feeling that the supply of money to be invested was small enough (because people were reluctant to save), and the other demands on it were so great (because all businesses needed money for their own projects), that the government could cover its demands for the $40 billion only by pushing interest rates through the roof. High interest rates were good news for people who bought Treasury bills at 14, 16, 18 percent interest, but disastrous news for the bond market, which had been accustomed to doing business in the comfortable realm of interest rates at 7 or 8 percent. People spoke, without hyperbole, of the potential destruction of the long-term capital market. The Administration was backed into an embarrassing reversal of its policy, and it came up within weeks with a new, austere budget that would supposedly reduce the deficit to zero.

"If anyone had been able to tell the President that, as a near-certainty, his choice was the collapse of the capital market or taking heat for budget reductions, I'm sure he would have chosen the latter," says a man who participated in the budget plans. "From now on, Presidents will realize that this *is* the choice."

Part of the reason the government has been so sharply reminded of the limits on its reach is that the private economy is far sicker than it was in the days of Eisenhower, Kennedy, and Johnson. Economic productivity—output per worker—rose by nearly 2.5 percent each year between 1953 and 1969. Since 1973, it has gone up only one-fifth as fast.[1] The unemployment rate averaged less than 5 percent through nearly all of the fifties and sixties; the average inflation rate was only 2 percent at that time. Now inflation dips but rarely into the domain of single figures; unemployment persists at about 7 or 8 percent.

There are as many theories about the origins of these problems as there are economists, but there is one common element in every proposed cure: more money, lots of it, must be invested in productive capacity. Directly or indirectly, this will mean in the short run less money for consumption, and less for the government. The steel industry, which today employs 400,000 fewer workers than in 1969, is trying to revamp its furnaces and casters to match those of the Japanese. According to a government study of the industry, steel companies will have to find more than $6 billion in financing each year until 1984 to restore their competitive position—or about $2 billion more than they are likely to generate through profits, new stock issues, or other standard sources of finance.[2] If the steel industry is to raise all this money through normal investment, people will have to start spending less and saving more. If—as is more likely—the steelmakers get tax breaks from the government, then the government will have to cut back its other spending by that amount, or take the difference from the public (through either taxes or inflation).

The auto makers have been impoverished by their failure to turn out large numbers of competitive small cars. No one agrees on the villain, but all proposals for saving the auto companies involve large new infusions of capital. Even the semiconductor industry, which in manufacturing silicon "chips" for computers wrought the technical and economic miracle of the 1970s, now is full of warnings that its companies may be undone by a shortage of finance. As in many other cases, this industry's most intense competition comes from Japan, and the major Japanese edge has been a better supply of capital, made available by a cooperative government and a citizenry that saves one quarter of the money it earns (as opposed to the American public, which saves about 5 percent). With funds easier to obtain, and at lower rates, the Japanese have kept up investment in research and development, and automated more of their assembly plants. Andrew Grove, the president of probably the most successful American semiconductor firm, Intel, said in 1980 that "the development cost for the total system of the early 70's may have amounted to a million dollars for a company such as Intel. Today, the cost is in the $25 million range, and in the 80's it will be over $100 million."[3] He predicted that the equipment used to manufacture "chips" will rise in price fortyfold during the eighties. It would be catastrophic to lose the technical and economic edge the semiconductor industry has given the United States, but to sustain it will require still larger shares of long-term capital. This is not even to mention the largest single demand on capital over the next few years: money to drill oil wells, open coal mines, insulate houses, devise solar converters, build (or reinforce, or inspect) nuclear plants, explore fields for natural gas, and anything else that has to do with increasing supplies and reducing demand for energy.

The point of this exercise is to suggest that through the first few years of this decade, the government will not find it easy to expand its share of the national income by shrinking the shares for consumption and investment. To increase the government's share at the expense of consumption would mean either raising taxes or permitting inflation to erode the public's purchasing power. Those are the two things any elected government will be least eager to do. Will industry be able to tighten its belt and let the government have a little more money to build up the army? On the contrary, industries have a lot of making up to do for their low investment rates through the seventies, and one way they'll try to do it is through tax breaks and other government incentives. What's left is a competition in which some, or all, will come up short. The government's efforts to spend more for defense will run head-on into the resistance of the taxpayer and the claims of industries whose health also has something to do with "national security." (To use the most obvious example, economists may muse that the American steel industry should be allowed to fall to competitors from Korea and Taiwan, but how much military sense does it make to rely on imports for our supply of steel?)

There is, of course, one other possible way to make ends meet. If all government spending except defense could be slashed, then there would be more for the military without skimping on the share for steel, semiconductors, and oil. This is the enterprise on which the Reagan Administration embarked in 1981. The difficulties of such an undertaking became clear when the details of the budget came into view.

About 60 percent of all federal spending falls in the category of "entitlements," or the "uncontrollables," as they are often called. Uncontrollables are benefits offered, by law, to anyone who meets certain conditions: farmers who are entitled to price supports when the market reaches certain levels; unemployed workers who are entitled to assistance if a federal panel determines that they have lost their job because of foreign competition. Many of these programs, including the biggest, Social Security, are "indexed" and go up automatically with inflation.

The term "uncontrollable" has grown familiar in recent years, with the unfortunate result of suggesting that these programs are entirely beyond the reach of man's control. Technically, they are "uncontrollable" only for the President and his assistants as they prepare each year's budget. A President cannot say "Let's spend ten billion dollars this year for welfare" and stick to it, because widespread unemployment could make so many people eligible for the program that existing laws would require the government to spend $15 billion. In order to change or limit these expenditures, the Congress must act to alter the laws that now specify how the money should be spent.

The technical sense in which the programs are "uncontrollable," however, may mask the real intractability in the budget: the political barriers to reducing these payments, which are a far greater obstacle than the practical requirements of changing the law. Of the nearly $400 billion that is spent each year in entitlements, the great majority goes to *everybody*—that is, to groups that no politician can rationally write off. Social Security payments, at $138 billion,[4] stand atop the list of entitlements, and also at the head of any list of programs that politicians hesitate to attack. Interest on the national debt, at $79 billion, is second largest and is completely uncontrollable, since it is payment for debt already incurred. Medicare is next, about $39 billion a year. Another important entitlement, support payments to farmers, is about $3 billion. Together, these four programs—one of them (interest) impossible to reduce, and the rest the closest thing to it for political reasons—come to $259 billion, or more than 40 percent of the entire federal budget, and more than two thirds of the "entitlements" programs. By comparison, the "welfare" elements of the budget are fairly small. The most familiar welfare program, Aid to Families with Dependent Children, costs about $8.5 billion, and Supplemental Security Income a little less than $8 billion. Medicaid, a medical insurance program for the poor, is nearly $16 billion, and food stamps roughly $10 billion. Their sum, $42.5 billion, is no small figure, but it represents only about 6 percent of all federal spending, or 11 percent of all entitlements. In the fifteen years since entitlements became a substantial portion of the federal budget, no Administration, Republican or Democratic, has found it possible to keep them from growing faster than all other items, let alone reduce them. Even if Social Security were not propelled upward by a cost-of-living adjustment figure that exaggerates the effects of inflation, it would rise because each year the proportion of old people in the population is greater than the year before.

To be clear about this point, an intelligent dissection of entitlements is probably the major task of domestic policy in this decade. Although no politician has yet had the gifts as a teacher and leader to explain how Social Security can be reduced without terrifying those who truly depend on it, someone will find a way to teach such lessons someday. Perhaps the Reagan Administration's approach to reducing the budget will prove to be a historic breakthrough. Nonetheless, any significant change in entitlement programs is likely to be both difficult and slow.

On top of these entitlements, with their 60 percent of the budget, comes defense, with another 25. Everything else the federal government does, *everything*, comes out of the remaining 15 percent.[5] This includes: trips to the moon, the interstate highway system, all federal salaries, the construction of dams, agricultural conservation projects and the agricultural experiment system, the Congress and its staff, the State Department, foreign aid, the National Endowments for the Arts and Humanities, the Peace Corps and ACTION, Basic Educational Opportunity Grants, the Library of Congress, the "synfuels" program, the Law Enforcement Assistance Administration, federal subsidies for buses and subways, occupational safety programs, environmental protection, the CIA, solar energy development, nearly all nuclear energy projects, aid for elementary and secondary education, energy conservation programs, the Secret Service, the IRS, the federal judiciary, the National Forests and Parks, the FBI, the National Labor Relations Board, and the salary of the President and Vice President of the United States. Here too, no doubt, there is waste; and perhaps the Reagan Administration will master the trick its predecessors found so elusive: to mobilize a general political will that can overcome the fervent support each government program enjoys from its client groups. Even so, if it then transferred the savings to extra spending for defense, it would destroy the very benefit of a smaller federal budget that the Administration has so often stressed.

"IN THE TIME of Lyndon Johnson, you could do anything you wanted," says Larry Smith, an assistant to Senator Gary Hart of Colorado who was formerly the nuclear weapons expert for the Senate Armed Services Committee. "You could have guns and butter. You could have guns and guns. You could destroy North Vietnam and provide the money to rebuild it. You did not have to choose between ships and planes, or among different models, because you could have them all, or at least we believed we could." In 1967 Robert S. McNamara, then Secretary of Defense, was asked at a Senate hearing how long the United States could afford "the gigantic financial cost [of] this major ground war in Asia, without its economy becoming nonviable." "I think forever," McNamara replied.[6]

Supporters of "more" defense act as if we still were operating in that world. Shortly after the election of Ronald Reagan, a panel of his advisers recommended that the new Administration add $20 billion to the 1981 defense budget, on top of the $160 billion the Congress had appropriated.[7] Another of the new President's panels released a report that concluded that "no area of the world is beyond the scope of American influence," and that the United States must have "sufficient military strength to cope with any level of violence" at any spot on the globe.[8] Senator John Tower of Texas, the chairman of the Senate Armed Services Committee, said that the defense budget should go up by 9 to 13 percent in each of the next few years, on top of adjustments for inflation.[9]

Late in 1980 a defense consultant named Edward Luttwak, who writes with perception more often about tactics and strategy than about economic matters, contended that "defense outlays set at, say, 10 percent of the gross national product (still less than the Soviet fraction, and *entirely tolerable*), even if kept up for only three years, would amount to $700 billion. . . . These costs are, of course, high, yet what a surge effort could achieve is still most impressive [emphasis added]."[10]

"High" they certainly are; they are also unattainable under any circumstances short of wartime rationing and enforced savings. Speculations about "surge" efforts that are utterly indifferent to economic realities lead to self-deception, rather than "strength." Chuck Spinney, a civilian employee at the Pentagon, points out that in the three decades from the beginning of the Korean War through 1980, defense spending never increased more than three years in a row. Through those thirty years, the median change from one year's defense budget to the next was actually a slight decline in real terms (−0.4 percent, to be precise), not the steady increase that advocates of more defense are now predicting. Spinney says, "When you think back over the Korean War, John Foster Dulles, McCarthyism, the Russians getting the bomb, Sputnik, Hungary, the 'Missile Gap,' Berlin, the Cuban missile crisis, Czechoslovakia, and the Vietnam war, it is not realistic to think that the Ayatollah and Afghanistan are going to have more cumulative effect than everything else that has happened in thirty years."[11]

And if the historical pattern is broken and defense spending does suddenly increase in the eighties, that too could have its perils. "The worst thing that could happen is for the nation to go on a defense spending binge that will create economic havoc at home and confusion abroad and that cannot be wisely dealt with by the Pentagon," said Melvin Laird, who was Secretary of Defense under President Nixon, shortly after the election of Ronald Reagan.[12]

UNPREDICTABILITY

THE SECOND REALITY is the disproportion between the pace of international change and the slow, cumbersome response of our military programs. There is a related disproportion between the most immediate threats to our security and the crude fashion in which military forces can control them. If these facts are not taken into account as we make our military plans, the result will be a force whose size and structure are ill matched to the world in which it must operate.

In 1969, when the American government made its decision to build a large new nuclear-missile submarine called the Trident, there was no OPEC; China was still embroiled in its Cultural Revolution; the Shah of Iran seemed impregnable; and the United States was years from its ultimate extrication in Vietnam. As of springtime 1981, the first Trident submarine had not yet entered the fleet, and the latest schedule called for the first operational cruise in 1983. The "major surface combatants"—the largest naval ships, especially aircraft carriers—that Congress authorizes in 1981 will be with us in the year 2011, allowing ten years for construction and twenty for life in the fleet. Over those thirty years, the ships will tie up prodigious financial and material resources. A nuclear-powered aircraft carrier now costs about $3 billion to build and about $100 million per year to operate. The ships that accompany it—two or three nuclear-powered cruisers, plus one nuclear submarine—cost about as much again to build and operate. The carrier group requires a crew of about 6,000 men. Will the assumptions that were in congressmen's minds when they voted to build the carrier still hold by the time its keel touches water? Those assumptions are that the United States may need to "project power" in a conflict that is serious enough to draw in American troops, but not serious enough to mean full-scale war with the Soviet Union, since in that case the carriers would be among the first targets sunk. In 1981 the Reagan Administration proposed refurbishing several battleships left over from World II. When first designed, the ships were intended to destroy heavily fortified installations, by launching large shells, at a relatively slow rate of fire. Is that task likely to be appropriate in the eighties and nineties? When congressmen vote money to increase troop levels or buy machine guns, their foresight is less crucial. A foot soldier can be trained for a new mission in a matter of months, and he can use a machine gun wherever he goes. The carrier is a large, lumpy investment that must remain useful for thirty years, whether or not the conditions that originally justified it still apply.

The Army's equivalent of the carrier is the helicopter; since the early sixties, the Army has lobbied for one generation of armed "attack" helicopters after another. The helicopters had their uses in Vietnam, even though thousands of men died while operating them; but there they were used against an enemy that had no air force and virtually no antiaircraft weapons deployed against helicopters. How relevant will that assumption be for another war? "The helicopter is an awfully vulnerable piece of equipment," says retired General Bruce Clarke, a renowned tank commander in World War II. "It is not fast—60, 70, 80 miles an hour—and I think that anybody that can go to the moon can come up with a piece of equipment to keep the helicopter from flying."[13] Even a nation that cannot go to the moon can probably figure out how to exploit a helicopter's many vulnerabilities.

Since the end of World War II, the United States and its allies have girded themselves for the titanic struggle in Central Europe. Perhaps those very preparations have made the struggle less likely; but if there is anyone who, in 1945, foresaw that the next two wars in which the United States would be involved would both be on the littoral of the Pacific, his name is no longer known. "History suggests that it is possible to spend great sums and actually weaken one's defense," Senator Hart said in a speech at the National War College. "Britain spent 60 million pounds on the pre-war defenses in Singapore, but the defenses all faced the sea, and the attack which took Singapore came from the land."[14]

In addition to those cases, like the British mistake in Singapore, in which quickly changing situations can erode the rationale for weapons before the weapons themselves can be changed, there are other situations in which the threat is easy to discern but difficult to stop by military means. Can anyone doubt that a likely strike against American interests—not the ultimate threat, which is nuclear war, but the one whose effects we are most likely to feel—is a disruption in oil supplies from the Middle East? The Middle East's share of the world's oil supplies is shrinking, since almost every new discovery is someplace else, but a significant proportion of the oil on which the Western economies depends passes through the Persian Gulf or from other Middle Eastern ports. For the United States to lose those imports would be wrenching. For our principal allies, in Western Europe and Japan, a cutoff of Middle Eastern oil would mean catastrophe, since virtually all the oil they use comes from abroad. Most wars in history have been fought for smaller material stakes.

But in this case, what good would fighting do? Of course, it is possible that the Soviet Union would send troops to seize the oil fields of Iran, or blockade the Gulf with warships, or intimidate the Arab regimes by its brooding military presence. In those cases, a military threat would prompt a military response from the United States. But a betting man, asked to pick the most probable reason that the flow might slow down, would read recent history and conclude that the odds favored some agent other than Soviet troops. There has already been a 40 percent reduction in oil shipments from the Persian Gulf. They fell from 20 million barrels a day in 1979 to 12 million in 1980, not because of foreign battleships or tanks, but because the pious rulers of Iran decided to raise their price $5 above the world market level. It is all too easy to imagine a revolution in Saudi Arabia or Abu Dhabi bringing new groups to power, with similar disruptive plans. In fact, it is harder to imagine favorable circumstances, in which the oil will keep flowing dependably, than those in which it will not. Continued shipments of oil depend on stability in the Arab empires, no more battles like those between Iraq and Iran, no further successes by guerrillas in attacking tankers, terminals, or pipelines. If one or more of these things goes wrong, 5 million to 10 million barrels of oil per day might disappear from the market while the customers watch helplessly.

"Helpless" they would be, in standard military terms, because sending troops to seize and run the oil fields would be the most difficult of military operations. The troops would be fighting in the desert, ten thousand miles from home—and that would be the smallest of their obstacles. No matter how many troops were involved in the effort, their objective—to sustain the flow of oil—could be undone by a handful of guerrillas. In 1980 an article in *Armed Forces Journal*, no organ of appeasement, bore a headline saying: "The Key Message: Military Forces Can Do Little to Help Reduce the Risks of Western Dependence on Oil Imports." The article pointed out the obvious—that the oil must move through special, ever so vulnerable terminals, "where one bomb could halt tanker loading for six months to a year"; that it must then be borne by tankers, "which one $250 . . . anti-tank rocket can turn into an inferno"; that the ships must move through waters now controlled by Iran; that the only alternative route for Saudi oil, by pipeline across the desert, has a much smaller capacity and is nearly as vulnerable to disruption. The two most urgent steps it recommended were to reduce the imports and to work for an Arab-Israeli settlement. The other three steps were to shift from "a single-minded focus on power projection to meet a direct Soviet military threat to a parallel focus on helping the conservative Gulf states build up their own internal security"; to build reserve supplies of energy; and to improve intelligence sources about the sources of instability in the region.[15]

The limits on straightforward military solutions also apply for items two and three on any list of realistic threats to American security. They are terrorism and the proliferation of nuclear weapons. Yes, there are circumstances in which normal military methods might have some application against these threats. Tanks or helicopters might be designed specifically to break terrorist operations. The best tool for dealing with prolonged hostage situations might be a gas that would disable people temporarily without killing them. American forces in some troubled region might conceivably prevent the start of a small war, and thereby forestall the circumstances under which Pakistan or Israel or South Africa would explode a nuclear bomb. But terrorism and proliferation must be dealt with on their own terms, with the combination of military, diplomatic, economic, and psychological pressure each situation calls for. These threats, and the appropriate responses, almost never find their way onto the lists of new weapons requested by those who are concerned about the "present danger" or get mentioned in appropriations hearings.

Even in dealing with the ultimate threat, a showdown with the Soviet Union, we should remember that situations change. Given the Soviet missile force, no sane man would feel safe unless the United States also had an utterly invulnerable deterrent. But that should not lead automatically to the conclusion that this competition is predestined and eternal. "I could imagine such drastically changed international political relations with the Soviet Union that nuclear weapons would seem anachronistic," says Robert Pranger, an official of the Defense Department in the Nixon and Ford Administrations who directs national security studies at the conservative American Enterprise Institute in Washington. "When you are talking about the future of the nuclear arsenal, you have to postulate the political circumstances in which it occurs. It is a matter of the way political space is arranged in the world, and that is very much a matter of the political leadership of the United States and the Soviet Union. Any logician may be impressed by the orderliness of his war-game scenarios, but they will take place in a political environment that is most disorderly. To forget to allow for that disorder is to undermine our defense."[16] Our military plans should be based on the assumption of unpredictability, rather than on carefully drawn, static models of the world. They should not lose sight of the distinction between the full range of threats to American interests and the smaller number in which military force can usefully be applied; for if they do, our sense of peril may lead us merely to increase the defense budget while neglecting the other steps— such as developing new supplies of energy—that would make us more secure.

THE INTANGIBLE

THE THIRD reality is that the things that count most in combat are also the things most often omitted from political discussions about defense. If there is one recurring theme in the reminiscences of generals, privates, strategists, it is the importance in battle of the intangible, the moral, the human. General Bruce Clarke has said:

What constitutes the effectiveness of the armed forces our country produces?
I believe there are three factors:
First, their strength, arms, equipment, supplies, and transportation;
Second, their morale, esprit, training, leadership, information, motivation, conditioning, and confidence in mission;
Third, the ability of the government to employ them wisely and effectively. The second and third factors are far more important than the first.[17]

Officers repeat Napoleon's chestnut that in battle, the moral is to the material as three to one. In an article for *Infantry Journal* published in 1931, George S. Patton, then a major, wrote:

Success in war lurks invisible in that vitalizing spark, intangible, yet as
evident as the lightning—the warrior's soul. . . . It is the cold glitter of the
attacker's eye, not the point of the questing bayonet, that breaks the line. It
is the fierce determination of the driver to close with the enemy, not the
mechanical perfection of the tank, that conquers the trench. It is the cataclys-
mic ecstacy of conflict in the flier, not the perfection of his machine gun,
which drops the enemy in flaming ruins. Yet volumes are devoted to arma-
ment; pages to inspiration.[18]*

Clarke's statement is couched in the outline-thought that is one
typical form of military expression; Patton's, in the grandiloquence that
is another. Both insist on a point that almost never appears in debates
about defense. Clarke recalled an exchange with William J. Perry, the
director of the Defense Department's Research and Engineering division in the Carter Administration:

When we come out and say how we compare with the Russians, we only
add up those things that can be turned to numbers. There was a study by Dr.
Perry . . . in which he said we are superior to the Russians 18 to 12. I wrote
to him and I said, "You left out 60 percent—you did not cover the intangibles." Well, his answer was, "How do you do that?" I do not know how you
do it, but that does not mean that we can neglect it. . . . We must not let
the developers say we can develop equipment that cancels out these intangibles.[19]

As Edward Luttwak, the defense consultant, says,

technology or no technology, in the reality of warfare, as opposed to paper
calculations, the intangibles of leadership, command experience, tactical ingenuity, and skill of troops are much more important than matériel factors—your
firepower, mobility, and so on. From everything we know about warfare,
ancient and modern, those intangibles easily dominate. It's not 10 percent
around the margin, it's more like 200 or 300 percent.[20]

The intangible factor that looms largest in first-hand memoirs of
war,[21] but which is left out of most discussions about the B-1 bomber
or the newest model of tank, is the ingredient Karl von Clausewitz

---

*Patton wrote this nearly ten years before the Germans, with tanks inferior in number
and armor to those of the French and British defenders, sent their panzer divisions
to overrun most of Europe with a fantastic discipline for battle and the brilliant concept
of blitzkrieg.

called "friction." Friction, he said, is the difference between plans and reality—between war as it imagined and debated and war as it actually occurs. Clausewitz wrote in *On War:*

As long as we have no personal knowledge of War, we cannot conceive where these difficulties lie. All appears so simple, all the requisite branches of knowledge appear so plain, all the combinations so unimportant, that in comparison with them the easiest problem in higher mathematics impresses us with a certain scientific dignity. But if we have seen War, all becomes intelligible. . . .

Everything is very simple in War, but the simplest thing is difficult. These difficulties accumulate and produce a friction which no man can imagine exactly who has not seen War. Suppose now a traveller, who towards evening expects to accomplish the two stages at the end of his day's journey, four or five leagues, with post-horses, on the high road—it is nothing. He arrives now at the last station but one, finds no horses, or very bad ones; then a hilly country, bad roads; it is a dark night, and he is glad when, after a great deal of trouble, he reaches the next station and finds there some miserable accommodation. So in War, through the influence of an infinity of petty circumstances, which cannot properly be described on paper, things disappoint us and we fall short of the mark.[22]

Friction is bad weather. From *On War:*

Here the fog prevents the enemy from being discovered in time, a battery from firing at the right moment, a report from reaching the General; there the rain prevents a battalion from arriving at the right time, because instead of for three hours it had to march perhaps eight hours; the cavalry from charging effectively because it is stuck fast in heavy ground.[23]

Friction is fear and confusion. It is the feeling of terror, recounted in histories of war in every century, that seizes men when the enemy "looms up" and attacks—from the hills at the Little Bighorn, from the fog on the Marne, from the jungle in Vietnam. Friction is imperfect knowledge. "A general never knows anything with certainty, never sees his enemy clearly, never knows positively where he is," Napoleon said.[24] It is the difficulty of distinguishing between friend and foe. It is Jeb Stuart being gone at the crucial moment in the preparation for Gettysburg. It is deaths by "friendly fire."

Friction is plans going awry. It is the knowledge that if the statistical probability of a mechanical breakdown is one in ten, the actual probability of a breakdown in time of crisis is far greater. It is machines

operating at the low end of their range of reliability rather than at the
top. It is a hostile environment, which looks for the weak link in a
system rather than a benign setting in which baling wire will suffice.
"Friction is the only conception which in a general way . . . distinguishes real War from War on paper," Clausewitz said;[25] it is a concept that much of the American defense debate ignores.

As applied to defense planning, this third reality means that we suffer
if we overlook the importance of leadership, morale, discipline, simply
because they are difficult to measure, and that we delude ourselves if
we forget to discount all plans and technical predictions for the likely
effects of friction.

MY ARGUMENT so far is that the realities of economic constraint, of an
unpredictable future, and of the special nature of combat should shape
our plans for war. The next step is to contrast those factors with the
prevailing ethic of modern American defense. That is the "managerial"
view of the military, which assumes that organizing for conflict is
similar to organizing for other activities and that the most important
choices about defense can be justified by the same tools of rational,
often economic analysis that might be used in adjusting the federal
budget or developing a new style of car. That mentality leads to tactics
based on oversimplified, abstract models; to an emphasis on machinery
rather than on men and strategies; and to a tendency to neglect the
human elements that, through history, have often determined the
outcome of conflict.

TWO

MANAGERS

THE "MANAGERIAL" approach to the military means the desire to make defense a more straightforward and efficient business, by applying the disciplines of economics and management to military plans. It is often associated, correctly, with Robert S. McNamara, who became Secretary of Defense under John Kennedy in 1961 and resigned under Lyndon Johnson in 1968. It is less correctly identified with the "systems analysts" that McNamara brought with him to the Pentagon. Although the analysts, the "whiz kids," rubbed nerves raw throughout the Pentagon, and although they added an economic accent to the rhetoric of defense, their lasting influence was far less significant than the impact of another group that came in under McNamara's wing. These were the impresarios of high technology, who with McNamara's blessing made the Research and Engineering division of the Pentagon the power center for decisions about new weapons, and who used the analysts' economic calculations as cloaks for each new project they proposed.

The failing of managerial defense is usually described as its inability to distinguish between efficiency, in the economic or technological sense, and effectiveness on the battlefield. That covers the point, but too crudely. The real problem is the use of an oversimplified, one-dimensional form of analysis, often based on simulations and hypotheses, in place of more complicated judgments, based on data from combat or realistic tests, that take into account the eight or ten qualities that must be combined to make a weapon effective. The worst kind of management seeks a single optimum, a one-scale index of efficiency, like the mindless scales of 1 to 10 for grading a woman's beauty or one or four stars for a movie's appeal. For example, the huge, complex Trident submarine is "efficient" as a carrier of nuclear missiles, since each one will hold 24, compared to 16 for its predecessor, the Polaris. (The missiles are known as SLBMs, for submarine-launched ballistic missiles. They usually carry between 8 and 10 warheads apiece. The other kind of nuclear missile is the ICBM, or intercontinental ballistic missile, which is based in underground silos on land.) But a missile submarine's effectiveness finally depends on its ability to escape detection and survive attack so that its missiles will be safe and available for use as a deterrent. By that standard, the Trident is a senseless step down in effectiveness, since it greatly reduces the number of hiding points among which the missiles are dispersed. When the conversion is complete, the United States will have gone from 41 Polaris submarines to about 20 Tridents. Beyond that, because the Tridents are bigger, each of them may be more vulnerable to discovery by nonacoustic means (such as magnetic detection) than would smaller subs. The simplest kind of managerial logic has added many such weapons to our force.

McNAMARA AT THE PENTAGON

THERE IS much to admire in Robert McNamara's record. For instance, he ran the Pentagon, instead of being run by it. If there is a surprising degree of residual bitterness toward him among professional military men, much of it comes from their frustration that McNamara was so effective in making civilian control stick.

On arrival from the Ford Motor Company in January 1961, McNamara found a budget shaped more by the courtesies and traditions of organizational politics than by a detached view of who needed what. The money was divided among the services, which were usually left to spend it more or less as they chose. There was overlapping and squabbling; there were no forests, only trees. The logistics system was a mess. In one essay, "Managing for Defense," in his book *The Essence of Security,* McNamara said:

We found that the three military departments had been establishing their requirements largely independently of each other. The results could be described fairly as chaotic: Army planning, for example, was based primarily on a long war of attrition; Air Force planning was based, largely, on a short war of nuclear bombardment. Consequently, the Army was stating a requirement for stocking months, if not years, of combat supplies against the event of a sizable conventional conflict. The Air Force stock requirements for such a war had to be measured in days, and not many days at that.... Before we organized the Defense Supply Agency, the various elements of the Department—to cite a typical example—were using slightly different forms for requisitions, no less than sixteen in all. As a result, nearly every time a piece of property was transferred from one part of the Department to another, a new requisition form had to be typed. By the simple expedient of establishing a common requisition form and system, we eliminated literally tens of thousands of man-hours of labor formerly wasted in having clerks retype the forms. Other minor but colorful instances of improvement were the consolidation of eighteen different types and sizes of butcher smocks, four kinds of belt buckles and six kinds of women's exercise bloomers.[1]

Two of McNamara's disciples, Alain Enthoven and K. Wayne Smith, optimistically summarized his achievement as "decision making based on explicit criteria related to the national interest, as opposed to decision making by compromise among various institutions and parochial interests."[2]

Many of the fights McNamara chose are still good fights. The supply systems remain out of sync with one another. As of early 1981, the military stockpile contained enough Phoenix missiles to last about a day and a half in combat—and enough vanadium and chromium to last two years. The main difference between the Defense Supply Agency, which McNamara created in the early sixties, and the separate service supply bureaucracies it replaced often seems to be that its troubles are centralized, and therefore larger.

Each of the services is as parochial in defending its interests as ever. The Army has built a new armored personnel carrier and the Air Force has built hundreds of assault transport planes. The new armored vehicle is larger than the ramp opening of the planes, so that the planes cannot carry the infantry's most important vehicle. The Air Force "owns" the Minuteman and Titan nuclear missiles that sit in silos, aimed at the Soviet Union, but the Army is in charge of defending those silos against attack, whether from saboteurs or from enemy missiles. During the mid-seventies, when the supposed "vulnerability" of the missiles in their underground silos to enemy attack became a matter of first principle in nuclear planning, the Air Force developed its plans for a new, mobile "MX" missile without ever formally consulting the Army about other means of defending the sites. To one proposal for the future of America's nuclear force—getting rid of the silos and putting the missiles on ships and submarines—a frequent answer, advanced in dead earnest, is that this is too big a job to leave to the Navy.

McNamara also carefully insisted on the analytic difference between strategic nuclear weapons and everything else.* A B-52 bomber from the Strategic Air Command equipped with nuclear weapons is not just another airplane; the warhead atop a Minuteman III missile is not just another explosive device. The consequences of their use would be different from those of any other weapon, and therefore so must be the rules for their control and the strategy for their deployment. "Systems analysis led McNamara to consider strategic weaponry apart from other arms, to compare the merits of various strategic weapons, including the Polaris submarine, the Minuteman missile, and the B-52 bomber, apart from the service to which they were attached," says Eliot Cohen of Harvard's Center for International Affairs. "He deserves credit for considering strategic nuclear problems as distinct from conventional ones."[3]

Yet the distinctions that managers drew in some areas did not prevent the confusion between simple economic efficiency standards—cost per ton-mile, bang for the buck—and the more complex, more empirically proven measures of what kinds of weapons actually work. Since at least the early sixties, defense managers have predicted great things for new generations of "precision-guided munitions," which are meant to take much of the worry and messiness out of war. One such weapon is a missile called the TOW (the acronym stands for "tube-launched, optically tracked, wire-guided"). The theory of its operation is that a soldier will stand and fire the missile at a far-off tank. By keeping the sight on the launcher aligned on the tank during the ten seconds or so of the missile's flight, he can adjust its course as the tank maneuvers, theoretically ensuring a hit. These weapons are said to be marvelously "cost-effective," since a missile that costs $7,000 can theoretically destroy a Soviet tank that costs half a million dollars. Many groups that favor more defense spending think much of the money should be invested in precision-guided weapons. Some groups

---

*In U.S. defense language, "strategic" nuclear systems are the warheads and bombs targeted on the Soviet Union and intended to deter an attack on the United States or retaliate if one occurs. "Tactical" or "theater" nuclear weapons are the ones which, in the minds of some, could be used in battles restricted to one theater, such as Central Europe. The Soviets recognize no such distinction between "strategic" and "tactical" nuclear weapons.

on the left, who would not agree with the right on any other point, share the enthusiasm for precision-guided weapons, for they believe that the weapons will give a huge advantage to the side defending against an attack, and therefore will deter war and ultimately permit a reduction in military spending.

"Anyone who likes the TOW has never seen a battlefield," said one man who has studied the weapon. "To guide the thing, you have to stand exposed from here up"—motioning to the lower chest—"for at least ten seconds. The people who think these things up don't realize that there's all the difference in the world between a two-second exposure on the battlefield and ten seconds."

Although the TOW has never really been tested in combat, it is bulky enough that in wartime TOW gunners would probably not be able to protect themselves by lying down or hiding behind cover and still keep the missiles from hitting trees, bushes, or the ground. "To fire the TOW, you've got to stand there, practically naked," a Marine officer told me at Camp Pendleton. "A soldier's just not going to do that."

Tom Kelly, a veteran of Vietnam era, says, "Soldiers will throw a weapon away if they don't have faith in it. The soldier is the guy making the ultimate decision on weapons systems, and he is going to throw it out if he can't count on it. There was that Sheridan tank— you knew it was a coffin, so you wouldn't stay in."

The analytic error was to concentrate on one value only—the "probability of kill," or Pk, for each shot from the TOW—and to ignore several others, such as the gunner's ability to survive, and the rate at which he can fire missiles. The single-shot "Pk" means less than the rate of fire to a platoon that is facing not one tank at a time, but fifty. By ignoring these complications, the managers and technologists spent hundreds of millions for a weapon that is likely to litter the ditches of the first battlefield where it is really used. It is easy to sneer at this error, until you consider how much of modern life—college board scores, price/earning ratios, presidential "approval" ratings—is run on similar reductionist principles.

The same mistake applies to the modern radar-guided missiles, which have added so much to the cost of modern fighter planes. When the missile is flying toward its target, the pilot must stay locked in a pattern with the other plane, flying a predictable course that lays him open to destruction from any other planes that happen to be in the area. (Most aerial combat involves large numbers of planes, instead of one-on-one duels.) In their haste to equip planes with these precision-guided missiles, the managers passed up the opportunity to refine a weapon that had proved, in combat in Israel and Vietnam, that it did work. This was the 20-millimeter air-to-air cannon, a gun of Korean War vintage, which left the pilot much freer to maneuver to safety, which was hard for the enemy to spoof, and which had a better overall "probability of kill." Similarly, the high hopes attached to the TOW have pre-empted the effort—and the money—that might have been used for improving simpler antitank cannons, which soldiers could fire more quickly without exposing themselves to near-certain death.

Tom Kelly, the veteran of Vietnam who later worked as a civilian in the Pentagon, has described yet another precision-guided weapon called the Dragon. The guidance system, which consists of a heavy, shoulder-mounted sight, requires a soldier to stand very still, like a photographer taking a picture in dim light, while the Dragon is in flight, because any small movement is translated into larger variations in the missile's course: "The TOW's designed for long-range shots, but where in Europe are you going to get a two-thousand-yard clear shot? So instead they have the Dragon, which is for shorter ranges. When they fire these things on the test range, a guy can guide it for a couple of hundred yards. Then he breathes, and the thing goes up and down in flight. Assuming that the ground is perfectly flat, he may recover in time to guide it back to the target, but if the ground is rough, it won't make it. It turns out that what you really need to do it right is a guy who's about five foot eight and weighs two hundred and fifty pounds. There aren't many people built like a fireplug."

This managerial logic contributed to the growth of ineffective weapons in another, less direct, but perhaps more important way. Robert McNamara led the services toward the policy of "fixed force structure," which meant there would be thirteen aircraft carriers for the Navy, sixteen divisions for the Army, and so on down the list. In each case, impartial analysis would determine how much was enough—and that was how much the services would have, for all the foreseeable future. The intention of fixed force structure was, somewhat naïvely, to set rational limits and keep the services from asking for the moon. The effect was to give them an irresistible incentive to buy only at the top of the line. When the Navy knew it had thirteen carriers, no more, no less, why shouldn't it pack everything it could onto each carrier? From the services' point of view, the only virtue of simpler, cheaper weapons (apart from the fact that they work) was that they could buy more of them. Fixed force structure denied them even that incentive.

There was also a gap between the managerial approach and the real, human history of combat when it came to motivating and controlling men at war. Successful military commanders have understood that lies are built into news as it moves from the battlefield up the chain of command. Napoleon is supposed to have told subordinates that the only way to know for sure what was going on at the front was to "go look." The great German tank tactician of World War II, General Hermann Balck, mused in a recent interview, conducted by Battelle Laboratories, that he was irritated when his subordinates were rotated because he'd spent time learning the degree of lying to allow for in each one's reports. However dubious the causes in which it served, the combat leadership of the German army must be regarded as the most consistently excellent military establishment in modern times. In his history of the German military leaders, A Genius for War, T. N. Dupuy points out that German generals devoted extraordinary efforts to finding ways of getting realistic, accurate, first-hand information from the field.[4]

The German generals' efforts were dictated not by the convenience of internal routine, but by the need to perform on the battlefield. Some of the most successful enterprises—businesses in their hungriest phase, successful political campaigns, public agencies in extraordinary periods like the early New Deal—manage to enforce the same insistence on external results. The vast majority do not. All that the typical government executive knows about his programs is what he reads in reports and computer print-outs from his subordinates. The typical business executive never goes to a branch office of his company and sees what the customer sees. That is why the first casualty in any large organization is realistic information from the field. It is far more convenient to know only the facts that are easy to measure and that reflect well on those in the chain of command. Therefore, while the human cost of this practice was far greater in Vietnam than in nonmilitary organizations, there was nothing atypical in the managerial techniques the Army adopted to measure its progress there. In a book called Self-Destruction, an Army officer, writing under the pseudonym "Cincinnatus," says:

Since progress could not be measured by such traditional yardsticks as miles gained or cities won or armies destroyed, both Secretary of Defense McNamara and the upper echelon of his military followers sought other ways to compute the relative advantage of the United States over its adversaries . . . The "solution," acclaimed by both military and civilian parties, was to apply statistics to the battlefield: search for significant factors that would lend themselves to statistical manipulation; tabulate relative position semiannually, or monthly, or weekly, or daily, or hourly, then do it again and compare results with those previously determined.[5]

"Cincinnatus" quotes a paper prepared at the Army Command and General Staff College by Major William Lowry:

Duplicity became so automatic that lower headquarters began to believe the things they were forwarding to higher headquarters. It was on paper; therefore, no matter what might have actually occurred, the paper graphs and charts became the ultimate reality.[6]

The culmination of this logic was the body count, of which "Cincinnatus" says:

It has always been natural for one side in an armed conflict to estimate the number of casualties it has inflicted upon the other side. Not until Vietnam, however, did "estimated enemy casualties" become an all-encompassing obsession of the army. The feverish pursuit of this talisman actually led to increased American losses, brought dishonor upon those who espoused the practice, and generally lessened the stature of the army within American opinion. . . . Officially it was U.S. policy to claim as enemy dead only those bodies that had actually fallen on a battleground and had been physically counted by an American commander. Any man who has ever been to war, particularly anyone who ever fought in Vietnam, knows that such a policy was impossible to implement or enforce and consequently was conducive to "estimates" which could easily be falsified. Yet once entered on a report form, such estimates took on a reality of their own, transcending anything that might have actually happened. No matter how arrived at, the figures themselves became real.[7]

ATTRITION WARFARE

THE DESIRE to simplify and rationalize and the pursuit of one-dimensional measures suggest the second major drawback of managerial defense. Its effect on military strategy is to reinforce a style of "attrition" warfare that has dominated American military practice since at least the Civil War, but which is at serious odds with the military reality of the 1980s.

Attrition is a toe-to-toe slugging match in which each side assumes that the other will abide by predictable rules and that sheer weight of numbers and matériel will determine the outcome. Its equivalents in sports are tug-of-war contests and "demolition derbies"; its equivalent in nature is the sea wearing down the stones. It was the approach that all sides took during the trench warfare in World War I, and that the Allies followed to victory at the end of World War II, when the arsenal of democracy crushed its adversaries.

The purest operational description of attrition came from David Hackworth, a retired Army colonel, as quoted in Stuart Loory's book, *Defeated:*

I remember a German lieutenant captured at Salerno who I was guarding in 1946 in a prisoner of war camp. He was a real tough looking kraut and I was a young punk, a pimply-faced kid. He could speak perfect English, and I was riding him. I said, "Well, if you're so tough, and if you're all supermen, how come you're here captured and I'm guarding you?"

And he looked at me and said, "Well, it's like this. I was on this hill as a battery commander with six 88-millimeter antitank guns, and the Americans kept sending tanks down the road. We kept knocking them out. Every time they sent a tank, we knocked it out.

"Finally, we ran out of ammunition, and the Americans didn't run out of tanks."[8]

From Grant to Eisenhower, the United States has been the side that would never run out of tanks and didn't need to worry about anything else. "We gin up the production lines and crush the enemy with steel safes," says William Lind, a military historian who works on the staff of Senator Hart.[9] But attrition was also applied in Vietnam, through the search-and-destroy missions and the repeated attempts to draw the enemy into "decisive" battles, and there it failed. The reason has to do with an alternate view of conflict, and an alternate strategy known as "maneuver war."

THE DISTINCTION between "attrition" and the "maneuver" approach might best be introduced through the story of John Boyd.

During the Korean War, Boyd was flying the F-86 Sabre against the Soviet-built MiG-15. He had grown up in Erie, Pennsylvania, and after attending the University of Iowa, had been called up as a member of the ROTC to go to Korea. After his service there, Boyd became one of the most renowned pilots in the Air Force. As a tactics instructor at Nellis Air Force Base in the late fifties, he produced the "Aerial Attack Study," a manual that revolutionized the theory of air combat, laying out, with the conceptual elegance of a chess manual, the theory of move and countermove in combat between fighter planes. Modern air forces that teach combat tactics base their theories on his work. Later, after going to Georgia Tech to study engineering, he quantified his tactical approaches, leading to his "energy-maneuverability theory" of air combat. As the next chapters will explain, his "maneuverability" theories played a crucial role in the development of two modern American fighters, the F-15 and the F-16.

Boyd also reflected on an anomaly of aerial combat, as he had observed it in Korea. The F-86s consistently destroyed the MiGs, even though the MiG was a "better" plane by most conventional measures. It could climb faster, hold a tighter turn, and accelerate more rapidly than the F-86. But the F-86 could *change* from one maneuver to another far more rapidly—reversing its turns or rolling and diving away —so that as each plane maneuvered around the other, the F-86 would accumulate a greater and greater advantage in firing position off the tail of the other plane. This led Boyd into another, more broadly significant inquiry, into the patterns that dominate conflict at all levels, from the unit struggling to cross a battlefield to the general devising a strategy for the defense of the nation.

Boyd's theories are available in the form of a four-hour briefing, illustrated with 160 charts, that he has delivered tirelessly to audiences of military men and politicians over the last few years. His examples cover combat from the battle of Marathon twenty-five hundred years ago to the guerrilla warfare of the twentieth century, and military theorists from the Chinese master of the fifth century B.C., Sun Tzu, through the Swiss general Henri Jomini, Karl von Clausewitz, and Mao Tse-tung. His point of entry is to bring up those surprisingly frequent situations in which forces that were numerically weaker ended up carrying the day. The common pattern he extracts from those victories is that the commanders exploited the intangible factors of deception, surprise, confusion, to stay one step ahead of the enemy's thinking at all times, and then to attack the enemy where he was least prepared and weakest, rather than wade in head-on to match strength against strength.

The most familiar specimen of this approach is the German blitz-krieg attack of World War II. It is not generally known that on the eve of the war, the Germans had fewer tanks than the French and British forces stationed in France, and that the German tanks were more thinly armored and had less powerful guns. What the Germans did have was a new concept of how to use their tanks to exploit the weaknesses in their enemy's force, introduced and implemented by General Heinz Guderian. One of Guderian's disciples, General Hermann Balck, said thirty-five years after the war:

The decisive breakthrough into modern military thinking came with Guderian, and it consisted not only of a breakthrough in armor weapons, but also a breakthrough in communications weapons. . . . Guderian made two very important contributions in the area of panzer warfare communications. The first contribution was to add a fifth man, a radio operator, and a radio to each tank in the tank division. This allowed both small and large tank units to be commanded and maneuvered with a swiftness and flexibility that no other army was able to match. As a result, our tanks were able to defeat tanks that were quite superior in firepower and armor.

Guderian's second contribution was to give the panzer division a signal organization that allowed the division commander to command from any point within the division. . . . When Guderian first tried to explain the concept and organization to General Fritsch, Fritsch asked him, "And how do you intend to control this division?" and Guderian replied, "From the front using radio!" Fritsch replied, "Nonsense. The only way to command is from a desk at the rear, using telephone."[10]

This is of a piece with Boyd's larger contention that in any sort of conflict, what matters is "getting inside an adversary's O-O-D-A loop." This "loop" consists of cycles of *observing* (O) the enemy's actions, *orienting* (O) oneself to the unfolding situation, *deciding* (D) on a counter, and then *acting* (A). The principle is that the side which can complete these cycles more quickly will ultimately prevail. The enemy will shell the left, but you will already be moving to the right. When he launches his attack on the center, you will be ready to fall back and destroy him from the flanks.

The ultimate purpose of these maneuvers, in Boyd's view, is not to wear down the enemy's forces, but to destroy his view of the world. In order to operate in conflict, an army or an individual soldier must rely on its "paradigm"—its understanding of reality, its sense of the circumstances to which it must respond. This is true of the soldier in the foxhole trying to discern enemy riflemen, and of a general deploying tens of thousands against his foe. Boyd says that if the paradigm can be destroyed—by sending ambiguous or deliberately misleading signals, by moving faster than the enemy can respond—then the enemy's effectiveness is finished. You do not need to bomb or slaughter him, for his forces will fall apart. From Clausewitz, Boyd took the principle of reducing one's own "friction" (through simple equipment, decentralized commands, etc.) as one key to success. From Sun Tzu, he took the premise that the enemy could be destroyed if *his* friction was sufficiently increased.

The significance of Boyd's theory is that these principles, based on the records of combat over more than two millennia, lead to a demand for a military establishment that is very different from the one the United States has created.

In weaponry and equipment, this approach places a premium on simple, reliable, flexible tools that can be produced quickly, whose functions can be adapted rapidly in response to changing tactics, and that do not depend for their effectiveness on narrowly defined, fixed circumstances. The French spent roughly as much money as the Germans arming for World War II, but the French spent much of it on the Maginot Line, which was effective only as long as the Germans chose to attack it frontally with massed, slow-moving infantry. The Germans spent their money on tanks and trucks they could use anywhere.

In systems of communications and command, the maneuver approach emphasizes setting a clear, central goal—overrun Poland; destroy the morale of American troops in Vietnam—but then allowing local teams and commanders the maximum leeway to seize whatever opportunities they see. The orders given to Dwight Eisenhower were to invade France and liberate the continent; the details were left to him. Because of the profligate use of modern communications, the commanders of the failed American rescue missions to Iran and the *Mayagüez* both had to clear each minute tactical move by radio with the Joint Chiefs of Staff on the other side of the globe.

In battlefield tactics, maneuver dictates an emphasis on deception, unpredictability, surprise. The British troops who were sent to put down the American revolution walked in serried ranks, wearing red. The Americans wore mufti and fired from behind trees. So did the Boers, for it took the British troops until the middle of the Boer war to learn the lesson of the American revolution.* This is another illustration of the persistence of pure, abstract reason in resisting evidence from real life.

---

*The seizure of the American hostages in Iran provided a textbook illustration of the importance of ambiguity and deception in staying "inside the adversary's O-O-D-A loop." A few days after the hostages were released, George Wilson of the Washington *Post* reported that American military planners had contemplated a second rescue mission to Iran, after the failure of the first in April 1980. The plans were called off because the unpredictability of Iranian behavior left the Americans in constant uncertainty about where and how to attack. Wilson wrote:

The biggest obstacle, intelligence sources said, was the fact that the fractured command and erratic behavior of the Iranian militants screened both their intentions and the locations of some of the hostages. There was no one command center to put under human and electronic surveillance. . . .

Although electronic eavesdropping and spy satellites helped U.S. intelligence officials see through the claims of Iranian militants that the hostages had been scattered widely around Iran, the so-called "fine grain" information on the Americans' whereabouts remained elusive. . . . Intelligence officials continued to press for a breakthrough on the locations. But the hostages proved to be a moving target, even though most of the shuttling was in Tehran rather than to the distant countryside as the militants kept declaring. At most, about three quarters of the hostages were pinpointed for any length of time.[11]

And in the area of "intangibles"—where Boyd's maneuver theory places so much more emphasis than does the attrition approach—it stresses that no enemy should ever be viewed as a stone to be pulverized by repeated blows, but as a functioning organism whose overall effectiveness can be destroyed by attacks on the elements that give it cohesion. In the first real book of military theory, *The Art of War*, written about 400 B.C., Sun Tzu said that of the ways to conquer an enemy, the most desirable was to destroy his mind, that is, his plans, his intentions, his view of the world. Next best was to disrupt his alliances—which make his own world stable, which provide the moral bonds to sustain his effort. Worse was to attack his armies, and worst of all to attack his cities. On the level of grand strategy, this is Russia being "defeated" in World War I by its own revolution. On the level of individual combatants, it shows up in the harrowing accounts of the panic that disables fighter pilots, long before their planes are shot down, when they realize in a dogfight that they are certain to be outmaneuvered and killed. Attrition does not account for these effects. It would reverse the order of Sun Tzu's list. The predilection toward fire power and attrition, Stephen Canby has written, "is like that of the novice at the game of chess," whereas maneuver "aims to collapse the integrity of the system" and thereby resembles the approach "of the expert who aims immediately for the king and his entourage in order to terminate the game in a few moves."[12]

Viewing the enemy as an integrated organism rather than an undifferentiated mass also suggests fundamentally different measures of success. For example, in attrition warfare, enemy dead are the most reliable indicator of progress. In a maneuver approach, enemy *prisoners* are a more telling indicator. Their capture suggests that the enemy has not been able to adapt to changing situations, that "friction" has overwhelmed him, that his internal systems of discipline and command have broken down.

Finally, maneuver also suggests a different view of one's own vulnerability—which can be summed up as: an army (or nation, or weapon) is only as strong as its weakest link. If the opposing force is also an adaptable organism, it will probe for weaknesses and exploit them. At the beginning of the Soviet invasion of Afghanistan, Russian soldiers rode in armored personnel carriers called BMPs. The BMPs had fuel tanks in the hollows of their doors. "How long do you think it took the Afghans to figure out that one shot in the door would send it into flames?" one defense analyst asks.

There was a time when American forces fought with maneuver principles: in the Revolutionary War. Since then, the American military heritage has been long on the Ulysses S. Grants, the champions of the crushing, ponderous attack, and short on the Stonewall Jacksons and Douglas MacArthurs and George S. Pattons, who made quick, unexpected end runs around enemy forces rather than attempting to ram them head-on.

Vietnam was war waged in the attrition style, at least from the American side, and it was an illustration of how attrition can fail. As the anonymous "Cincinnatus" writes in his book:

American military leaders naively accepted guerrilla military units as the real problem they had to combat. They concentrated on identification and location of VC troop units and mounted operations to destroy them when found. While dissipating American men, matériel, and money in such efforts, the generals failed to recognize that the prime force behind those enemy troops remained intact. Viet Cong organizational, administrative, leadership, and control elements could thus continue to refill, refit, retrain, and resupply the units decimated by American military actions.[13]

Despite its failure in Vietnam, attrition remains embedded in current American military philosophy, kept in place by managerial logic. The Army's current field manual instructs officers on how to identify the "Forward Edge of the Battle Area," a line that simply never existed in maneuver operations like the blitzkrieg or the Inchon invasion. It tells commanders of divisions in the field that

The chief mission of these forces must be to fight with sufficient strength and tenacity to force the enemy to disclose the size and direction of his main attack, and to buy time while defending forces concentrate *in front of the main thrust* . . . In mounted warfare, armored and mechanized elements [tanks and trucks] must be set in motion toward the battle positions *in the path of* the enemy thrust [emphasis added].[14]

The American Air Force and Navy both pursue the ultimate in attrition warfare—"interdiction" bombing, far behind enemy lines. The Navy does so under the label "power projection," and designs its fleet to that end. (The Soviet navy, by contrast, is designed to sink the American navy.) Military historians may debate whether or not the two atomic bombs dropped on Japan in 1945 had a "decisive" effect in that war. Apart from that special case, it is hard to make a serious argument that deep interdiction bombing, far from the battlefield, has ever had a significant military effect—except possibly to harden the will of the bombed civilian population to persevere. After World War II, the U.S. Strategic Bombing Survey, a team on which John Kenneth Galbraith

and George Ball worked alongside Paul Nitze, found virtually no correlation between how heavily different regions of Germany had been
bombed and how much their morale or productivity had declined.
Complex-weapons buffs often point out that the Thanh Hoa bridge in
Vietnam was finally destroyed by a guided missile, after more than fifty
planes had been lost in the effort. They rarely add that this technical
achievement could not be converted into a strategic success because
there was a ford just up the river.[15] The military problem with day-in,
day-out bombing is that people get used to it. The first time a city is
bombed, people are shocked, trapped, caught in the open and killed.
After that, they learn to anticipate, hide, survive. Bombing is effective
under two circumstances: when used suddenly, in combination with
other maneuver tactics that force armies to move and expose themselves; and in the special, hideous case of nuclear bombs.

"Wars of attrition worked in the past because of our phenomenal
industrial base," says Larry Smith. "There was always time. The seas
kept us separate. We could get the 'arsenal of democracy' running. We
could gear up in time. I'm not sure that our industrial capacity has that
self-evident surge capability now—especially for this different kind of
production. You can change a farm truck line to one making military
trucks by changing the paint job. Retooling Boeing to make fighter
planes is a different story."[16] Smith's employer, Senator Hart, said in
1980:

Our highly technical and specialized peacetime economy is not as easily and
quickly converted to war production as it was in World War II. A Soviet
invasion of Western Europe might prevail before we could surge to meet it
—if it is fought in the traditional firepower/attrition manner.

Maneuver warfare, on the other hand, could attack important Soviet weaknesses. Their command structure is highly centralized and cumbersome. Little
discretion is permitted to unit commanders. The stresses in their ranks due
to the fusion of divergent nationalities, the language barriers which often exist
between a Russian officer corps and enlisted men of other nationalities, and
the uncertain reliability of Warsaw Pact units—all suggest a vulnerability to
a maneuver warfare designed to disable through disorientation.[17]

"The American national style of warfare remains unchanged," Edward Luttwak has written. "It still presumes a net superiority in material, for it is a style based on the methods of attrition."[18] Luttwak's
point is not simply that attrition is a habit carried over from a day when
the United States enjoyed a cushion of time and distance from foreign
conflict and was endowed with an unparalleled resource base, but also

that the managerial approach to defense encourages an attrition strategy. Attrition, he says, is "war in the administrative manner . . . in which the important command decisions are in fact logistic decisions. The enemy is treated as a mere inventory of targets, and warfare is a matter of mustering superior resources . . ."[19]

"War in the attrition style has the great advantages of reliability [of results], of functional simplicity, and analytical predictability, and it is this that allows such great scope for the use of objective ('systems analysis') methods of evaluation and allocation decisions."[20] Luttwak might have said that attrition gives the *illusion* of predictability and reliable results. The outcome of the war of attrition in Vietnam was anything but what its managers had predicted. Maneuver, by contrast, requires skill and daring on the part of the officers, and a willingness from their superiors to tolerate the risk of an occasional sloppy loss when the calculated risks don't pay off.

Eliot Cohen, in an article called "Systems Paralysis," says that the simplistic, too typical approach to systems analysis discourages "the study of one's opponents, his language, politics, culture, tactics, and leadership. The unit of analysis is the mission or the object: The enemy is therefore often regarded as a passive collection of targets. The attitude is that of an engineer building a bridge across a river, who does not for a moment think that the river will act deliberately in order to thwart him. Alternatively, systems analysis assumes that the enemy resembles us."[21]

AS IF IN PARODY of the managerial approach to defense, one analyst wrote in a book about air power, published in 1974, that "waging war is no different in principle from any other resource transformation process, and should be just as eligible for the improvements in efficiency that have accrued elsewhere from technological substitution."[22]

The natural legacy of viewing war as a "resource transformation process" is an overreliance on technology and an underemphasis on the intangibles of leadership and esprit. The consequences of this mentality for the officer corps of the army and its enlisted ranks will be the subject of chapter 5. The next two chapters are devoted to its effects on the machinery the military acquires. They explain, first in general terms and then through two case studies, what happens when the military designs and buys weapons without allowing for the realities and "friction" of war.

THREE

MAGICIANS

The DISTINGUISHING feature of modern American defense has been the pursuit of the magic weapon. In the years since "research and engineering" came to dominate the Pentagon, more and more of the resources available for defense have been invested in the search for weapons that will make victory automatic, that will give ten men the power of ten thousand. American troops are said to be outnumbered; therefore, only technology will save them. Extreme battle scenarios are conceived, for which only an all-capable plane or tank will do. The pursuit of more exacting technical specifications takes on a life of its own. Aircraft engines are designed, at ever steeper costs, to withstand higher temperatures and internal pressures. Tanks and ships must carry more and more complex computer systems, whether or not there is reason to think that the computers will help on the battlefield, and often when there is reason to think they will hurt. The outlook is like that of a hi-fi aficionado who is attracted by the ultrahigh frequency capabilities he reads about in his brochure and pretends that he can hear. In the case of the aficionado or of the defense planner, the manufacturer is only too happy to give him reasons to buy.

The effect of this pursuit has been a lineage of weapons in which each generation of plane, tank, missile, ship, costs between two and five times as much in constant dollars as the previous one. The process, if unchanged, will render much of the debate about defense spending moot. It makes little difference whether the defense budget rises by 1 percent each year or 10 if the cost of weapons doubles every few years. No amount of spending can keep up with the rise in costs. This makes another discussion far more urgent: whether these weapons will survive in combat, and whether their cost will leave any residue for such vital work as training troops. The outlines of this pattern are suggested by the story of Tac Air.

The Air Force's Tactical Air squadrons comprise those planes not designed for strategic nuclear assault on the Soviet Union. They include fighter planes, attack or bombing planes, radar planes, reconnaissance planes, radar early-warning planes, and electronic countermeasures planes. Their purpose is to provide "air superiority"—denying the enemy's aircraft the ability to operate in his homeland or over the battlefield; "close air support" of ground combat operations; and "deep interdiction," or bombing well behind enemy lines.

The forces of Tac Air represent a substantial, and growing, part of the resources we invest in defense. During the late seventies, the United States has devoted as much as one quarter of its total defense budget to Tac Air.[1] Compared to the early sixties, the Air Force now spends less for the Strategic Air Command (mainly nuclear bombers) and the Air Defense Command (to defend against Soviet bombers) than it used to, and much more for Tac Air. In the early sixties, about 20 percent of the total Air Force budget was devoted to Tac Air; it takes 40 percent now. Over those same years, the Tac Air share of the Air Force's investment budget—the money for new equipment—roughly tripled, from 21 percent to 62 percent.[2]

Tac Air's era of expansion is probably at an end. In the next few years the competition from other, very costly programs—particularly strategic missiles and a field called "C³I" (which will come up again later in this chapter)—will be intense. If the MX missile is built, it could cost the Air Force more than $10 billion each year through the middle eighties.[3] The Navy wants to build more ships. There is pressure for a general pay increase for soldiers. There will be pressure for even further expansion of strategic nuclear systems: submarines, cruise missiles, new bombers, elaborations of the MX.

In short, if there ever could be a test of the principle that more money, by itself, will ensure better defense, it would be found in the last fifteen years' history of Tac Air. And yet, as the Pentagon employee Chuck Spinney has demonstrated in an extraordinary study, which has built on earlier work by a predecessor of Spinney's in the Pentagon named Pierre Sprey, more money has not necessarily made Tac Air any better prepared for battle—and quite possibly, the reverse.

With very few exceptions, the riches devoted to Tac Air have been used to finance a progression toward ever more technically complex aircraft and weapons. The aircraft engines have been pushed toward the extremes of high internal pressure and temperature, which requires many more compressor stages, and more exotic materials to withstand the tremendous heat and stress. Aluminum will not do for the airframe of a plane designed to travel, however briefly, at two and a half times the speed of sound. It must be strengthened by such expensive materials as titanium, stainless steel, and beryllium. The fighter planes have acquired more complex "avionics" systems, consisting of large radars to detect enemy planes and a variety of computerized "fire control" systems meant to launch guided missiles to their targets. Extremely "capable" planes—such as the F-14, known as the Tomcat, which is built by Grumman and based on aircraft carriers, and the F-15 Eagle, built by McDonnell Douglas for the Air Force—are "all-weather" fighters, theoretically able to locate and destroy targets at night, or in fog or rain. The missiles they carry, with names like Phoenix and Sparrow, are supposed to be able to home automatically on targets well beyond the range of the pilot's sight, and to destroy them without fail.

With each of these developments, the cost of the planes has also gone up. In 1980 dollars, the F-14 costs somewhere between $26 million and $35 million apiece, depending on the accounting system you use.* The F-15 costs between $15 million and $25 million, compared to about $6.5 million for an simpler attack plane known as the A-10 and about $4 million for a simple fighter, the F-5. In the twenty-five years after the end of World War II, the cost of first-line American fighter planes rose by a factor of 100, in constant dollars.[4] (Over the same period, the cost of a tank went up by a factor of about 10 in constant dollars, while the defense budget has remained roughly the same in real terms since the Korean War.[5])

The driving force behind these cost increases has been the pursuit

---

*The sizable difference between these figures depends on whether you take the "program cost" for the airplane—the total cost of the program divided by the number of planes actually built (which gives high figures); or the marginal cost of building the next plane off the assembly line (which is low); or some hypothetical cost for a standard "buy" of 1,000 or 1,500 airplanes (which is often lowest of all). In discussions of defense, there is no equivalent to the Securities and Exchange Commission to prohibit such accounting games. The gap between the figures shows how difficult it can be to develop realistic projections for the costs of complex weapons. It also suggests how dramatically unit cost estimates can change if, as will be explained later in the chapter, the military is not able to buy as many of the planes as it originally planned.

of technical complexity. During the quarter century after World War II, the cost per fighter for avionics rose from about $3,000 to roughly $2.5 million, and the cost of the engines from about $40,000 to about $2 million.[6] During the seventies the cost of civilian electronics—calculators, radios—dropped through the floor as manufacturers took advantage of solid-state technology to reduce the complexity, size, and cost of their equipment while increasing its reliability and usefulness. In those same years, military avionics rose sharply in both complexity and cost. The difference is that the civilian market, unlike military contracts, did not support products that became more and more costly, and less and less reliable.

The most immediate effect of rising cost and complexity has been on the numbers of planes in the force. No conceivable amount of funding, not even the comparative riches of Tac Air, could keep up with unit-cost increases of 30 or 40 percent every year, so the number of planes in the inventory has gone down. In 1944, at the peak of wartime production, the United States turned out 100,000 airplanes (not all of them fighters). In the mid-fifties the military purchased 3,000 fighters (including planes for air defense) a year. The typical yearly rate in the late seventies was about 400[7] and dropped to fewer than 250 in the 1982 budget. Since the mid-fifties the total American inventory of fighter planes has fallen from 18,000 to 7,000. Norman Augustine, a vice president of Martin Marietta Aerospace, says: "From the days of the Wright brothers through the F-18 [a current Navy fighter], aircraft costs have been increasing by a factor of four every ten years." If the trend continues, he says, "in the year 2054, the entire defense budget will purchase just one tactical aircraft. This aircraft will have to be shared between the Air Force and Navy, three and a half days each per week."[8]

This decline in numbers is only the first step. The second is that, with a smaller base of planes, each individual plane has been used less often than its simpler, cheaper alternatives. Instead of fewer planes doing more, fewer planes can each do less. In the modern Air Force the "sortie rate"—which is the number of flights per plane per day—has also fallen steadily with the progression toward more complicated weapons.

Why? The main reason is that as an airplane or missile becomes more complicated, the probability that *all* its parts will be working at the same time goes down. In simple mathematics, if you are dealing with parts each one of which has a 99 percent reliability rate, a system with just one part will work 99 percent of the time. But as more elements are added to the system, its overall reliability will be .99

multiplied by itself as many times as there are parts. By the time there are 70 elements, the likelihood that the whole system will work is less than 50 percent.

This model does not perfectly predict the performance of a modern jet plane, but it suggests some of the problems that arise with aircraft that have as many as 45,000 component parts. In specific, consider just one small part of the airplane's equipment, which Spinney analyzes in his brief: the "fuel controls" (essentially, the carburetors) used in two different jet engines.

One is the control for the mid-fifties vintage J-79 engine, which is used in the F-4 Phantom jet; the other, for the mid-seventies F-100 engine, which is used in the F-15 and F-16 planes. The F-100 is an engine built to operate at higher temperatures and pressures; those requirements, and several others, make its fuel control much more complex. The F-100's fuel-control system has about 4,500 parts, versus about 1,000 for the other system. The result? The "mean time between depot repairs"—that is, how long the engine goes between breakdowns that can't be handled right on the air base—is 386 hours for the more complicated engine, versus 3,049 for the simpler one. Man-hours per repair are 328 for the F-100, and 47.8 for the J-79. That is, the more complex fuel control breaks down eight times as often as the simpler one, and takes six times as long to fix when it does. The price for higher complexity is equipment that is less often on line.

What is true of fuel controls is true, on a larger and more disturbing scale, of the planes themselves. The clearest official acknowledgment of the problem came early in 1980, in the "Consolidated Guidance" that Harold Brown, then Secretary of Defense, issued to the Air Force, Navy, and Marine Corps as they prepared their Tac Air requests for the 1981 budget. This document, which was based on Spinney's analysis, was not meant to be made public, but it was leaked, like so much else, to *Armed Forces Journal.* Its most striking element was a chart (see page 41) comparing the "readiness" rates for different planes with their levels of complexity.

The costs of buying and operating our tactical air forces are taking an increasing share of the defense budget [Brown said in the "Consolidated Guidance"]. Their increasing complexity is a significant factor not only in this growth, but also in an increasing difficulty in maintaining the combat readiness of our aircrews and their equipment. These trends, if continued, could jeopardize our ability to maintain a force that is large enough, that is modern enough, and that is ready enough to carry out our war plans.[9]

The implications of more and more complex weaponry lead in directions that may not immediately be apparent. On any list of factors that have proven decisive in air combat, the skills and tactics of a cadre of experienced pilots always come at the top. This was one of the advantages the Germans possessed in the early days of the Battle of Britain: their pilots had trained in realistic, "swarm"-type encounters, in which many planes tangled with many others all at once. The British had instead emphasized precision flying and one-on-one encounters in their pre-war training, which left them better prepared for Air Show exhibitions than for combat. Bitter British pilots have recalled that the RAF only came into its own when flight leaders trained in the pre-war formations had been killed and replaced by those who had been taught in battle.[10]

In the modern American Air Force, the main barrier to the formation of a cadre of experienced pilots is that so many of them quit. Fighter pilots are the very model of people who do a job because they like to do it. The pay, the recognition, are important, but not as much as flying the planes. Those accustomed to a civil service view of life think that because the pilots leave a military job paying less for a commercial airline job that pays more, they must be going because of the pay. In fact, pay becomes more and more important when the pilots grow less and less satisfied with the other rewards of their jobs. In 1980 the American Psychological Association released the results of a study of pilots that asked what they did and did not like about their job. After interviews with 3,300 Air Force pilots and 2,250 from the commercial airlines, the researchers determined that by far the most important reason pilots left the Air Force was that they didn't get enough chance to fly and to keep flying jobs.[11] They joined the Air Force in the first place because they liked to fly, and left when they couldn't. The first to leave under the conditions are the enthusiastic pilots the Air Force needs most—particularly in combat.* According to Chuck Spinney's analysis, the average pilot's flying time has dropped by more than one third in the last ten years, from twenty-six hours per month to sixteen. Spinney points out that in 1978, pilots were asked how many hours of

---

*In a number of recent air-combat exercises, pilots from the Air National Guard have regularly outflown pilots from the active-duty Air Force, even though the National Guard flies older and less souped-up planes. The apparent explanation is that they are experienced pilots who have left the Air Force and then joined the guard for one reason only, which is that they love to fly and get more opportunity to do so. Also, they are not diverted from that function by the weapons-buying business that has become so central an aspect of regular military life.

CHART I

Aircraft Model	Complex. Level	NMC%	MFBHF	Maint/ Sortie	MMH/ Sortie	Cann/100 Sorties	Work-load
(Air Force:)							
A-10	Low	32.6%	1.2	1.6	18.4	16.7	20.9
A-7D	Med.	38.6	0.9	1.9	23.8	9.3	20.3
F-4E	Med.	34.1	0.4	3.6	38.0	13.3	28.7
F-15	High	44.3	0.5	2.8	33.6	29.3	23.5
F-111F	High	36.9	0.3	9.2	74.7	44.9	26.5
F-111D	High	65.9	0.2	10.2	98.4	58.5	30.5
(Navy and Marine Corps:)							
A-4M	Low	27.7	0.7	2.4	28.5	12.0	41.0
AV-A8	Low(?)	39.7	0.4	3.0	43.5	13.4	51.8
A-7E	Med.	36.7	0.4	3.7	53.0	27.1	60.6
F-4J	Med.	34.2	0.3	5.9	82.7	22.2	77.4
A-6E	High	39.3	0.3	4.8	71.3	39.4	67.9
F-14A	High	47.1	0.3	6.0	97.8	69.6	74.5

The first column on the left names the airplanes; the second describes their comparative level of complexity. There is a question mark after the AV-A8, known as the "Harrier," because it is part of a class of "very short take-off and landing" planes that are inherently more complex than normal planes.

The next three columns describe the reliability of the different models of plane. The column headed "NMC" describes what percentage of the planes are "not mission capable" at any given moment—that is, not fully ready for combat because of repairs, parts shortages, etc. "MFHBF" stands for "mean flight hours between failure," or how often breakdowns of one sort or another occur. The "Maint/Sortie" column lists how many "maintenance events," or repairs, are necessary each time the plane flies.

The last three columns describe the maintainability of the plane—the resources that must be invested in keeping it flying. "MMH/Sortie" means "maintenance man-hours per sortie"—how much maintenance work must be done per flight. "Cann/100 Sorties" refers to the "cannibalization" rate—how often maintenance crews must take parts from one plane to repair another. For the Air Force planes, this column includes dipping into the "war reserve" of spare parts that are supposed to be set aside for combat. "Workload" combines a number of figures (how often each plane flies per month, how much maintenance work it requires per flight, how many planes each repairman must handle) to determine the monthly load of maintenance hours per worker.

The Air Force keeps its records by slightly different rules from those the Navy and Marine Corps use, so planes from one service should not be compared with planes from the other. But the pattern within each service is clear. The more complex the plane, the less often it can fly, and the more time it takes to repair breakdowns when they occur.

---

flying per month it took to be adequately ready. More than two thirds felt that the amount they were getting, sixteen hours, was not enough.

Training realism is related to complexity and to the higher costs that complexity induces [Brown said in the "Consolidated Guidance"]. The greater the technological complexity, the less the realism. For example, because of prohibitive costs, we have never conducted realistic operational training with the F-14 firing Phoenix missiles in the presence of jamming and tactical countermeasures. [Brown was saying that the biggest question about sophisticated, precision-guided weapons—whether they can overcome the efforts any competent adversary would make to thwart them, by jamming or deception or anything else—has never been answered in realistic practice.] Nor have we ever demonstrated that we can load and launch the large number of Phoenix missiles against multiple targets that would be required to defend against a determined . . . attack. Safety considerations preclude training with the complex F-111 in Central Europe in the bad weather for which it was specifically designed; the crews have to deploy to the Mediterranean, where they simulate all-weather operations in clear weather. Although 1400–1500 Air Force aircraft are tasked to fire them in combat, Maverick missiles are so expensive that we fire only about 200 per year in training. On the other hand, training realism for the less complex A-10 is much higher: pilots are practicing low level tactics and are actually firing live ammunition.[12]

Bear in mind that Brown is describing the most richly funded part of the American military establishment through the last generation.

To carry the situation just one step further, the combination of high price and low reliability not only inhibits training and reduces the number of airplanes in the inventory but also makes a far more dramatic reduction in what fighter pilots call "presence in the sky." A retired Air Force colonel named Everest Riccioni, who now works for Northrop, has written about the difference between the "real fleet" and the "phantom fleet." The real fleet is the one that can be put in the air at any given moment, and the phantom fleet is composed of all the planes that are confined to the runway, for reasons of repair, unreliability, lack of crews. "The enemy doesn't give a damn about the phantom fleet," he says. "The only force that matters to him is the one in the air."[13]

The connection between cost, complexity, and the growth of the "phantom fleet" comes out in a comparison that Riccioni has developed for three representative planes. The first of them is the F-5, one of the simpler aircraft now in the American inventory; the second, the F-4 Phantom, a very large fighter of medium-level complexity; and the third, the even larger and more complex F-15. (It should be noted that Riccioni now works for Northrop, which builds the simplest plane on this chart, the F-5. But he had been advancing his argument about simpler planes within the Air Force for years before he went to work for Northrop.)

The first difference is cost. By Riccioni's estimates, the F-15 costs about four times as much as the F-5 and twice as much as the F-4, so for the same amount of money, you will end up with a force this size:

Model:	F-5	F-4	F-15
Planes:	1,000	500	250

These figures include the "phantom force." To find the real force, we must multiply the number of planes by the "sortie rates." The rates are roughly as follows:

Model:	F-5	F-4	F-15
Sorties/day:	2.5	1.5	1

The product is a "real force" of:

Model:	F-5	F-4	F-15
Planes in the air/day	2,500	750	250

From patterns like these, Riccioni developed a set of "Laws of Recondite Economics." One of them is: "The number of weapons systems that can be employed in battle varies inversely as the *square* of the level of sophistication."

"The typical contractor's question is, 'Would you rather go to war in an Eagle [the F-15] or a F-5?,' " says an aircraft designer. "The more realistic question would be, 'Consider a confrontation between one F-15 and six MiG-21s. Would you rather be the pilot of the F-15 or one of the six MiG pilots?' "

To carry the logic yet another step, consider how well these new, more complex airplanes are adapted to the likely circumstances of combat. Each F-15 contains forty-five "black boxes"—computer systems that run the avionics and other functions of the plane. The pilot has indicators that let him know when one of the boxes is malfunctioning. When that happens, the offending box is removed *in toto* and a new box is snapped in. Then, in the service bays, the box is tested with another computer system known as the Avionics Intermediate Shop, or AIS. As anyone who has worked on computers knows, tracking down a defect can be a maddening and lengthy process. In theory, the AIS tells which computer card has gone wrong and needs to be replaced. In practice, it has problems of its own. In 1979, according to Spinney, the testing system worked only 50 percent of the time; the following year, it improved to 80 percent. Moreover, even when the AIS computers are working, about one quarter of the time they yield "Cannot Duplicate" signals—that is, they can't find anything wrong with the box that was pulled from the plane. Those boxes are generally put back on the shelf, to see if they can fit into a different plane without tripping the malfunction signal.

The typical "wing" of 72 F-15s has three AIS systems, which divide up the forty-five black boxes on each plane. The computers can only check one box at a time, which takes an average of three hours and can run as long as eight. To be able to support 72 planes, with a total of more than three thousand boxes, requires a smoothness of scheduling that is difficult to sustain even when there are no bombs falling on the hangars. As a result, the Air Force has started talking about "computer supportability" as a big problem in its own right. Since no one air base could possibly afford to stock the thousands of costly spare parts that might be needed to repair the black boxes and the AIS itself, there are now proposals for two centralized computer depots, one on each coast, to take care of the airplanes. In time of need, such as wartime, a special transportation system, dedicated to this purpose alone, would ferry the computers from one air base to another. "One thing you do not have in combat is a dedicated transport system," Spinney says.

There is a similar pattern in repair of the sophisticated engines for the F-15. They are designed to make it easier for crews to pull them out and ship them to the depot than to repair them on the flight line. "It is so easy to pull an engine that they get rid of it if there's a gurgle," says an aircraft analyst. There are peacetime regulations to control the pulling of engines, but these rules would almost certainly be ignored in time of war. That would merely move the bottleneck from the flight line to the depot. The analyst says, "To generate sorties, you end up swamping the engine shop. It takes half an hour to pull the engines, but four or five hours in the shop to check it out, even if nothing is wrong. The whole system depends on a smooth flow, and if that's disturbed, as it would be in war, it completely falls apart." The wartime experience of the F-4 jet suggests the dimensions of the problem. The F-4 is a less complex plane, and the intensity of air combat in Vietnam was far lower than the projections of all-out air war in Europe that were used to justify the F-15. Even so, during the Vietnam war there was a two-year backlog for repair of battle-damaged F-4s at the depot in Utah.

IN THE FALL of 1980 the public relations director for McDonnell Douglas, John J. McGrath, wrote a letter of complaint to the editor of *Newsweek* magazine. He took exception to a report that questioned the effectiveness of the F-15, which McDonnell Douglas produces. Specifically, he objected to the (accurate) statement that in Air Force tests, three F-5 airplanes had shown that they could shoot down one

F-15. "In combat exercises against many types of aircraft (all having combat ability equal to or greater than a F-5), the F-15 exchange ratio was 88 to 1," McGrath said.[14]

This is, of course, the case for high technology. If those new planes really are 88 times better, then who cares if you can put only one tenth as many of them in the sky as you could, for the same money, simpler planes? But there is another way to look at the question of "exchange ratios" and comparative "capabilities," which is to ask just what the achievements in complexity and electronics add up to in combat.

As for a plane's top speed, obtained at such cost in high-pressure engines, rare materials, and mechanisms always in need of fine tuning, the fact is that pilots hardly ever use it in combat. The pilot's saying is that an airplane will reach Mach 2 just in time to run out of fuel. Fuel consumption rises sharply as a plane approaches Mach 1, the speed of sound (738 mph at sea level). When the pilot turns on the afterburners to maximize thrust and reach supersonic speeds, fuel consumption rises even more. As Everest Riccioni explained in a paper in 1978:

> Despite more than 100,000 sorties flown by Mach 2 capable aircraft over the skies of Vietnam—
> Not one second of flight combat time at Mach 2.2 speed (or above) was recorded.
> Not one second of flight combat time at Mach 2.0 speed (or above) was recorded.
> Not one second of flight combat time at Mach 1.8 speed (or above) was recorded.
> Almost no time at 1.6 Mach (or above) was recorded. (Seconds)
> Extremely little flight time at 1.4 Mach (or above) was recorded. (Minutes)
> Remarkably little time at 1.2 Mach (or above) was flown. (Hours)
> The vast majority of military operations and all heavy combat maneuvering was done in the domain of speeds below 1.2 Mach . . .[15]

"Even the time at 1.6 proves my point," Riccioni said later. "They became prisoners, pilots who ran out of fuel." He mentioned, as an example, that three American F-4 fighters, carrying a total of six men, ran out of fuel while chasing MiGs at Mach 1 6 into North Vietnam. The pilots were captured after they bailed out and became prisoners of war at the "Hanoi Hilton."

As for the complex avionics systems, they have two drawbacks. One (which is discussed in more detail in the next chapter) is that they vitiate the most important single factor in aerial combat: the ability to take another plane by surprise. Surprise has accounted for more "kills" in aerial warfare than all other advantages combined, but a plane with a powerful radar gives away that edge. For the same reason that automobiles equipped with a "fuzz-buster" can tell when police are running a radar speed check, pilots with passive radar warning systems are instantly aware when another plane has turned on its radar to look for them. In the words of one analyst, radar amounts to a "beacon in the sky," alerting all to a plane's presence. The laws of physics add an extra twist. A plane with a radar warning receiver will be aware that another plane is beaming radar at it long before that other plane comes close enough to see the first plane on the radar screen. In computer simulations or practice dogfights, this may not matter; no one's going to be surprised in a test, anyway. In real combat it has been the dominating force. Everest Riccioni recalls the metaphor that Charles Myers, a former official of the Pentagon's Research and Engineering division, used: "Imagine yourself holding a gun and a flashlight in a pitch-dark room, with a lot of other guys with flashlights and guns. Who's going to turn on his flashlight first? Well, radar is that flashlight."

The real world degrades the advantages of high technology in yet another way, because of what is known as the "IFF Problem." IFF stands for "identification friend or foe" and refers to the difficulty a pilot has telling whom he is shooting at. Modern radar and avionics systems are advertised as giving planes an "all-weather" and "beyond visual range" capability, which should enable the pilot to detect other planes in the dark, through clouds and rain, and from much farther away than he could see with the naked eye. But until the pilot can *see* the other plane, he normally cannot be sure which side it's on. In one-on-one mock battles, a pilot has no doubt about who the blip on the screen is, and can lock missiles on him as soon as he shows up. In real combat there are likely to be dozens of planes coming from unpredictable directions, which prevents him from firing at any of them until he is sure which plane is which. In almost every case, the pilot is only sure when he sees the other plane. Through the history of aerial combat, including the night combat of World War II and engagements involving radar-guided missiles over Israel and Vietnam, the vast majority of pilots who have scored "kills" have first identified, with their own eyes, the planes they hit. A pilot can see out of a simple plane at least as well as from a complex, expensive one with its batteries of radar.

These principles were demonstrated in a series of tests called AIM-VAL/ACEVAL, held in 1976 and 1977 over the desert at Nellis Air Force Base in Nevada. In these tests, when a more "capable" plane like the F-15 was matched one-on-one against a simpler plane, the F-15 almost always won. But when the match-ups were four-on-four, the differences between the planes essentially washed out. With eight planes in the sky, things moved too quickly and chaotically for the avionics to be of much use. When surrounded by enemies, a pilot who took eight or ten seconds to get a computer "lock" on another plane to target his missile gave other pilots an opportunity to lock on to him. McDonnell Douglas spokesmen contend that the tests were not "fair" to their F-15, since pilots were required to identify enemy planes visually before firing, instead of going after the first blip on the radar screen. In that limitation, however, the tests resembled the likely circumstances of combat. Moreover, the tests showed that the "capability" of a weapon and its "probability of kill" are not firm, technically determined values, but depend very heavily on the circumstances in which they are used. After the tests, two Air Force officers summarized the evidence:

There was not a single ACEVAL 4-versus-4 trial in which the Blue [F-15] side managed to target a missile against all four Red machines at the outset of the fight. This outcome is rather sobering given the high costs of F-15/F-14 avionics, together with the fact that air combat in a future war in Central Europe is likely to be more on the order of 50-versus-20.[16]

There is a final exemplary lesson to be drawn from Tac Air. The real message of Chuck Spinney's analysis, which is one of the most significant documents in modern American defense, is that unrealistic military planning, which chronically pays too little attention to the economic and military effects of complexity, constitutes a "form of organizational cancer." The pattern, in essence, involves four steps:

First, the planners are eternally optimistic about the amounts of money they will be able to spend to buy new equipment. The history of military budgets is a series of zigs and zags around an essentially constant level; yet year after year the long-range spending plan predicts a smooth, steady increase in funding for the five years that are about to begin. These predictions, in turn, shape decisions about the kinds of weapons to buy. That is, the military might decide to build a new, complex fighter plane in the belief that it can purchase 1,500 of them, even though it would never choose that plane if it knew in advance that it would be able to afford only 500. Although the clearest lesson of the past is the unpredictability of military budgets, the plans are premised on a certain and predictable future.

Second, in their desire to buy more equipment for the force, the

planners forget or fool themselves about how much money they need
to set aside for "operations and maintenance" (known as O&M) of new
equipment, especially the more complex varieties. For example, Spinney points out that in 1968, Secretary of the Air Force Harold Brown
endorsed a new avionics system for the F-111D, saying that despite its
complexity, it would be extremely reliable. He predicted that the system would go 60 hours between breakdowns (technically, "mean time
between failure"), and that it would require less than 1.5 man-hours of
maintenance per sortie. In 1980 the system went about 3 hours between breakdowns and averaged 33.6 maintenance man-hours per
sortie. That is, it required about twenty times as much maintenance
as predicted on both counts. Such unpleasant surprises are most frequent in the most complex systems because they break down more
often, their parts are more numerous and expensive, and—more than
a trivial factor—it is so hard to train people to repair them and keep
the repair specialists in the force. By the time they have mastered the
technical skills needed to work on complex equipment, these people
can make two to three times as much money in the civilian world. In
the last quarter of 1980, thirty-three specialists in the AIS computer
system for the F-15 came up for re-enlistment. Not one of them chose
to stay. The result of similar patterns throughout the military is that,
when the complex new systems actually go into operation, the Pentagon discovers that it has seriously underestimated the money it needs
for operations and maintenance.

Third, as a natural consequence of the second step, the military has
to make unexpected cuts in its "investment" budgets—the money it
has set aside for new equipment—in order to make up the cost of
maintenance and the overruns on previous programs. No matter what
the weapons system, whether ships, planes, helicopters, or missiles, the
military ends up buying a smaller number than it originally projected
simply because it doesn't have the money to buy more. This means,
among other things, that the cost for each plane or ship is much higher
than expected, since the overhead is spread over a smaller force.

Fourth, when certain parts of the military do enjoy momentary
prosperity, they tend to use the money not to bail out the projects they
have already started, but to get yet another complex system, with yet
another inadequate maintenance budget, under way. This, of course,
is much of the story of Tac Air.

"In a general sense, this pattern reflects a tendency to reduce our
current readiness to fight in order to modernize for the future," Spinney says in his presentation. "However, because of rising operating
costs, the price of even *low* [emphasis in original] readiness is rising

inexorably over the long term. . . . This pattern of behavior can be expected to continue as long as costs, particularly operating costs, grow faster than the budget."*

The Pentagon's "Five Year Defense Plan," which projected spending from 1980 to 1985, demonstrated exactly the self-delusion Spinney described. The Air Force projected a 5 percent increase for its total budget in those years—but the increase was distributed as 10 percent for investment and only a 2 percent increase in O&M. The Navy projected a 4 percent overall increase—but a 7 percent increase for investment and a 1 percent increase for O&M. For the Army, the figures were a 3 percent overall increase, 5 percent increase for investment, and 1 percent increase in O&M. Eventually the services will be forced to put the money back into O&M. It would be far better, Spinney says, to recognize that fact from the beginning, and choose weapons accordingly.

RISING COSTS

THE SHADOW cast by Tac Air falls over much of the rest of the Pentagon. In nearly every weapons system, designers have pushed technology as the solution to American military problems, without distinguishing between the innovations that simply breed extra layers of complexity and those, like Guderian's radios, that represent dramatic steps toward simplicity, flexibility, and effectiveness. As a result, the cost of military equipment keeps going up, the number of units in the inventory goes down, and their reliability becomes open to serious question.

The Army's latest tank, the XM-1, costs at least seven times as much as the Sherman tank of World War II. (All comparisons in this section are in constant dollars, adjusted to remove the effects of inflation.) The Main Battle Tank—a proposal from the early seventies that was junked because of technical problems and resistance from the Congress—would have cost ten times more than the Sherman. Modern aircraft carriers, with their nuclear propulsion, cost four to five times as much as those built at the end of World War II. The first guided missile used for aerial dogfights, and still the most reliable, is the heat-seeking

---

*It is impossible to do full justice to Spinney's analysis here. At the urging of Senator Sam Nunn of Georgia, the Pentagon released the study early in 1981. It is available from the Public Affairs office of the Defense Department (Washington, D.C. 20301), under the title "Defense Facts of Life," by Franklin C. Spinney, December 5, 1980.

Sidewinder, which originally cost about $3,000 apiece, or about $10,-
000 in today's dollars.[17] Its less reliable radar-guided competitors, the
Sparrow and Phoenix, cost ten and one hundred times as much, respectively.[18] (The latest model of the Phoenix goes for more than $1
million.) The nuclear-powered attack submarines, whose creation Admiral Hyman Rickover has overseen, are different from other complex
weapons in that they work. But at roughly $300 million apiece, the
Navy can buy only one-fourth as many of them, for the same money,
as of diesel-electric subs. As one study after another has pointed out,
these increases have come in precisely the areas, especially electronics,
in which the cost of civilian products has plummeted.*

---

*Jacques Gansler, a former Deputy Assistant Secretary of Defense, compared civilian
and military equipment on a case-by-case basis and found that a military videotape
recorder cost three times as much as a commercial model, a military diesel generator
four times as much, a military shipboard tape recorder forty-seven times as much as
the equivalent civilian model.[19] The difference was largely due to the more elaborate
specifications for military models, such as those illustrated in the story of the Air Force
flashlight, below. "In 1973, the Army tried buying commercial vehicles in a program
called 'Project Wheels,'" Gansler says in his book, The Defense Industry. "It found
acceptable performance in vehicles that cost $3,000 to $4,000 each, versus military-
unique vehicles that cost $8,000 to $18,000 each. In addition, the military-unique
vehicles had R&D costs, and the commercial vehicles came with a one-year war-
ranty."[20] According to a study at the end of 1971, the average commercial airline radar
had a "mean time between failure" of 800 hours, compared to 5 to 10 hours for military
radars.[21]

A retired Air Force colonel tells what happened when the Air Force decided to build
its own flashlights: "During the time when Curtis LeMay was the Air Force chief,
there was a big movement to develop the Air Force flashlight. Flashlights never work,
so they decided to develop their own. It's nice to have one to read maps in the cockpit,
to count the turbine blades before you take off at night, things like that. Well, people
started thinking about all the extra things it should do. Somebody said, wouldn't it be
great if it were a *signal* flashlight, so you could use it to send messages in code. And
if it had a red light along with the white, so you could read maps at night and protect
your night vision. And there were the usual military specs about performing after two
weeks on the North Pole, or in the Sahara. Finally it became the Tri-Command
Flashlight: the Strategic Air Command, the Tactical Air Command, and the Air
Defense Command all added their requirements. By that time, the thing was so huge
that you couldn't fit it in your flight suit—hell, if you had to bail out, you'd never take
it with you, so what was the point of all the signal flashing or the heat and cold
requirements?

"The Air Force turned out about 100 of the things and left them around Andrews
Air Force Base for pilots to try out. General LeMay came out one time, saw one of
them all wrapped up, and asked what it was. 'That's the new Air Force Flashlight,

To measure against another standard, in 1976 a U.S. government report contrasted an American military jet engine with a Soviet engine built to do the same job. The report said that the Soviet model would be inherently less costly, by between 50 and 67 percent, even if it had been built by workers paid the American wage and made of materials purchased at American prices, because of differences in its design and technical specifications.[23] The Soviet Union has built cruder, cheaper tanks than the United States. But after inspecting a captured one, the late General Creighton Abrams told Elmo Zumwalt, "I got in the goddamn tank, and it didn't have all the fancy things the colonels want in our tanks, you couldn't push a joystick and make the thing turn around, but it could do every damn thing you want a tank to do."[24] The XM-1, by contrast, was designed to be the world's most "advanced" tank. Everything about it, from its night vision and fire-control systems to its mechanism for stabilizing the tank, was the most complex ever included in a production-model vehicle. Its engine was a gas turbine, similar to those usually found on aircraft. But turbine engines cannot tolerate dust, and since the day the first prototype was built the manufacturers have been fiddling with one heavy, bulky air filter after another, trying to convert the XM-1 into something that could survive on a dusty, dirty battlefield. When the Sheridan tank—which, remember, was simpler than the XM-1—was introduced to Vietnam, "the performance marks were not high. . . . It had to do with the highly sophisticated mechanisms. The first official report lists 16 major equipment failures, 123 circuit failures, 41 weapons misfires, 140 ammunition ruptures, 25 engine replacements, and persistent failure of the 152 mm main gun."[25] Many soldiers considered the Sheridan a death trap. Among other things, it employed "caseless ammunition," which sprinkled flammable material onto the floor of the tank and endangered the lives of any crew called upon to operate the tank in combat.

As was the case in Tac Air, the progression toward higher and higher costs degrades real military readiness in two ways. The first is simply that it diverts resources. When so much money goes for computers and complex engines, there is less for training sessions, extra rounds of ammunition, realistic preparation for combat. The pattern is most

General!' the supply officer said. He asked LeMay if he wanted to take one on his flight, and LeMay said sure. So they peeled the airtight wrapping off one of them, got out a new battery—and it just wouldn't work. The lights wouldn't even turn on. They opened up a second one, with a second battery, and it wouldn't work either. Finally they got the third one to work, but that was the end of the Air Force Flashlight. Most pilots use the $1.50 Japanese plug-in model now."[22]

clearly demonstrated by the "Command-Control-Communications-Intelligence" networks in which the military now invests so much effort and money. The "cee-cubed-eye" systems, as they are known (in written form, it is "C³I"), are radio and computer hookups designed to carry out the dream of controlling military maneuvers from one central point. To that end, the military has invested somewhere between $10 billion and $15 billion in the Worldwide Military Command and Control System (or WWMCCS, pronounced "wimmex"). Another network, called the Joint Tactical Information Distribution System, or JTIDS, is designed to feed information from one computer to another on the battlefield. From a technical standpoint, even the partisans of C³I will admit that, yes, there are still a few bugs in the system. Once or twice a month, the newspapers carry a story about the WWMCCS computers breaking down. When the system was thoroughly tested in 1977, attempts to send messages ended in "abnormal terminations"—that is, breakdowns—62 percent of the time. One part of the network, the Readiness Command, broke down 85 percent of the time. But even if the systems did work, in time of crisis they would be of dubious value. One study of the NATO central command bunker in Europe pointed out that to keep up with the flow of information and orders coming in over its communications system, the commanders would have to keep reading 790 words a minute, around the clock. The accompanying diagrams of the JTIDS system and another C³I network give a sense of where the problems might arise. (The JTIDS diagram comes from a contractor's presentation; the other chart is from the Defense Department.) As chapter 5 will discuss, the wild expansion of C³I also undermines the very qualities of leadership and initiative that are essential to success on the battlefield, since officers must operate in time of crisis with a commander looking over their shoulder from miles away. Nonetheless, since 1977, there has been an Assistant Secretary of Defense charged with no other responsibility than promoting C³I. He has been so successful that the United States is now spending billions of dollars every year on centralized command networks that are useless when they don't work and may be actively harmful when they do.

In addition to consuming resources, the costly and complicated systems harm military readiness in another way: by making it too expensive, or too impractical, for soldiers to spend much time in realistic training. For example, John Fialka has reported in the Washington *Star* that the Army's gunners who are stationed in the front-line areas of Europe and Korea, where they would presumably be charged with stopping the Soviet tanks with TOW missiles, get to fire at most once a year with a live round. The rounds now cost $6,000 apiece.

CHART II

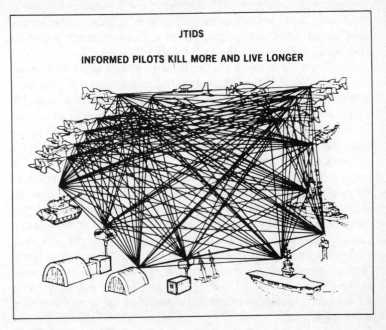

CHART III

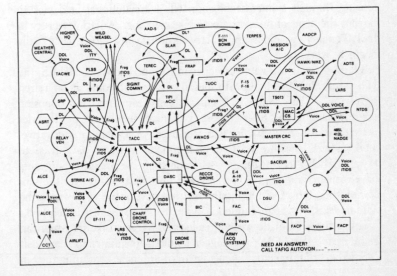

The question must be asked, here as with the complex airplanes: Do the virtues of "advanced" systems offset these drawbacks? In general, the answer is no, because in designing more "capable" weapons and dreaming of the advantages they will bring, planners usually avert their eyes from the "friction" that is the only certainty of war.

The Rapid Deployment Force planned for the Middle East would, as George Wilson of the Washington *Post* has pointed out, most likely encounter its greatest difficulties not from enemy aircraft or tanks, but simply in figuring out how to find enough water to keep its equipment functioning and its men alive for more than about one day.[26] In the Saudi desert, each soldier and his supporting equipment would require about 12 gallons of water per day. A GI canteen holds one quart. The engines of a KC135 tanker plane must be injected with 670 gallons of distilled water each time they are started up. The military planners Wilson interviewed said that it was impossible to carry enough water onto the scene, and difficult to imagine distilling it from seawater on the spot. Wilson recalled a report from one of Rommel's associates, Generalmajor Alfred Toppe, who said that if in World War II the German forces had ever moved away from the coast to "the interior of the desert, water would undoubtedly have been the decisive factor which would have determined the strength of the troops and their radius of action."

And these are merely the vagaries of nature. The real challenge comes from adversaries who can alter their behavior. A colony of bacteria will not change its tactics to avoid detection by a scientist looking through a microscope, nor will a gravitational field plot to disrupt the plans of builders erecting a skyscraper. An army will try to fool its enemy's weapons, and will try hardest against those that actually begin to work.

During recent war-game exercises in Europe known as MILES, the U.S. Army equipped tanks with special sensors that would set off a siren signifying a "kill" when struck by a laser beam from the opposing team's weapon. John Fialka reported: "One of the Army's pet theories is that the American soldier is better because he is more innovative. The soldiers have proved that in Germany. Privates have tried to thwart MILES by smearing Vaseline on their laser sensors. Sergeants have casually draped ponchos, helmets, and plastic bags over the sensors on their tanks."[27] During the first few days of the 1973 war in the Middle East, Egyptian gunners had great success against Israeli tanks by using a Soviet-made weapon called the Sagger. Like its American counterpart, the TOW, the Sagger required its gunner to stand half exposed in order to guide the missile in toward its target during the ten seconds or so of its flight. Soon the Israelis discovered that all they had to do was shoot at the Sagger gunner. Whether they hit him or simply made him duck, they accomplished their purpose, which was to keep him from guiding the missile to the tank.

All "precision-guided" weapons depend on sensors to home on their targets or to direct them to a desired path. All the sensors depend on making mechanistic, yes/no comparisons to distinguish the target from its surroundings. Infrared sensors choose between hot and cold; radar guidance measures the relative strengths and frequencies of waves reflected from the target and the background; some systems use television cameras to search for black/white contrasts in the target images. The sensors will fail if they have to deal with small differences between the target and its background—and such small differences are what soldiers instinctively strive for with camouflage. When the "smart" missiles went to Vietnam, most of them were flops. One of these, the Falcon, had been produced at a cost of $2 billion. On paper, its predicted "probability of kill," or Pk, was 99 percent. In combat, it was effective about 7 percent of the time, only slightly less than another "smart" missile, the Sparrow.[28] Eventually pilots refused to carry the Falcon on their planes.

The most highly touted prospect in the catalogue of high technology is "millimeter wave" radar guidance, a process that will supposedly enable each missile to tell a tank from a car and an artillery piece from a rock, and pick out, with pinpoint precision, the targets it was programmed to destroy. According to optimistic predictions from the Pentagon's Research and Engineering officials, these weapons could be launched, in a swarm, over a battlefield, and then could be relied on to fly around, spot Soviet tanks, and track them down to certain death. "What would I do if I were on the other side, and those things started to work?" asks one Pentagon official skeptical of the approach. "I'd get a bunch of corner reflectors [devices that send back disproportionately strong radar reflections] and put 'em in a lake, or mount them on a bunch of motorcycles going the other way. You'd see the missiles take out after them."

HOW IT HAPPENS

IN THE SUMMER of 1980, *Business Week* carried a major story about the American military. Its title was: "The New Defense Posture: MISSILES, MISSILES, MISSILES."[29] The story concerned new techno-

logical development projects in an increased defense budget. It quoted
at length from Norman Augustine, the man who, earlier in this chapter, was warning about the dramatic rise in the cost of military airplanes. Augustine is a former Assistant Secretary of the Army for
Research and Development who, in an oft-repeated pattern, had left
to become a vice president of Martin Marietta Aerospace, producer of
such Army missiles as the Pershing, Patriot, and Copperhead. Shortly
after the *Business Week* article was published, he became chairman of
the Defense Science Board. One section of the story, which begins with
a discussion of a missile called Maverick, is a fundamental document
for understanding modern defense. Not only does it suggest the effect
on weaponry of the high-technology juggernaut, but it also provides a
window into the mentality of magic weapons that has done so much
to pervert the proper functions of defense:

Maverick went into development 10 years ago as an electro-optically guided
missile that carried a tiny television camera in its nose. The theory was that
its camera would photograph a potential target, and the missile would then
lock on it. But the camera did not work well in clouds or at night. So, three
years ago, the Air Force turned instead to the development of an infrared
guidance system for the Maverick.

The infrared device helped make Maverick an all-weather missile,* but it
also left a lot to be desired. Its sensors spotted targets imprecisely, and its
signal-processing computers were too often uncertain about where to steer it.
Sometimes the hot spots it saw turned out to be flares fired as decoys. Because
it did not see full shapes or images, Mavericks still could not distinguish among
real and spurious targets well enough to make it a truly one-shot
weapon. . . .

But the air to ground Wasp and a new missile called AMRAAM (for
advanced medium-range air-to-air missile), now in development, should be
vastly better systems.

Embodying the latest in miniaturized electronic components, large-scale
integrated circuitry, and minicomputers for signal processing, the new missiles
will pack many thousand times more computing power and sensory capability
than did their predecessors. Such advances in electronics will permit the
missiles to see whole shapes of targets and select the right ones to hit.

"We're beginning to see seekers that make a list for their signal-processing
computers as they fly," says Martin Marietta's Augustine. "They say, 'I see
a tank, a bridge, and an armored personnel carrier.' The computer is programmed to kill tanks, so it chooses tanks as its first-priority target."

---

*Not really—the infrared sensor still does not work in rain, fog, or high humidity.

Augustine predicts that by the end of the decade, the computers in missiles will come very close to comparing with the human brain. "Our missiles," he says, "will be not just smart, but brilliant."[30]

Change a few of the names, and this could have been any account of any exciting new weapon written in the last twenty-five years. The voice of reality is heard in description of such systems in the past. They didn't work quite right; the clouds got in the way; the sensors were fooled by flares. The voice of the huckster is heard in the predictions. Yes, you had problems before, but wait till you see these new, brilliant items.

What makes this passage so valuable is that it illustrates both sources of pressure that carry the military toward more "advanced" and more expensive weaponry. One is the force of seeming logic. In this category are the extreme battle scenarios that call for wonder weapons as the only appropriate response; the technical visions of how easy and automatic warfare might be if new inventions work out; and the argument that American forces are "outnumbered," and therefore must exploit their advantage of high technology. The natural corollary of this reasoning is tolerance for rising cost, and a lack of interest in the seamy business of seeing which weapons actually work. The other major force is that of primitive self-interest. A culture of procurement has been created in the Pentagon, which, as I will argue through the rest of this chapter, draws the military toward new weapons *because* of their great cost, not in spite of it.

THE REALM OF REASON

ON ITS RATIONAL side, this culture reminds doubters that technical changes have repeatedly altered the nature of war. In World War I, the machine gun gave an edge to forces on the defensive; twenty years later, the tank restored the old dominance of maneuver and attack. In 1937 the U.S. government commissioned a study on "Technological Trends and National Policy." Among the developments its experts failed to foresee were the military applications of helicopters, jet engines, radar, computers, nuclear weapons, missiles, satellites, nuclear submarines.[31]

It is also possible to argue, when dealing wholly in thought or on paper, that certain hypothetical situations cry out for special new weapons. What would happen, for example, if several aircraft carriers operating off the coast of Africa were attacked by Soviet "Backfire" bombers firing missiles from a hundred miles away.* (In today's version of the scenario, these would not be planes from the Russian air force itself, since that would suggest a total war in which the carriers would already have been sunk by Soviet submarines. Rather, the Backfires would carry the colors of some small, reckless nation. Years ago, when the scheme was first dreamed up, the idea was that the American carriers would actually be attacking Russia.) The best way to counter the Backfires, the reasoning goes, would be to shoot them down before they had a chance to fire their own "smart" missiles,† and to do that you'd need a plane with a lot of speed, electronics, and guided missiles. Reasoning of more or less this sort lay behind the creation of the Navy's F-14 Tomcat fighter.

Or what would happen if the Soviet Union, in addition to destroying all the nuclear missiles that lay buried in American silos, also figured out how to destroy the submarines and bombers that carry four fifths of the total American nuclear arsenal? What if you want to be sure not only that the different elements of your nuclear system together constitute an invulnerable deterrent but also that each part of it, on its own, could survive any conceivable attack? Reasoning of this sort (which will be explored in chapter 6) leads directly to the MX missile.

---

*"Backfire," of course, is not the Russian name. It is the title NATO assigns to the latest Russian bomber. There are other anglicized names for Russian equipment—for example, the "Foxbat" fighter, the "Oscar" submarine, the "Galosh" missile system, the "Sagger" antitank missiles. The names seem to be catching on. Recently, the *Dial*, the PBS monthly magazine, reported: "Rather than disclose the actual names of their own missiles, Russian military specialists have adopted NATO terminology and use it when speaking to those 'Not entitled to know.' Thus, they write out the NATO-named Backfire bomber as 'Bekfeier.' "

†Consider how this problem might look if you stepped back and applied the reasoning about deception and maneuver that was laid out in the previous chapter. Instead of preparing to slug it out with the Backfires in the sky, American planners might look for the vulnerable point in the Soviet system—primarily the sensors that will guide their missiles to the targets. Those sensors home in on radar reflections. The scenario assumes that the missiles will be launched from so far away that the pilot will not be able to see the ships he is attacking. Suppose the carrier towed a small boat behind it, equipped with a "repeater jammer." This device sends back a very strong radar return, and the guided missiles would have no sure way of distinguishing it from a carrier. If a convoy of ships carried several such decoy boats, it would greatly reduce the odds that the missiles would strike the proper targets. Like other solutions, this one should not be viewed as the only answer, but it suggests the different avenues a more flexible approach opens up.

Instead of hypothesizing threats, such speculation can also run to marvelous wish-book solutions. Wouldn't it be great to have a tank that went from zero to 60 like a hot rod? What if we had a missile with a .99 "probability of kill" or one that would assure American forces a 955-to-1 exchange rate against Soviet airplanes? (The promoters of a recent missile actually made that claim.) What if we could build an electronic "fence" across Vietnam and Laos to keep all the Communists out? Wouldn't it be wonderful if, instead of leaving aerial combat to a group of pilots trying to figure out for themselves which enemy planes to destroy, the whole enterprise could be automatically controlled from the ground? If you had a huge radar and computer complex, it might be able to identify all the "friendly" and "enemy" planes in the sky and rationally distribute assignments for shooting them. Then it could transmit commands to each fighter plane, guiding it precisely to its target. Visions of this sort lay behind a $20 billion radar complex of the sixties known as SAGE—which, after countless revisions, finally foundered due to the technical complexity of devising a computer program that could keep the friendly and enemy planes straight.* Nonetheless, the Air Force and Navy have invested further billions in radar planes known as the AWACS and E-2, which face the far greater technical challenge of doing the same thing from a single plane in the air.

Running through all arguments in favor of high technology is the idea that the United States really has no choice. Since we are a modern nation, "quality," not "quantity," is the obvious way to go. "Given our disadvantage in numbers," Harold Brown said in the "MISSILES, MISSILES, MISSILES" article, "our technology is what will save

---

*The real problem was that since planes in a dogfight fly in unpredictable patterns, when two "blips" from two planes crossed on the radar screen the computer could not be sure which plane was which when they separated again. The civilian air traffic control systems run by the Federal Aviation Administration can keep their planes straight—but that is because commercial planes carry cooperative "transponders," which, when struck by the radar beam, send back a signal that includes data on their identity.

As a child in California, I grew up five miles from SAGE headquarters at Norton Air Force Base. Each year our classes would take school field trips to Norton. The dramatic conclusion came when we were ushered into the SAGE control room. The commanding general would appear at this point and attempt a demonstration of how quickly and reliably his system worked. In every instance I can remember, there was a technical screw-up of some kind, and the general would lead us out, assuring us that, heh heh, this sort of thing did not happen very often.

us."[32] More Americans probably understand this about our armed forces than grasp any other single concept. That is unfortunate because the concept is wrong. It is not "wrong" in the sense that American Seabees should attempt to build airfields with hand tools like the Chinese; but it is wrong in implying that high technology always, or even usually, increases the usable military "quality" of a weapon.

The "we are outnumbered" argument is also wrong in concealing the fact that if the United States has fewer tanks and planes than the Soviet Union, it is because American planners have chosen to build fewer. There may be a parallel with Larry Smith's description of the "throw weight" question in nuclear weapons. American nuclear strategists have consciously decided that instead of following the Soviet pattern of building large, heavy nuclear-armed missiles, they would concentrate on lighter, smaller missiles by exploiting American technological advances in accuracy, warhead design, and propulsion systems. Yet, when it comes time to compare U.S. and Soviet forces, they complain about the ominous Soviet advantage in throw weight, i.e., how big a load the missile can lift. In conventional weapons, American planners keep pushing at the frontiers of technological complexity—and then complain that since we are falling further and further behind the Soviet Union in numbers, we must push the frontier further still. *

If being outnumbered is really the problem, why not solve that problem directly? The Soviets now add about 500 tactical fighters to their force each year, about twice as many as the United States does. If a sensible plane could be built for $5 million instead of $25 million to $35 million, then it would cost about $2.5 billion to match the Soviet output. Are they building 2,000 tanks a year, to our 1,000? If planners concentrated on building a tank for $800,000 instead of $2 million, then it would cost $1.6 billion to match the Soviet output, and $3.2 billion to double it. These are not trivial sums, but they are hardly in the ballpark with the total procurement budgets being thrown around. One nuclear-powered aircraft carrier and its escorts cost about $6 billion. For the same money, we could easily eliminate the entire Soviet advantage in production of fighter planes and tanks.

In addition to making the military tolerant of ever rising costs, the logic of "advanced" weaponry has several other effects on the internal priorities of the Pentagon. For one thing, it makes planners far more interested in paper projections of how a weapon should work than in realistic reports of how it actually performs. Much of the weapons-procurement system is designed precisely to shield projects against unflattering data from the field. Cripples such as the XM-1 are nursed toward survival, their problems regarded as mere growing pains that do not blemish the ultimate potential of the weapons.* The emphasis on paper projections also tempts planners to show more passion for making weapons conform to their own regulations than to shaping them to perform in combat. Any defense contractor can tell tales of the endless, pettifogging revisions he had to make in his product before it could be accepted as up to military specifications. Most soldiers would be hard put to it to see a connection between those specifications and the qualities that matter in combat. The M-16 rifle (whose development is described in the next chapter) was converted from an uncannily reliable weapon into one that betrayed its users not by an enemy plot, but by the small-minded machinations of a development bureaucracy that was damned if it was going to let a privately developed, unconventional weapon compete with the products of its own system.

Further, the wonder-weapon mentality generates hostility to small, sensible steps that will not revolutionize the battlefield, but might do some good tomorrow. Hand-held calculators, the reliable $6 kind, might be a big help to artillery men. Instead, the Army has the TAC-FIRE system, a huge, cumbersome, unreliable, and quite vulnerable computer designed to control artillery. Richard Garwin, a physicist who works at IBM and Harvard and has long served on the Defense Science Board, suggests that the United States might look more closely at the use of mines, for example, to help slow the Soviet fleet's passage through the "Greenland-Iceland-U.K. Gap" between their home ports and the open sea. "But no one can command a mine," he says. "You don't get promoted for procuring them. There's no glamour to them."

---

*In fairness to the modern army, it should be said that an aversion to honest testing is one of the chronic maladies of a peacetime military. In the first two years of World War II, submarine crews from the German, Japanese, and American navies withstood hardships and performed acts of incredible daring in order to carry out their missions. Captains would drift into shallow harbors, keel barely clearing the bottom; subs would go as deep as they dared into concentrations of enemy force, all to get a clear, close shot. And when they pushed the button and saw the torpedo churning toward the doomed target ship, they would wait in the sweaty fastness of their craft, only to hear a loud *clunnk*, or nothing at all. All three navies had produced torpedoes that didn't explode. Defective depth-control systems also meant that many of the torpedoes would not even hit their targets. In all three countries, self-contained research and development bureaucracies had been making and testing the torpedoes through the thirties. By the standards of these bureaucracies, the torpedoes were ready for action, but when they were put to the test in combat, they chronically failed in all three navies. In each country, naval officers protested and in some cases were threatened with court-martial to keep them quiet. Submarine warfare began in earnest only when a new generation of weapons was developed and subjected to harshly realistic tests.

Might there be a familiar note in Gulliver's description of the scientific academies that abounded in Laputa?

In these colleges, the professors contrive new rules and methods of agriculture and building, and new instruments and tools for all trades and manufacturers, whereby, as they undertake, one man shall do the work of ten; a palace may be built in a week, of material so durable as to last for ever without repairing. All the fruits of the earth shall come to maturity at whatever season we think fit to choose, and increase an hundred fold more than they do at present, with innumerable other happy proposals. The only inconvenience is, that none of these projects are yet brought to perfection; and in the meantime, the whole country lies miserably waste, the houses in ruins, and the people without food or clothes. By all which, instead of being discouraged, they are fifty times more violently bent upon prosecuting their schemes, driven equally on by hope and despair.[33]

THE CULTURE OF PROCUREMENT

THE FORCE of logic only goes so far toward explaining the trend toward costly, complex weaponry. The real reason American forces are "outnumbered" and high technology is king has to do with the culture of procurement in the Pentagon. In thirty years of peacetime operation (even Vietnam qualified as that, since almost no one except the soldiers ever viewed it as total war, in which the weapons and strategies *had* to work), the central function of the military has been perverted. Yes, the Pentagon is in business to devise war plans and understand the enemy and protect the nation; but before any of those things, it is in business to spend money. Many people have come to recognize this reality as it applies to, say, the Department of Housing and Urban Development. Indeed, many of the voices that are now crying most stridently for "more" defense belong to those "neoconservatives" who have shown an acute understanding that employees in the Office of Economic Opportunity may sincerely want to help the poor, but will fight poverty less fiercely than they will fight a threat to their program or their jobs. Why can't the conservatives, neo- or otherwise, see the same thing in the Pentagon? Between 1977 and 1979, the catch phrases for America's most urgent military priority shifted from "NATO modernization" to "rapid deployment force." The purchases that the services listed as "essential" to carry out these very different missions were virtually the same.

This is corruption, but not in the sense most often assumed. The bribes, the trips to the Caribbean in corporate aircraft, do occur, but they distort the essence, as Abscam distorts the essence of congressional irresponsibility, and payoffs in the General Services Administration distort the pathology of the civil service. The real damage is not spectacular but routine: it is the loss of purpose in the daily operation of the military machine, the substitution of procurement for defense. This is the true corruption, and it affects all the relevant groups: soldiers, who are converted into sales agents, rewarded for skills that count in real estate; contractors, whose productive core is corroded by contact with the nonperformance culture; and finally the rationality and civility of public discussion about defense, which are sabotaged by the hidden purpose of continuing to spend money.

It was striking to me that whenever veterans of the defense business —the ones with "dissident" tendencies, the kind in any organization who stop to look carefully at things everyone else takes for granted— reached the point, after hours of talk, where they wanted to move beyond the details to explain what *really* troubled them about defense, it was always this theme they emphasized: the corruption of military purpose by procurement. Consider the testimony of two such men. The first comes from a man who has worked for both sides, the Department of Defense (DOD) and the aircraft industry:

Any program [for improving defense] needs to start with the recognition that DOD is not different in nature than, say, the HEW or Interior Department bureaucracies. All three are primarily concerned with increasing their budgets and their perquisites, and only secondarily concerned with more effective accomplishment of their intended missions. . . . It is now clear that HEW's problems can only be aggravated by more money. Is there any reason to believe that DOD is fundamentally different?[34]

The second is from Dr. Thomas S. Amlie, who worked for nineteen years at the Naval Weapons Center at China Lake, California, and became its Technical Director:

There is no amount of money, even exceeding the GNP, which could redress the imbalance [between Soviet and American force structures] unless fundamental changes in the organization and its operation are made. . . . We could have significantly better defense for 3/4 of the present budget . . . The basic reason for the problem is incredibly simple and will be incomprehensible to anyone who has not spent time in the system: there is no profit and loss sheet. Thus, there is no competition and incentive to produce. The goal of every good bureaucrat is to get an exclusive franchise on what he is doing. If nobody else is doing it, no one can measure how well or poorly he is doing it. If he supervises more people, his grade level goes up. The only requirements are to stay busy, generate paper, and make no mistakes. The reader tempted to criticize this behavior is invited first to imagine himself in this situation, complete with a large mortgage and children in college.

Nobody cares much what is bought so long as the money gets spent. . . . The DOD has all the symptoms of being corrupt, incompetent, and incestuous, and is so to an alarming degree. This is not because of some sinister plot but because the present structure forces millions of players to act like rational human beings and do what is necessary for their survival or perceived best interests. Many of the players are aware that things are going badly and are unhappy they do not have meaningful jobs where they contribute. They are not, in the main, dishonest or incompetent, just caught in a very bad situation. All pressures are to maximize mediocrity. . . . To the [large] extent that the DOD performs non-competitive procurement, it forces the industry into the same habits. Indeed, the larger corporations have to separate those divisions which do business with the Government from those in the competitive market because of the corrupting effect of Government procurement policies and practices.[35]

The culture of procurement teaches officers that there are two paths to personal survival. One is to bring home the bacon for the service as the manager of a program that gets its full funding. "Procurement management is more and more the surest path to advancement" within the military, says John Morse, who retired as a Navy captain after twenty-eight years in the service. When the cruise-missile was gathering steam in the early seventies, there were two promising young officers, one in the Air Force and one in the Navy, who were in charge of their respective service's cruise-missile programs. The Navy liked the cruise missile from the start, seeing in it ways to add more missions to the fleet. The Air Force saw the cruise missile as a potentially threatening alternative to its plans for a new bomber, and dragged its heels. The Navy man became an admiral and directed the combined cruise-missile program when the Navy and Air Force programs were merged. The Air Force man resigned, his career in a stall.

The other path that procurement opens leads outside the military, toward the contracting firms. To know even a handful of professional soldiers above the age of forty and the rank of major is to keep hearing, in the usual catalogue of life changes, that many have resigned from the service and gone to the contractors: to Martin Marietta, Northrop, Lockheed, to the scores of consulting firms and middlemen whose offices fill the skyscrapers in Rossyln, Virginia, across the river from the capital. In 1959 Senator Paul Douglas of Illinois reported that 768 retired *senior* officers (generals, admirals, colonels, and Navy captains) worked for defense contractors.[36] Ten years later Senator William Proxmire of Wisconsin said that the number had increased to 2,072.[37]

Under legislation sponsored by Senator Proxmire, defense contractors are now required to report on retired senior officers and civilian defense officials who transfer to the company, or company officials who move the other way. The Council on Economic Priorities (CEP), a private organization based in New York, has followed these reports and compiled totals.[38] Between 1971 and 1979, according to the council, 1,455 more officers over the rank of colonel went to work for defense contractors, along with 335 civilian employees of equivalent rank from the Pentagon, and 31 from the National Aeronautics and Space Administration. (The NASA figures cover only the period between 1975 and 1979.) At the same time, there was also a smaller traffic in the other direction, with 223 company officials going to work for the Defense Department, and 47 for NASA. Boeing led the list with 398 transfers, Northrop was second with 360, Lockheed was third with 321, and General Dynamics fourth with 239.[39]

The study also cites what it is careful to call "appearances" of possible conflict of interest—officers or defense officials hired to work on projects that overlap their previous duties in the Pentagon. To give just one example: in the early seventies, at a time when General Dynamics had frequent disputes with the Navy over shipbuilding claims, a man named Edward Drake worked for the company as assistant general counsel for contracts, claims and litigation. In 1973 Drake went to work for the Navy, as assistant counsel handling legal review of shipbuilders' claims.* The CEP lists 114 such "appearances" for eight of the largest defense contractors (Boeing, General Dynamics, Grumman, Lockheed, McDonnell Douglas, Northrop, Rockwell, United

---

*This case is particularly interesting because shipbuilding litigation has become such a colossal headache for the Pentagon. Ships are like no other military project. They can take ten years to build, and it is impractical to have the kind of competition with prototypes that make sense for tanks and airplanes. As a result, the contracts are usually let on the basis of initial bids. Some contractors have turned this into a bait-and-switch procedure, in which they bid low to get the contract, put in a few years' work, and then ask to have the contract renegotiated because of increased costs or some other excuse. At the same time, Navy officials—most notably Admiral Hyman Rickover— harass the contractors with ceaseless, detailed changes in the specifications. The Navy can't cancel the contracts, because it needs the ships. A whole legal bureaucracy has grown up to handle these contract claims.

Technologies). Four of the companies, the CEP report said, made job offers to large numbers of civilian employees before they left the government. The companies were Rockwell (16 offers), Northrop (16), Boeing (16), and Lockheed (14).

J. Ronald Fox, a former Assistant Secretary of Defense, has said of this process:

> The availability of jobs in industry can have a subtle, but debilitating effect on an officer's performance during his tour of duty in a procurement management assignment. If he takes too strong a hand in controlling contractor activity, he might be damaging his opportunity for a second career following retirement. Positions are offered to officers who have demonstrated their appreciation for industry's particular problems and commitments.[40]

Thomas Amlie says:

> It is when an officer reaches his forties that his real problems begin. Like his civilian counterpart, his expenses are at a maximum with mortgage, children in college, etc. Unlike the civilian, he has no security. He realizes that he will not make COL/GEN/Chief of Staff, and that he will have to find employment to keep up his standard of living. In addition, there is the problem of "psychic income." He is at the peak of his powers, works very long hours, is emotionally involved in what he is doing and doesn't want to quit. Yet, for reasons beyond his control, he will be forced out. These officers are honorable and decent men, yet they are forced into supporting the present system which supplies post-retirement income for them.
>
> The military is a closed society that takes care of its own. If a retired general representing a client goes in to see an old classmate still on active duty, he will get a very attentive hearing. The officers on active duty are also thinking ahead. Fighting the system gets one blackballed and future employment prospects are bleak. In this way the industry has come to completely control DOD even more than its political appointees. This control is acquired with relatively little money and, to add insult to injury, the industry uses Government money to get control of the Government. As in the case of the civil servant, there is no vast and sinister plot; the system grew that way because nobody was in charge or cared.[41]

The money at stake is considerable. In 1978, for example, ten companies each did more than $1 billion worth of business with the Pentagon. The leading firm, General Dynamics, which makes the F-16 and F-111 airplanes, the Tomahawk cruise missile, and nuclear submarines, held contracts worth $3,492,100,000. The next, McDonnell Douglas, which makes F-15 and F-18A fighters and Harpoon missiles, had $3,229,200,000. United Technologies, which makes helicopters and jet engines, among other things, received $2,553,600,000. Until the beginning of the Reagan Administration, the president of United Technology was Alexander Haig—former four-star general, former Supreme Allied Commander of NATO forces, Reagan's Secretary of State, and perhaps the single most dramatic example of the traffic between defense contractors and the government. The other companies in the top ten were General Electric (jet engines, nuclear warheads, etc.), $2,042,500,000; Lockheed (large transport planes), $1,796,600,000; Hughes Aircraft ("smart" missiles like the Falcon and Phoenix), $1,556,900,000; Boeing (cruise missiles, B-52 bombers, Minuteman nuclear missiles), $1,514,500,000; Grumman (F-14 fighter and other planes), $1,364,200,000; Raytheon (Sidewinder, Patriot, Hawk, and other missiles), $1,249,400,000; and Tenneco (shipbuilding), $1,092,600,000.[42]

After the election of Ronald Reagan, the contractors announced that those sums were sure to soar. Defense stocks led the rally on the stock exchange after the election; Raytheon went from 85 before the election to 102 1/4 one week after, Rockwell International from 30 7/8 to 42 1/2, McDonnell Douglas from 34 5/8 to 42 5/8, and General Dynamics from 59 to 77 3/4.[43] If the new Administration decides to approve the B-1 bomber, that would mean some $10 billion for Rockwell; Boeing has recently received a $2 billion contract for cruise missiles. Northrop is trying hard to sell its F-5G fighters to the foreign market, on the theory that $5 billion of business may await it there. The list could go on and on.

IF THE MOST obvious thing about this list is the huge sums involved, the most interesting aspect is that such huge contracts generate comparatively little *profit*. Business, yes; they generate a lot. Also jobs, political influence, support of overhead, cash flow. Still, defense contracts by and large create a lower profit level than normal commercial business. Partly that is by definition; much defense business is on a cost-plus basis, which means that the contractor states his costs and adds a standard markup. A great deal of hidden profit is certainly buried in the "cost." But more, the lower profit rates reflect the fact that exposure to the soft world of cost-plus contracting and sky's-the-limit specifications corrupts even the industry that is its most obvious beneficiary. Corruption in this case means eroding the disciplines of efficiency, innovation, and sound business practice that are, in the long run, essential to the firms' survival. David Packard, a renowned Deputy

Secretary of Defense, ran his (very successful) electronics firm, Hewlett Packard, on the principle that it should stay as far from government business as possible.

During the last decade, small subcontracting firms that needed to retain the ability to compete in the private market stayed away from the defense business, despite the money involved. There are now only two companies making airborne radar systems for the military, two making jet fighter engines, one making the castings for tank hulls.[44] (This thinning out of the contractor base, although secondary to the increasing complexity of all weapons, is one reason people doubt that the United States could quickly gear up for war production if the need arose.) Apart from the harassment of meeting government specifications, the smaller companies also fear the "lumpiness" of investment that comes as a result of more expensive weapons. A $2 billion submarine like the Trident means feast or famine for the contractors. Rockwell won't get half, or one third, of the B-1 contract; it will get $10 billion or almost nothing.

In France, the Dassault firm is the only manufacturer of military fighter aircraft; it makes the Mirage jet. Yet conditions of French contracting are such that Dassault has retained small design teams, and a reputation for efficiency and excellence.[45] American firms—bowing to the book-length specification lists for new military projects, the cadres of retired officers they have taken aboard to generate business, and the line-by-line scrutiny of designs practiced by the Congress— suffer from inefficiency in direct proportion to the willingness of the Defense Department to pay their bills. Charles Bernard, an official in the Research and Engineering office of the Pentagon, says, "The U.S. industry has a lot of dilettantes in it—guys who are aircraft designers one day, torpedo designers the next. You'd say that's impossible, but I've seen it. Guys with zero experience in something would get interested, write a brochure, get the contract, and then figure out what the hell to do.

"What we've lost in this process is the discipline of the project engineer. If you hired an architect for a building, you'd let him draw the plan, let him supervise the work, and then hold him responsible for the results. If you ask who the 'architect' is for most defense projects, you won't find one. All they have are 'program managers' who don't know squat about weapons.

"To give you an example. The Sidewinder is the best air-to-air missile we've ever had. It was developed in the fifties, and we still have it. It was the product of one engineer, Bill McLean. There was a man obsessed with simplicity. He was *one guy* making sure that the system didn't go out of control. Today we'd break it up into 'interface managers' and 'engineering groups.' Why? I think this kind of 'matrix management' was developed as a way to keep everybody on direct charge for the project, not indirect charge."[46]*

Nearly everyone involved with defense contracting says it now captures the worst of both worlds. It permits neither cooperation between government and business, in the pattern of the French government and Dassault, nor the genuine arm's-length relationship and freedom from specifications that might permit companies to be more efficient and innovative. The one clear exception is the long-time collaboration between the Lockheed Corporation and the Special Projects Bureau of the Navy for the production of submarine-launched ballistic missiles (the Polaris, Poseidon, and Trident models). Special Projects is run on the same principles as one of the design bureaus of the Soviet military establishment, with a cadre of officers that stays year after year and trains one crop of leaders after another from within. There is also little turnover among its counterparts at Lockheed. Management experts who have studied these organizations consider it no accident that the record of the missiles has been so much better than the Pentagon's average, in both performance and cost.

"For as long as we have written records, the major improvements [in weapons] have come from outside this system," says one civilian expert. On his list are radar, the jeep, the first modern tank, the Browning automatic rifle, the nuclear submarines the regular Navy opposed—and the legendary P-51 fighter of World War II, which FDR had to force on the Army Air Force because it came from outside.

The priority of the system is to keep dollars moving, men on direct charge, management careers on track.

THREAT INFLATION

THE PURSUIT of high technology and the culture of procurement ultimately rest on democratic assent. There are many other claims on public resources; the people's elected representatives, in the Congress

---

*Bernard's explanation of direct and indirect charge: "Here's the difference. When you have to heat the building, that's indirect charge. You can't bill anybody for it. You tell yourself, if I have a big salaried professional force, they're going to be on indirect charge whenever they're out of work. If I have one guy in charge of a whole operating group, he's going to need a lot of different people at different times. It's going to be wasteful to have them sitting around when they're not needed. But if I have an 'aerodynamics group,' their manager can sell their talents to different projects and keep them all busy and on direct charge."

and the White House, theoretically possess the power to deny the Pentagon its money if it is serving only the needs of technology rather than of defense. The importance of one further form of corruption is that it makes the others possible. Through "threat inflation," the public is stampeded into an embrace of expensive, complicated projects.

This phenomenon has one trait in common with the weaknesses of the wonder missiles: it cannot be disproved in advance. Perhaps the "millimeter waves" will be a military breakthrough as fundamental as the longbow or the machine gun, and perhaps each new model of Soviet submarine and fighter plane will possess the dazzling capabilities now claimed for them by those agitating for "more" defense. But the record of high-technology weapons suggests a habit of overestimating their capabilities, and the pattern of reading enemy capabilities shows the same systematic error.

Consider the case of the "Foxbat," the "first-line" MiG-25 fighter of the Soviet Union. The capabilities of the Foxbat, as reported in the United States during the late sixties, were awesome: it could fly at Mach 3.2 or better, with a combat range of 2,000 miles. Stories written with the full authoritative tone of the background briefing said that the weapon promised to change the balance of air power; research-and-development officials let it be known that only with a correspondingly heroic effort could America counter the threat. For such a mission, only an aircraft like the F-15 would do. The Foxbat was, in fact, the principal threat used to justify the F-15's high speed, large radar, and great cost.

In 1976, half a dozen years after the contract was let on the F-15, a Soviet air force lieutenant named Viktor I. Belenko defected, and flew his Foxbat to a landing in Japan. At last the Western military had a chance to see the plane. Suddenly its capabilities dwindled. Its skin was not made of titanium, as in American versions, but plated with steel. The wings had rust spots; rivets protruded. John Barron, in his book *MiG Pilot*, describes the first astonished reaction of Western officials when they got a look at the plane:

"My God! Look what this thing is made of. Why, the dumb bastards don't have transistors; they're still using vacuum tubes. These engines are monsters! Maybe the Sovs have a separate refinery for each plane . . ."

The data Belenko supplied in response to the first quick queries also seemed surprising and, at first, contradictory.

"What is the maximum speed of the MiG-25?"

"You cannot safely exceed Mach 2.8, but actually we were forbidden to exceed Mach 2.5. You see, at high speeds the engines have a very strong tendency to accelerate out of control, and if they go above Mach 2.8, they will overheat and burn up."

"But we have tracked the MiG-25 at Mach 3.2."

"Yes, and every time it has flown that fast the engines have been completely ruined and had to be replaced and the pilot was lucky to land in one piece." (That fitted with intelligence the Americans had. They knew that the MiG-25 clocked over Israel at Mach 3.2 in 1973 had landed back in Egypt with its engines totally wrecked. They did not understand that the wreckage was inevitable rather than a freakish occurrence.)

"What is your combat radius?"

"At best, 300 kilometers [186 miles]."

"You're joking! . . . We thought the range was 2000 kilometers [1240 miles]."

Belenko laughed. "That's ridiculous. . . . Check it out for yourselves. I took off from Chuguyevka with full tanks and barely made it to Japan." Of the 14 tons of fuel with which he began, his flight of less than 500 miles consumed all but 52.5 gallons.[47]

The point of the Foxbat story is not that we should laugh at the Russians' weapons or ignore their areas of strength. Instead, the danger of threat inflation is that an unrealistic sense of the world we live in and the dangers we face will lead to ill-considered, desperate moves that may reduce our overall security rather than preserve it. The response to the Foxbat—making the F-15 into a costly, unmaintainable system —is a comparatively mild example of this syndrome.* The decision to build the MX missile (discussed in more detail in chapter 6) is a more

---

*Here is a recent parallel case. On January 9, 1981, the front page of the Washington Post carried the headline "Soviets Launch Huge New Attack Submarine." The story began: "The Soviet Union has stunned the U.S. intelligence community by launching a new cruise-missile firing submarine which will make American aircraft carriers 10 times more vulnerable than they are now, Navy officials disclosed yesterday.

"The jumbo submarine, code-named Oscar, is almost twice the size of the largest U.S. attack sub now at sea . . ." Throughout the story, the reader was led to think that a bigger submarine was automatically a better one.

The obvious implication of the story was that the Russians had stolen another march on American forces, and that the United States had to gear up with more ships and better sonar to meet the threat. Nowhere did the story mention that in a serious conflict between the United States and the Soviet Union, the carriers were likely to be destroyed very quickly whether or not "Oscar" existed, nor that the critical question about submarines is not how big they are, but how noisy. It also involved a careful calibration of the threat that "Oscar" supposedly presented to American carriers: serious enough to justify a new building program, not serious enough to suggest that the carriers were obsolete.

serious case. Within this century, there has been an illustration of the gravest consequences of threat inflation:

In terms of sheer senseless, preventable tragedies, who can but weep at the forces that pushed all sides into World War I? An immediate cause of friction between England and Germany was the dramatic build-up of the German navy under the young Kaiser Wilhelm; that build-up, in turn, was directed by Admiral Alfred von Tirpitz, under the German Navy Laws of 1898 and 1900. These laws promoted the creation of a fleet that would rival England's. The contracts they provided meant a dramatic expansion of business for steel-producing firms and the great arms establishment of Krupp. Tirpitz, no less skillful a politican than a naval organizer, struck a deal with the manufacturers. In return for the contracts, the firms agreed to devote a certain portion of the money to generating propaganda for a larger German fleet. That propaganda, and the military build-up it helped sustain, constituted a significant part of the war fever that swept Germany in those days.[48]*

How familiar it all seems to open an American newspaper and see a full-page ad placed by the Bath Iron Works, producer of naval vessels, showing Soviet ships being deployed across the Atlantic and warning of the danger that the ocean will become "a Red Sea." Or to find in magazines another full-page ad, from Todd Shipyards, depicting the United States as an isolated, insular power, and asking "How Will We Keep This Island Functioning Without Ships?" Or to find in *Time, Business Week*, and *Fortune* an advertisement from Lockheed, also full-page, about the advantages its S3A transport would provide in getting supplies from the American base on Diego Garcia, in the Indian Ocean, to the mouth of the Persian Gulf.

Or, more redolent still of Krupp and Tirpitz, to hear the explanations that arms company officials gave George Wilson of the Washington

---

*The Krupps practiced in rawest form the business of threat inflation. William Manchester, author of *The Arms of Krupp,* describes Fritz Krupp's system of *Schutz- und Trutzwaffen Schaukeln*—"the offensive/defensive weapons seesaw":

    Having perfected nickel-steel armour, Fritz advertised it in every chancellery. Armies and navies invested in it. Then he unveiled chrome-steel shells that would pierce nickel steel; armies and navies invested again. Next he appeared with a high-carbon armour plate that would resist the new shells. But just when every general and admiral thought he had equipped his forces with invincible shields, Fritz once more produced good news for advocates of offensive warfare. It turned out that the improved plate could be pierced by "capped shot," with very expensive explosive noses. The governments of the world kept digging deep into their exchequers; altogether, 30 of them were caught in Fritz's arms game.[49]

Post when he asked them about such advertisements. Robert J. Daniels, public relations director of Todd Shipyards, said of his firm's advertisements, "That is an advocacy ad. We're trying to influence the Congress to beef up the merchant marine and the Navy." Wilson said that "another defense company executive, who did not wish to be quoted by name, said contractors, as well as trying to cash in on higher defense budgets and the Pentagon's newly aroused appetite for weaponry for intervening in distant trouble spots, also are under pressure by the armed services to advertise more. 'The customer,' he said in referring to the Army, Navy, Air Force, or Marine Corps, 'often asks us to help sell the project to the administration and Congress through advertising.' "[50] Frank Kerr, the public relations director of the Bath Iron Works, gave me this explanation in an interview: "This is a very conservative shipyard that hardly ever advertises. The decision was made last year to alert the Congress to the fact that we are in serious jeopardy at sea. In addition to some columns and editorials we tried to generate, we ran four ads. All of them were addressed to the fact that our Navy is outnumbered. I've noticed other defense people doing it too."

Through much of 1980, readers of *Time* and *Newsweek* and other publications saw full-page ads for the Strike Eagle, a version of McDonnell Douglas' F-15 with added avionics. Within the Pentagon, in the corridors to which the public is denied entry, the company had set up a video display, in which a Russian military officer lamented with his colleagues about America's fearsome new weapon. The more the Soviet officials questioned him about the Strike Eagle, the more their spirits fell. America truly had devised the wonder weapon! They could only hope that the Americans would be foolish enough not to understand and exploit the advantage the new plane would offer. The ads were placed and the filmstrip run in the Pentagon before the Strike Eagle had ever officially been proposed in any Pentagon budget.

There is one other crucial element of the culture of procurement, which is that politicians of the left, when opposing new weapons, have embraced the same mechanical, technological view of warfare that their counterparts on the right have used when justifying new systems —and thereby have reinforced the flawed premises of the entire debate. During the late sixties and early seventies, a number of liberal senators boned up on the reasons why the Main Battle Tank, or the F-14 airplane, or the antiballistic missile system was a waste of money. Like those supporting the systems, they argued that machines were what ultimately mattered in military planning. They tried to rebut the Pentagon technologists on their own terms, which is why, during the ABM debate, the Senate floor was crawling with radar experts, advancing technical reasons why the system would or would not work. Such technical arguments do have a proper place in military decisions—but they are only one part of the question, and often a less important part than innovative strategies, morale, and training, and allowance for the friction of war. The left has been as uninterested in these *military* realities as any contractor beating the drum for his marvelous new weapon.

When convenient, liberals have embraced wonder weapons of their own, with eager credulity. When "stealth" technology was disclosed in 1980, senators such as John Culver of Iowa rhapsodized about how stealth would make our planes invisible to radar and thereby forestall the need for a new bomber, such as the B-1. A few years earlier, those who opposed the B-1 were skeptical about technical claims for the bomber, but entirely uncritical about similar predictions for the cruise missile, which they saw as the main alternative to the B-1. In a widely noticed study, published in 1979, a collection of academics known as the Boston Study Group argued that the United States should significantly reduce its military spending. One of their central premises was that precision-guided weapons would give an overwhelming advantage to whichever side was defending against an attack, so that NATO could hold off the Russians with a modest force. The emotional impulse behind these actions may be the desire to come up with a different machine to replace the ones you oppose. The effect is to distract attention from the complexity and unpredictability of battle as it really occurs, and from any factors other than those on the specification sheets for a machine.

THROUGH THE late sixties a Soviet official known as Colonel Kulish often came to visit the United States. A former army officer, he had fought at Stalingrad and was so badly wounded that he had to leave the service. He took a degree in history, and joined a Soviet research institution on political and economic affairs.

John Morse, who during his naval career had been an attaché in Moscow, says, "If you asked him what he was doing here, he'd give a plausible answer. 'I want to see if we can solve our differences without resorting to war.' My boss at the time said it sounded like Al Capone, 'I don't want no trouble.' " The general assumption was that Colonel Kulish was collecting intelligence in whatever way he could.

In 1971 John Morse met Kulish at a dinner party in Washington. "He was very calm and collected," Morse says; "he answered everyone's questions very politely, until someone mentioned that American strategic thinking was not the best. He smiled at that. 'You are right,' he said. 'You Americans leave your strategic thinking to mathematicians and economists, and that's not good.' Then the other guy made a slighting remark about Soviet strategy. Kulish got mad. He said, 'You Americans forget that for two hundred years you've been over here invulnerable to invasion. We've been invaded every twenty or thirty years for centuries, so we think about strategy. We have had one institute thinking about it for at least a hundred years.'

"I said at that point, 'Would you mind giving us an example of what you think of as a strategic triumph.' He said, 'Gladly. When you ended the last war, you had a one-sided ability to destroy us with nuclear weapons, and we survived with conventional superiority in Europe. I think that is a pretty good strategic achievement.'" Morse said he agreed.

Later Morse asked Colonel Kulish what he considered America's greatest strategic error. That, too, was easy, Kulish said. "You have consistently overestimated our capabilities."

The scholars of Laputa worried constantly that the sun would soon engulf the earth. So absorbed, they had no time to sleep, or laugh, or tend to the daily routine of life, or even to notice as their wives carried out assignations with their neighbors. So with American military forces. Preoccupied with an exaggerated view of Soviet capabilities, we have often forgotten to listen to our common sense.

THE MANAGERIAL ethic, the pursuit of high technology, the culture of procurement, and the indifference—of left and right—to the "intangible" aspects of combat have driven American forces toward more expensive, more complex systems, designed with less and less attention to the uncertain realities of the battlefield. The following chapter describes the way these forces played themselves out in the case of two weapons that broke the standard pattern: an infantry rifle and a fighter airplane that were designed to be more effective in battle, and lower in cost, than the systems they replaced.

FOUR

TWO WEAPONS

T HE DESIGN of every military weapon involves tensions among the imperatives of the battlefield, the habits and interests of supply agencies, the desire to save money, and the contradictory desire to spend it. The two weapons whose stories are the subject of this chapter were created with unusual attention, especially in the early stages of their development, to the requirements of reliable performance in combat and low price. By the time they entered production, some of their most striking virtues had been removed. The M-16 rifle had been a brilliant technical success in its early models, but was perverted by bureaucratic pressures into a weapon that betrayed its users in Vietnam. The F-16 airplane was designed as an "austere" fighter that would save money by eliminating every complication except those that had been proven to count in air combat. It too was altered into a less "austere" but still impressive form. In the two cases are signs of the best, and worst, tendencies in the way the United States selects its weapons.

THE M-16

BETWEEN 1965 and 1969, more than one million American soldiers served in combat in Vietnam. One can argue that they should never have been sent there, or that the strategy under which they were commanded ensured their demoralization and defeat. No one can argue that, while there, the soldiers should have been given inferior equipment. Yet that is what happened. During those years, in which more than 40,000 American soldiers were killed by hostile fire and more than 250,000 wounded, American troops in Vietnam were equipped with a rifle their superiors knew would fail when put to the test.

The rifle was known as the M-16; it was a replacement for the M-14, a heavier weapon that was the previous standard. The original version of the M-16, a commercial model developed by the Armalite company and known as the AR-15, was the most reliable, and the most lethal, infantry rifle ever invented. But within months of its introduction in combat, it was known among soldiers as a weapon that might jam and misfire, and could pose as great a danger to them as to their enemy. These problems, which loomed so large on the battlefield, were entirely the result of modifications made to the rifle's original design by the Army's own ordnance bureaucracy. The Army's modifications had very little to do with observation of warfare, but quite a lot to do with settling organizational scores. By the middle of 1967, when the M-16 had been in combat for about a year and a half, a sufficient number of soldiers had written to their parents about their pathetically unreliable equipment, and a sufficient number of parents had sent those letters to their congressmen, to attract the attention of a congressional investigating committee. The committee, headed by Representative Richard Ichord, a Democrat from Missouri, conducted an exhaustive inquiry into the origins of the M-16 problem. Much of the credit for the hearings belongs to the committee's counsel, Earl J. Morgan. The hearing record, nearly 600 pages long,[1] is a forgotten document, which received modest press attention at the time and calls up only dim recollections now. Yet it is the purest portrayal of the banality of evil in the records of modern American defense.

NEARLY A CENTURY before American troops were ordered into Vietnam, weapons designers, especially in Europe, had made a discovery in the science of "wound ballistics." The discovery was that a small, fast-traveling bullet often did a great deal more damage than a larger round when fired into human or (for the experiments) animal flesh. The explanation lay in physics: when the bullet passed from a medium of one density, such as air, into a medium of different density, the bullet became unstable and began to tumble. This was true for bullets fired through air into water, and it was equally true for bullets as they entered human flesh. What impeded the bullet from tumbling was its own weight and momentum; the lighter the bullet, the more rapidly and wildly it would tumble end-for-end in flesh. A large artillery round might pass straight through a human body, but a small bullet could act like a gouge. During the early stages of the congressional hearings Representative Ichord asked Eugene Stoner, the designer of the original version of the M-16, to explain the apparent paradox of a small bullet's destructive power.

ICHORD: One Army boy told me that he had shot a Vietcong near the eye with an M-14 [which uses a substantially heavier bullet] and the bullet did not make too large a hole on exit, but he shot a Vietcong under similar circumstances in the same place with a M-16 and his whole head was reduced to pulp. This would not appear to make sense. You have greater velocity but the bullet is lighter.

STONER: That is the advantage that a small or light bullet has over a heavy one when it comes to wound ballistics . . . What it amounts to is that bullets are stabilized to fly through air, and not through water or a body, which is approximately the same density as the water. And they are stable as long as they are in the air. When they hit something, they immediately go unstable. . . . If you are talking about a .30 caliber bullet [like that used in the M-14], that might remain stable through a human body . . . While a little bullet, being it has a low mass, it senses an instability situation faster and reacts much faster. This is what makes a little bullet pay off so much in wound ballistics.[2]

A far-sighted troop commander, General Wyman, had asked Stoner to design his rifle precisely to take advantage of the "payoff" of smaller bullets. The AR-15, the precursor of the M-16, used .22-caliber bullets instead of the .30 caliber that had long been standard for the Army.* As early as 1928, an Army "Caliber Board" conducted firing experiments in Aberdeen, Maryland, and then had recommended a move toward smaller ammunition, perhaps of the .27-caliber range; but the Army, for reasons that were partly technical but largely traditional (and that will be more fully explained as the story goes on), refused then and for the next thirty-five years to change from the .30-caliber bullet, which it preferred to describe as "full-sized."

*A word about "caliber." Ammunition is described in two ways, by millimeter measure or "caliber." Both are measures of the bullet's diameter, one expressed, obviously, in millimeters, and the other in inches. A ".22 caliber" bullet has a diameter of .22 inches, and is the same thing as a 5.56-millimeter bullet. That is what the M-16 uses. A .30-caliber bullet, or 7.62 millimeter, had been the standard for most Army rifles, including the M-1, which was used in World War II and Korea, and the M-14, which was introduced after the Korean War.

A second discovery about weaponry also lay behind the design of Eugene Stoner's AR-15. In his studies of combat units during World War II, S.L.A. Marshall found that nearly four fifths of combat soldiers never fired their weapons during battles. This finding, which also led to the "Fighter" studies (discussed in the next chapter), prompted a closer look at the weapons the soldiers used. It turned out that one group of soldiers was an exception to this rule: those who carried the Browning automatic rifles (BAR). These were essentially portable machine guns, which could spray out bursts of continuous fire. The M-1s that the other soldiers carried were "semiautomatic," and required a separate trigger squeeze for each round. Within a combat group, firing would begin with the BAR man and spread out from him. The nearer a soldier with an M-1 stood to the BAR man, the more likely he was to fire. The explanation most often suggested was that the infantryman carrying a normal rifle felt that his actions were ultimately futile. As John Keegan said in *The Face of Battle*, "Infantrymen, however well-trained and well-armed, however resolute, however ready to kill, remain erratic agents of death. Unless centrally directed, they will choose, perhaps badly, their own targets, will open and cease fire individually, will be put off their aim by the enemy's return of fire, will be distracted by the wounding of those near them, will yield to fear or excitement, will fire high, low, or wide."[3] The normal infantryman could not see the enemy clearly or have any sense of whether he had hit. The BAR man, by contrast, had the sense that he could dominate a certain area —"hose it down," in the military slang—and destroy anyone who happened to be there.

From the end of World War II, there was a demand from some Army officers for a new infantry weapon that would be light, reasonably accurate, and capable of fully automatic fire. The response of the Army's ordnance organizations was to build the M-14. This was basically an automatic-firing, less solidly made version of the Army's previous standard, the M-1. Like the M-1, it used a large .30-caliber round. Its disadvantage was that it was virtually uncontrollable when in fully automatic firing. The explosive charge needed to propel the heavy bullets was so great, and the rifle itself so flimsily built in an effort to make it lightweight that the kick was ferocious. A soldier who used it on automatic fire was likely to get a nosebleed, in addition to being unable to control the weapon's aim. It was with this rifle that American troops trained in the early and middle sixties, and with it they went to Vietnam.

The M-14 was a product of the Army's own arsenal system, an informal congeries of weapons laboratories, private contractors, and the Army Materiel Command that is often generically known as the "ordnance corps." The ordnance corps had been in charge of small-arms design for the Army for more than a hundred years. In questions of technology, it emphasized the outlook of the "gravel-bellies," the sharpshooters and marksmen who measured a weapon by how well it helped them hit a target four hundred, five hundred, six hundred yards away in peacetime rifle competition. "The M-14 had been developed on the premise that aimed·fire, the fire of the marksman, was of the utmost importance in combat," a Rand employee named Thomas McNaugher wrote in a study of the M-16.[4] "To the U.S. Army, it was more than a premise, it was a creed that had evolved over nearly a century since the service adopted its first rifle in 1855."[5] Giving generous credit to the element of rationality in the ordnance corps' practices, McNaugher says that the marksman's philosophy was appealing because the Ordnance Department, the agency that developed and produced the service's rifles and ammunition, preferred tactics that stressed slow and deliberate fire because it meant less waste of ammunition and hence less strain on the Department's supply lines and production facilities."[6]

For the marksman's purposes, a large, heavy round was ideal, since it remained steady in flight and was less sensitive to wind. Hand in hand with this mentality went an insistence on rigid technical specifications. If a round didn't leave the muzzle at 3,250 feet per second, it was no good; if it couldn't be fired in the Arctic and the Sahara and perform just as well in each place, it was not fit for army duty. These emphases had little to do with the experience of modern combat, in which most fire fights took place at a range of thirty to fifty yards or less, and in which speed and surprise were so important that it might often cost a soldier his life to take the time to aim his rifle, as opposed to simply pointing it in the right direction and opening up on automatic.

In its sociology, the ordnance corps was small-time, insular, old-fashioned. Its first instinct, when presented with a new technical possibility, was to reject it and stick to its own, traditional solutions. Twice since the Civil War, American Presidents have had to force the ordnance corps to adopt new rifles that had come from outside its own shop.*

---

*When the Civil War began, Union troops were equipped with a cumbersome muzzle-loading rifle. In 1860 a young inventor from outside the ordnance system named Spencer had come up with the first reliable repeating rifle for military use, a lever-action model similar to the Winchester .73, which later became famous in the Old West. Spencer could not get the Army to pay attention to his rifle, but he eventually wangled an appointment with President Lincoln. Spencer and the President went out behind

There was also an air of coziness in relations between the ordnance corps and the rifle and ammunition makers who supplied it. "Sole source" contracts, which gave one company a monopoly on the Army's business, were not unusual. One of the most important of these, which would prove to have an especially crucial effect on the development of the M-16, was with the Olin-Mathieson Corporation, which since the end of World War II had been the Army's supplier of a kind of gunpowder known as "ball powder."

The ordnance corps had every reason to dislike the AR-15. It came from an outside inventor and threatened to replace a product of their own arsenal system, the M-14. It was not a gravel-belly's or a technician's rifle. And it proposed using what was, by the standards of the corps, a laughably small round—a .22-caliber bullet, the size kids used to shoot at squirrels. A popgun was all it was. In the early fifties the U.S. ordnance corps had fought a grueling battle against European

---

the White House, where a target had been set up. Lincoln, who was a good shot, fired a few rounds from Spencer's rifle and saw its merits. He sent a note to the Secretary of War—who had been invited to the demonstration but had declined—ordering him to buy the rifle for the Union Army. The Army bought the minimum amount, 60,000 rifles, and assigned them mostly to the cavalry, saying that they were not suitable for infantry use. Nonetheless, several Union regiments bought Spencer rifles out of their own pockets, rather than use the government issue muzzle-loaders. When the war was over and the President was dead, Colonel Ripley, the long-time head of the ordnance corps, quickly declared the Spencer repeating rifle obsolete and ordered it sold. Many of the purchasers were Indians, who used it in their marauding raids—including their attack on George A. Custer at the Little Bighorn. Near the bodies of Custer's men were found their standard-issue Army rifles, the single-shot Trap-Door Springfields, which the ordnance corps had developed and which the Indians had not deigned to take.

By the time of the Spanish-American War, the Army had selected and issued to American soldiers a hard-to-load rifle known as the Krag-Jorgensen. When Theodore Roosevelt led his Rough Riders up San Juan Hill, they faced troops equipped with the finest rifle of the time, the Mauser. Three years later, Roosevelt was President, and he ordered the War Department to buy Mausers for American troops. There was little enthusiasm in the Army for a rifle that came not only from outside its own system but also from outside the country. The ordnance corps made some minor modifications on the Mauser design, named it the Springfield '03, and adopted it as the Army standard. This turned out to be so gross an infringement on the Mauser patent that the Army was forced to pay royalties to the Mauser company.[7]

The M-16 story was similar in its general dimensions to these two previous episodes, and it also involved a President's intervention. The decision to equip the Special Forces with the original version of the M-16, described later in this chapter, was largely engineered by President Kennedy and Secretary McNamara.

governments in NATO, who wanted to have a small bullet adopted as the NATO standard. The ordnance corps' struggle to impose the .30-caliber bullet as NATO standard had been successful, but it had left much ill will in its wake. Having won that bitter struggle, the Army was not likely to surrender meekly on the same point in its own home territory.[8]

The M-14 was adopted as the Army's standard in 1957. At the same time, Eugene Stoner was completing the design of the rifle then known as the AR-15. By that time Stoner was known as one of the great figures in this special calling. Like some of the other outstanding American rifle designers—including John Browning, inventor of the Browning automatic rifle, who had to sell his weapon to foreign governments after rejection by the American ordnance corps—Stoner had never seen his models win easy acceptance from the Army. Stoner was working for the Armalite Corporation when he finished developing the AR-15.

The rifle combined several advantages. One was the lethal "payoff" that came with its .22-caliber bullets. The smaller, lighter ammunition meant that the rifle could be controlled on automatic fire by the average soldier because its kick was so much less than the M-14's. The rifle itself was also lighter than the M-14. Together, these savings in weight meant that a soldier using the AR-15 could carry almost three times as many rounds as a man with the M-14. This promised to eliminate one of the soldier's fundamental problems in combat: running out of ammunition during a fire fight. The rifle had two other technical advantages. One was the marvelous reliability of its moving parts, which could feed, fire, extract, and eject 600 or 700 cartridges a minute and practically never jam. The other was a manufacturing innovation that drastically cut the cost of the weapon. The parts were stamped out, not hand-machined as in previous rifles, and they could be truly mass-produced. The stock was made of plastic, which further cut the cost. To traditionalists, this was one more indication that the AR-15 was not a real weapon. They said that you couldn't use a plastic rifle as a club. Stoner's reply, in effect, was that with the AR-15's reliability and its destructive power, you wouldn't need to.

The AR-15 was tested in 1958 at three military bases. The reports were favorable, but there were reservations from the ordnance establishment about the propriety of using such small-caliber ammunition. To reconcile the differences in opinion, the Army commissioned an extensive series of tests at the Army Combat Development Experiment Center, known as CEDEC, at Fort Ord, California. These tests ran from the fall of 1958 until the spring of 1959, and were designed not to follow the usual marksman's pattern, but to simulate the conditions of small squads in combat. In the tests, the AR-15 was matched against the M-14 and another lightweight rifle made by Winchester. The results, released in May 1959, included these findings:

a. With a total weight per man equivalent to that planned for a rifleman armed with the M-14, a squad of 5–7 men armed with the [AR-15] would have better hit distribution and better hit capability than the present eleven man M-14 squad . . .

b. By opinion poll, the experimentation troops preferred the [AR-15] because of its demonstrated characteristics of lightness in weight, reliability, balance and grip, and freedom from recoil and climb on full automatic (ease of firing). . . .

h. The attributes demonstrated by the prototype weapons of the lightweight high-velocity category indicate an overall combat potential superior to that of the M-14. Such advantages include: . . . lightness in weight of arms and ammunition, ease of handling, superior full automatic firing capability, accuracy of the Winchester, and functional reliability of the Armalite [AR-15].[9]

The report's conclusion was that the Army should develop a lightweight rifle "with the reliability characteristics of the Armalite" to replace the M-14. "Concurrent with the adopting of a lightweight high-velocity rifle," the report said, "serious consideration should be given to reduction in the size of the present squad," because of the increased fire power of the new weapons.[10]

The repeated references to the "reliability" of the AR-15 bear emphasizing, in view of the weapon's unreliability after it had been transformed into the M-16 and sent to war.

After the CEDEC tests, the Army admitted the theoretical "promise" of the lightweight system but rejected it as a practical proposition. It is important to remember that the ordnance corps had fought this battle before. In 1928 the special Caliber Board had conducted extraordinarily demanding and realistic tests, and ended up recommending that the Army move to a smaller, .276-caliber bullet. In 1932 Douglas MacArthur, then the Chief of Staff, turned down the recommendation, accepting the advice of the chief of ordnance that it would be too confusing to introduce a new bullet to the Army's supplies. Thirty years later, in the arguments over the M-16, that was still the ordnance corps' line. Emphasizing the importance of having all rifles and machine guns use the same ammunition, the Army ordered full scheduled production of the M-14 and its .30-caliber round.

However, advocates of the AR-15 enlisted the support of a redoubtable gun enthusiast, General Curtis LeMay, then the Air Force's Chief of Staff. Based on his interest, the Air Force conducted further tests and inspections and declared the AR-15 its "standard" model in January 1962. The Air Force then took a step whose later significance would be enormous. On the advice of the Armalite Corporation, which owned the design for the rifle, and of Colt, which had the contract to manufacture it, the Air Force tested a sample of the ammunition that the Remington Arms Company had developed for the AR-15. After the tests, the Air Force declared the ammunition suitable for its purposes. In May 1962 it ordered 8,500 rifles from Colt and 8.5 million rounds of ammunition from Remington.

At this point, decisions about the rifle moved from the world of tests and paper specifications to that of actual combat. In 1962 the Defense Department's Advanced Research Projects Agency, prompted by staff members who were advocates of the AR-15, managed to get 1,000 AR-15s shipped to Vietnam for tests by ARVN soldiers (ARVN stands for Army of the Republic of Vietnam). The rationale was that Vietnamese soldiers were too short and slight to handle rifles with full-sized ammunition. The reports were glowing, especially about the phenomenal reliability of the weapon. There were no broken parts reported in the firing of 80,000 rounds during one stage of the tests. In the whole period, only two replacement parts were issued for all 1,000 rifles. The report recommended that the AR-15 be shipped in bulk to South Vietnam as standard equipment for the ARVN soldier. But Admiral Harry Felt, then the Commander in Chief, Pacific Forces, rejected the recommendation, based on Army advice saying that it would create a complicated logistics problem to have different rifles using different rounds in the war zone. The Joint Chiefs of Staff supported his decision.

Through 1962 and 1963, there followed a series of tests, evaluations, and counterevaluations by the American military, the repeated theme of which was the lightness, "lethality," and reliability of the AR-15. The results of one test, conducted by the Defense Advanced Research Projects Agency, were summed up in September 1962 by the Comptroller of the Defense Department:

Taking into account the greater lethality of the AR-15 rifle and improvements in accuracy and rate of fire in this weapon since 1959, in overall squad kill potential the AR-15 is up to 5 times as effective as the M-14 rifle. . . .

The AR-15 can be produced with less difficulty, to a higher quality, and at a lower cost than the M-14 rifle.

In reliability, durability, ruggedness, performance under adverse circumstances, and ease of maintenance, the AR-15 is a significant improvement over any of the standard weapons including the M-14 rifle. The M-14 rifle is weak in the sum of these characteristics. . . .

It is significantly easier to train the soldier with the AR-15 than with the M-14 rifle.

Three times as much ammunition can be carried on the individual soldier within the standard weapon and ammunition load.[11]

Meanwhile the Army Materiel Command, home of the ordnance corps, was conducting its own evaluations of the AR-15. In these, too, there was consistency. The corps found little to admire in the AR-15, and many technical objections to it. It had poor "pointing and night firing characteristics"; its penetration at long distance was also poor. The ordnance corps' recommendation was to stick with the M-14 until a "radically" better model, based on advanced technology, emerged from research programs the ordnance labs had recently begun.

Early in 1963, with strong support from President Kennedy and Secretary of Defense McNamara, the Special Forces (Green Berets) asked for and got approval to use the AR-15 as their standard issue because they needed lightweight gear for mobility and stealth. The Army's Airborne units in Vietnam also got it, as did some operatives from the CIA. As the AR-15 attracted a greater and greater following among units actually operating in Vietnam, Secretary of the Army Cyrus Vance asked the Army's Inspector General to look again at the reasoning and evidence that had led the Army Materiel Command to reject the AR-15. His investigation found that the tests had been blatantly rigged. The M-14s used in the tests were all hand-picked, hand-made, "matchgrade" weapons (suitable for marksmen's competitions), while the AR-15s were taken straight from the box. The ammunition for the M-14 had also come from a special, coddled lot. The inspector found that various organizations of the ordnance corps had met beforehand to discuss how to fix the tests. They agreed to take a dry run through the tests, and then (according to the printed minutes of their meeting) include in the final tests "only those tests that will reflect adversely on the AR-15 rifle . . ."[12] The lines became more clearly drawn within the Pentagon, with the Air Force and the civilian leadership of the Defense Department (especially McNamara and his Secretary of the Army, Cyrus Vance) in favor of the AR-15 and the Army ordnance establishment opposed.

As the fighting in Vietnam grew more intense, procurement of the rifle began in late 1963, with 19,000 rifles for the Air Force and another 85,000 for the special Army units. Robert McNamara, in the interests of efficiency, designated the Army as the central procurement agency for all the services. It was at this point that the Army ordnance corps got hold of Eugene Stoner's AR-15, declared it to be inadequately "developed," and "militarized" it into the M-16.

The first of several modifications was the addition of a "manual bolt closure," a handle that would permit the soldier to ram a cartridge in manually after it had refused to seat properly by itself. The Air Force, which was to buy the rifle, and the Marine Corps, which had tested it, objected vehemently to this change. An Air Force document said, "During three years of testing and operation of the AR-15 rifle under all types of conditions the Air Force has no record of malfunctions that could have been corrected by a manual bolt closing device."[13] Worse, they said, the device would add cost, weight, and complexity to the weapon, thereby reducing the reliability that had been its greatest asset. Years later, during the congressional testimony, Colonel Harold Yount, who had been a project manager at the Rock Island arsenal in 1963, was asked how this change could have been justified. Not on the basis of complaints, or of prior tests, Colonel Yount said. It was justified "on the basis of direction."[14] Direction from where? a congressman asked. Direction from his superiors on the Army staff, was all he would say. The fact was that General Earle Wheeler, the Army's Chief of Staff, had personally ordered the useless handle.

The next modification was to increase the "twist" of the rifle's barrel, from a one-in-14-inches twist rate to one-in-12. More twist made the bullet spin faster as it flew, and therefore made it hold a more stable path; but by exactly the same process, it made the bullet more stable as it entered flesh, and thereby greatly reduced the shocking "lethality" that had so distinguished the AR-15. In the face of the logic that led the Army to this decision, it is difficult to avoid the conclusion that reducing the M-16's "lethality," along with its other advantages over the beloved M-14, was precisely the intention of the change. The Army's explanation for the increased "twist" of the barrel was that otherwise the rifle could not meet its all-environments test. To qualify as "Army standard," a rifle and its ammunition had to show that they would perform equally well at 65 degrees below zero and 125 above. On the basis of skimpy test evidence, an Arctic testing team concluded that the AR-15 did not do so well on the cold-weather portions of its test. Supposedly, the rounds wobbled in flight at 65 below. The Army's reaction was to increase the "twist" and thereby decrease the "lethality," even though the rifle was due for shipment to the steaming jungles along the Mekong.

The final change was the most important. Like the others, it was publicly justified by a letter-of-the-law application of technical specification, but it seems to have been motivated by a desire to discredit the AR-15 as a competitor to the Army's own M-14.

Weapons designers speak of automatic rifles as "resonant mechanisms," in which several different cycles must all work in harmony. One of the determining factors for synchronizing these cycles is the explosive characteristic of the ammunition. Some powders explode very quickly, others build up pressure more slowly. Depending on that pattern, certain other decisions follow—for example, the location of the "gas port," or the proper cycling rate for inserting and extracting the bullets. Eugene Stoner had designed his AR-15 around a powder known as IMR (for "improved military rifle"). It was produced by Du Pont, which sold it to Remington to fill the cartridges. It is made of nitrocellulose, sometimes known as guncotton, which is extruded like toothpaste and cut into little granules. All of the early tests of the AR-15 had involved IMR ammunition; it was the ammunition that the Air Force had accepted and that had proven so reliable in all field trials.

In June 1963 the Army Materiel Command conducted tests at Frankford Arsenal which showed that IMR powder would not do. Once again, it seems obvious that the test was designed to produce exactly this result. The problem, as with the barrel twist, was failure to meet a technical specification. For reasons that no members of the ordnance corps could ever satisfactorily explain to congressional investigators, the Army specified that the muzzle velocity for the rifle must average 3,250 feet per second, plus or minus 40. In all its previous tests, and in its successful performance in combat in Vietnam, the AR-15 had never attained that velocity. The Army had tested the weapon thoroughly enough to know that when it was fired with the gunpowder it had originally been designed to use, its velocity averaged about 100 feet per second less. No testing panel had complained about the lower velocity. No problems had shown up in combat—quite the contrary. But when the Army's "technical data package" for the M-16 was issued in 1963, it required the 3,250 fps muzzle velocity, and also specified that the pressure within the firing chamber could not exceed 52,000 pounds per square inch.

After a good deal of negotiation and haggling that lasted several months, the outcome of the Frankford Arsenal tests was that IMR ammunition could not meet the newly devised standards. To get the velocity up to 3,250 fps, it had to bring chamber pressure too close to the limit. In February 1964 the Army sent out a request to the manufacturers to come up with substitute powders. A few months later Du Pont said it would stop producing IMR, and Remington switched to the Army's "sole-source" supplier of "ball powder," Olin-Mathieson. By the end of 1964 Remington was loading only ball powder in its cartridges for the rifle, which by now had been renamed the M-16.

Ball powder was first adopted by the Army early in World War II, for use in certain artillery rounds. It differs from IMR in being "double-based" (made of nitrocellulose and nitroglycerine) and in certain other ways. Its most important difference is its explosive characteristics, for it burns longer and slower than IMR. Olin-Mathieson has long enjoyed a comfortable relationship with the ordnance corps as the "sole-source" supplier of ball powder for many ammunition jobs.[15] Olin-Mathieson received contracts for some 89 million cartridges in 1964 alone, and far more as the war went on. More than 90 percent of the cartridges used in Vietnam were loaded with ball powder.

After the Army had made the decision to switch to ball powder, it sent a representative, Frank Vee of the Comptroller's office, to try to get Eugene Stoner to endorse the change. Stoner had not been consulted on any of the modifications to his rifle, not the bolt closure nor the barrel twist nor the ball powder, and he thought that all were bad ideas. He recalled for the congressional committee his meeting with Vee:

He asked me my opinion [about the specs requiring ball powder] after the fact. In other words, this was rather an odd meeting. . . . I looked at the technical data package and he said, "what is your opinion?" I said, "I would advise against it . . ."

I asked, "so what is going to happen?" And he said, "well, they have already decided this is the way they are going to go." I said, "so why are you asking me now," and he said, "I would have felt better if you had approved of the package."

And I said, "well, we both now don't feel so good."[16]

The reason for Stoner's concern was that the change of powders destroyed most of the qualities he had built into his rifle. With ball powder, the M-16 looked better on the Army's new specification sheets but worse in operation. There were two problems. One was "fouling" —a powder residue on the inside of the gas tube and chamber that eventually made the rifle jam. The AR-15 had been designed so that its gas port stayed closed through the combustion of the powder, but that was for a different powder. The new ball powder was inherently dirtier; in addition, it burned longer, and was still burning when the

gas port opened and let it burn into the gas tube. The other effect of
ball powder was to increase the rifle's "cyclic rate." The AR-15, with
all its interlocking mechanical cycles, had been designed to fire between
750 and 800 rounds per minute. When cartridges loaded with ball
powder were used, the rate went up to 1,000 or more. "When the Army
said, 'No, we are going to use our ammunition,' the cyclic rate of the
weapons went up at least 200 rounds per minute," Stoner told the
congressional committee.[17] "That gun would jump from 750 to about
1000 rounds a minute, with no change other than changing the ammunition."[18]

The consequences of a higher cyclic rate were immediate and grave.
What had been a supremely reliable rifle was now given to chronic
breakdowns and jams. In November 1965, engineers from Colt fired
a number of rifles, some with the original IMR powder and some with
ball. They reported: "For weapons such as those used in this experiment, none are likely to fail with ammunition such as [IMR], whereas
half are likely to fail with ammunition such as [ball powder]."[19] In
December the Frankford Arsenal conducted another test for malfunctions. When M-16s were loaded with IMR cartridges, there were 3.2
malfunctions per 1,000 rounds, and .75 stoppages. When the same
rifles were fired with ball powder, the failure rates were about six times
higher (18.5 and 5.2, respectively). Under the central procurement
policy, the Army's decision also forced the Air Force to switch to ball
powder. The Air Force protested, pointing out that the rifles had been
extremely reliable when loaded with IMR. One Air Force representative described a test in which 27 rifles fired 6,000 rounds apiece. The
malfunction rate was one per 3,000 rounds, and the parts replacement
rate one per 6,200 rounds. The rifle and its original cartridge worked
fine, the Air Force insisted, even though they didn't happen to meet
the specifications of 3,250 feet per second from the muzzle.[20]

In May 1966 there was one more report, this one the result of an
extensive and unusually realistic series of tests held by the Army's
CEDEC field test organization at Fort Ord. In these tests, the soldiers
fired as squads, not as individuals; the targets resembled real battlefield
targets; in that they were hard to see, and obscured by brush and other
cover, there was simulated fire from the targets themselves, done in a
pattern resembling that of combat; soldiers were run through the
course only once, to avoid any familiarity with it. The conclusion was
that the M-16 was more effective than the M-14 or the Soviet AK-47
(which was also tested), but that it was an unreliable weapon. The
reason for the fouling, the jamming, and the breakdowns, the testers
said, was the switch to ball powder.[21] By that time the Army was

ordering ball powder in greater quantities than ever and shipping it to Vietnam.

IN 1965, after the years of the advisers and the Special Forces, American troops began full-fledged ground combat in Vietnam. The regular Army and Marine units carried the old M-14. On arrival, they discovered several things about their weapon. One was that in jungle warfare the inaccurate, uncontrollable M-14 was no match for the AK-47, made in the Soviet Union, which their enemies used. Both rifles fired a .30-caliber bullet, but the AK-47's cartridges had a lighter bullet and were packed with less powder, which reduced the recoil to an endurable range. They also saw that the old AR-15s that had been used by the Special Forces had been a big hit in Vietnam. On the black market the weapon was going for $600 (the original price was around $100), to soldiers who were willing to sacrifice several months' pay to get hold of one.

One of those who noticed these patterns was William Westmoreland, then the commander of American forces in Vietnam. He saw that his men were doing very badly in the fire fights against the AK-47 and that the casualties were heavy. He also saw how the AR-15 performed, and near the end of December 1965 he sent an urgent, personal request for the M-16, immediately, as standard equipment for units in Vietnam.

The ordnance corps met this request with grudging compliance. The rifle would be sent to Vietnam, but only as a special, limited purchase. It would not be issued to American troops in Europe or in the United States; it would not replace the M-14 as the Army's standard weapon. Nor would it go to Vietnam under circumstances likely to show off its merits, because there was no backing off the requirement that its cartridges be filled with ball powder.

The climactic struggle over ball powder had occurred one year before Westmoreland's request, in 1964. As test after test showed that ball powder made the rifle fire too fast and then jam, the manufacturing company finally threw up its hands. Colt said that it could no longer be responsible for the M-16's passing the Army's acceptance test. It could not guarantee performance with the ball powder. One of the provisions of test was that the rifle's cyclic rate not exceed 850 rounds per minute, and six out of ten rifles were far above that when using ball powder. Don't worry, the Army said in an official letter; *you can use whatever ammunition you want for the tests.* But we'll keep sending our ball powder to Vietnam. Beginning in 1964, Colt used IMR powder so that its rifles would pass the acceptance tests; the Army promptly equipped those rifles with ball-powder cartridges and sent them to soldiers who needed them to stay alive. The Army's official reasoning on the matter was that since it did not recognize the theories that ball powder was the cause of the problems, why should it care which powder Colt used? Colt delivered at least 330,000 rifles under this agreement. After uncovering the arrangement, the Ichord committee concluded in its report:

Undoubtedly, many thousands of these were shipped or carried to Vietnam, *with the Army on notice that the rifles failed to meet design and performance specifications and might experience excessive malfunctions when firing ammunition loaded with ball propellant* [emphasis in original]. . . . The rifle project manager, the administrative contracting officer, the members of the Technical Coordinating Committee, and others as high in authority as the Assistant Secretary of Defense for Installations and Logistics knowingly accepted M-16 rifles that would not pass the approved acceptance test. . . . Colt was allowed to test using only IMR propellant at a time when the vast majority of ammunition in the field, including Vietnam, was loaded with ball propellant. The failure on the part of officials with authority in the Army to cause action to be taken to correct the deficiencies of the 5.56-mm ammunition borders on criminal negligence.[22]

The denouement was predictable and tragic. In the field, the rifle fouled and jammed. More American soldiers survived in combat than would have with the M-14, but the M-16's failures were spectacular and entirely unnecessary. When they heard the complaints, ordnance officials said it only proved what they'd said all along, that it was a lousy rifle, anyway. The official Army hierarchy took the view that it was a question of improper maintenance. Officials from the Pentagon would go on inspection tours to Vietnam and scold the soldiers for not keeping the rifles clean enough, but there never seemed to be enough cleaning supplies for the M-16. The instruction leaflets put out by the Army told them that "This rifle will fire longer without cleaning or oiling than any other known rifle," and "an occasional cleaning will keep the weapon functioning indefinitely."[23]

At last the soldiers began writing letters—to their parents, to their girl friends, and to the commercial manufacturer of a rifle lubricant called Dri-Slide. The Dri-Slide company received letters like the following:

December 24, 1966

Dear Sir:

On the morning of December 22nd our company . . . ran into a reinforced platoon of hard core Viet Cong. They were well dug in and boy! Was it hell getting them out. During this fight and previous ones, I lost some of my best buddies. I personally checked their weapons. Close to 70 per cent had a round stuck in the chamber, and take my word it was not their fault.

Sir, if you will send three hundred and sixty cans along with the bill, I'll "gladly" pay it out of my own pocket. This will be enough for every man in our company to have a can.

—————, Spec. Fourth Class

March 9, 1967

Dear Sir:

I'm very much interested in your product, Dri-Slide. Being stationed here in Vietnam with the rain seasons coming, myself and other GI's I'm with, need something to keep our weapons from jamming up. The regular type oil that we are using collects too much dust, and the dust here is quite terrible.

—————, Spec. Fourth Class[24]

Parents in Idaho received this letter from their son, a Marine:

Our M-16s aren't worth much. If there's dust in them, they will jam. Half of us don't have cleaning rods to unjam them. Out of 40 rounds I've fired, my rifle jammed about 10 times. I pack as many grenades as I can plus bayonet and K bar (jungle knife) so I'll have something to fight with. If you can, please send me a bore rod and a 1 1/4 inch or so paint brush. I need it for my rifle. These rifles are getting a lot of guys killed because they jam so easy.[25]

One man wrote to a member of the Armed Services Committee staff, recounting what his brother had told him about his experience in Vietnam:

He went on to tell me how, in battles there in Vietnam, the only things that were left by the enemy after they had stripped the dead of our side were the rifles, which they considered worthless. That when battles were over the dead would have the rifles beside them, torn down to attempt a repair because of some malfunction when the enemy attacked . . . This man speaking has been shooting since he was 15 . . . He said, "part of me dies when I have to stand by and see people killed, and yet my hands are tied.[26]

A letter that ended up in the office of Representative Charles W. Whalen, Jr., of Ohio:

I was walking point a few weeks back and that piece of you know what jammed 3 times in a row on me. I'm lucky I wasn't doing anything but reconning by fire or I wouldn't be writing this letter now. When I brought the matter up to the Captain, he let me test fire the weapon—well in 50 rounds it double fed and jammed 14 times. I guess I'll just have to wait till someone gets shot and take his rifle because the Captain couldn't get me a new one.[27]

Another, referred to Senator Gaylord Nelson of Wisconsin:

The weapon has failed us at crucial moments when we needed fire power most. In each case, it left Marines naked against their enemy. Often, and this is no exaggeration, we take counts after each fight, as many as 50% of the rifles fail to work. I know of at least two marines who died within 10 feet of the enemy with jammed rifles. No telling how many have been wounded on that account and it is difficult to count the NVA who should be dead but live because the M-16 failed. Of course, the political ramifications of this border on national scandal. I suppose that is why the Commandant and all the bigwigs are anxious to tell all that it is a wonderful weapon.

My loyalty has to be with these 18-year old Marines. Too many times (yesterday most recently) I've been on TF's awaiting medical evacuation and listened to bandaged and bleeding troopers cuss the M-16. Yesterday, we got in a big one . . . The day found one Marine beating an NVA with his helmet and a hunting knife because his rifle failed—this can't continue—32 of about 80 rifles failed yesterday.[28]

When investigators from the congressional committee went to Vietnam, they confirmed another report: that one Marine had been killed as he ran up and down the line in his squad, unjamming rifles, because he had the only cleaning rod in the squad.[29]

THE TECHNICAL data that came out of the congressional inquiry convinced the members of the committee to release an unusually sharp report, charging that the M-16 had been sabotaged by the ordnance corps. Yet the most striking aspect of the testimony was its humdrum, routine tone. When representatives of the ordnance corps were pressed to explain their decisions, they fell back on citations from the rule books, like characters in a parody of the bureaucratic temperament.* They seemed to have a hard time remembering who was responsible

---

*This exchange between Representative Ichord and Colonel Harold Yount, who was the Army's project manager for the M-16, suggests the petty bureaucratic tone of the Army's explorations:

ICHORD: Has anyone in the Army Materiel Command made a study trying to relate malfunctions to cyclic rates using 5.56 millimeter ammunition, Colonel Yount?

YOUNT: The test, of course, that we conducted at Frankford Arsenal in December,

for crucial decisions; they tended to explain things by saying, "the feeling was," or "the practice has been . . ." They could list with careful bureaucratic logic the reasonableness of each step they had taken: if you didn't have Arctic test requirements, you might not have adaptable rifles. If you didn't change to ball powder, you would have had chamber pressures over the allowable limits—which might have been dangerous for the troops. They seemed not to see a connection between these choices and the soldiers who were dying with jammed rifles in their arms. They were certainly aware of the M-16's troubles, and bowed to no one in their concern. What it proved, they said, was that the rifle had always been a risky experiment—especially (as they pointed out several times) when it was being used by the kind of soldiers the draft was dredging up these days, who couldn't understand the importance of keeping their weapons clean.

Even the accusations of impropriety were small-time. In its report, the committee criticized one Nelson Lynde, Jr., a general who was in charge of the Army Weapons Command between 1962 and 1964 and approved purchases of the M-16 from Colt, and then accepted a job shortly after retirement with the parent company of Colt. The committee reprimanded General Lynde for an apparent conflict of interests—even though, as Lynde pointed out, the Army's counsel had not forbidden him to accept the job. The committee also urged an audit of the profits Colt had made on the rifle and of the "sole-source" relationship with Olin-Mathieson. In 1980 I asked the committee's investigator, Earl Morgan, whether more blatant corruption—bribes, kickbacks—had been involved. "Oh, I'd be amazed if there wasn't some, knowing how that business is done," he said. "But we never found anything we could prove."

The committee also recommended that the Army immediately conduct a thorough, honest test of the two kinds of ammunition, with the strong suggestion that it should switch back to IMR. That never happened. Instead of going back to the original powder, the ordnance

---

1966 was aimed at doing this . . . As far as other studies are concerned, are you referring to something like computer studies?

ICHORD: Any type of study, just trying to get a correlation. I believe we have had record statements that you had no way of knowing that increase in the cyclic rate of approximately 100 rounds per minute would increase the malfunctions of the rifle. That is why I asked the question. Has there been any study trying to correlate it?

YOUNT: Oh, yes, since that time we have found that if this weapon is fired above 850 rounds per minute you are going to run into malfunctions due to the higher cyclic rate. Prior to that time we did not have this number isolated.[30]

corps modified the ball powder and changed the mechanical "buffer" of the rifle, which slowed down the cyclic rate. That solved part of the jamming problem, but did not restore the rifle's original reliability or "lethality." (Nor was the change in the barrel "twist" ever corrected.) Through every day of combat in Vietnam, American troops fired cartridges filled with the ball powder that was the legacy of the ordnance corps. They still do.

The ordnance corps is still at work. Late in 1980, after Army troops went on exercises in Egypt, unattributed comments started showing up in news reports about the special circumstances of desert war. You could see for miles across the sand, the stories said. What you really needed was a rifle that would be sharpshooter accurate at 600 or 800 yards—not a popgun like the M-16. What you really needed was a weapon from the Army's own labs.

THE F-16

IN JANUARY 1979 the United States Air Force took delivery of the first operational model of a new fighter airplane known as the F-16. It was the first American fighter, and one of the very few American weapons of any type, that cost less than the preceding model. It was also the product of a fundamentally different approach to defining the purposes of combat aircraft and the means of producing them. As with the M-16 rifle, the novel approach its designers took accounted for the plane's most striking virtues, but that very novelty created resistance within the Air Force development bureaucracies. The result was a series of modifications in the original design of the plane, which showed up as defects and compromises in the plane that Air Force pilots were finally asked to fly.

IN DECEMBER 1978, as part of a celebration of the 75th anniversary of the first powered flight at Kitty Hawk, an engineer and analyst named Pierre Sprey went to Wright-Patterson Field in Ohio to present a speech. His subject was the evolution of the fighter airplane in the third quarter of a century since Kitty Hawk. Sprey's real theme was the analysis of air combat that he and a small group of associates known as the "Fighter Mafia" had been pushing from within the Defense Department for at least a dozen years. His talk summed up the lessons learned and the reasoning followed in the development of the F-16 in the beginning of the decade.

Sprey is a dapper-looking man in his forties, with silver hair combed straight back and a jaunty air. He had been trained as an engineer at Yale and as a statistician at Cornell, had worked for the Grumman Aircraft Corporation, and had come to the Pentagon as an analyst during the regime of Robert McNamara. His approach at Wright-Patterson was to compare the major U.S. fighters that had been built between 1950 and 1975, starting with the F-86, which had been so successful in air combat in Korea, and ending with the most modern, expensive, and "capable" American fighters, the F-14 and F-15. He included planes from Russia, France, and Sweden as well.

The novelty in Sprey's approach was to judge the planes not by their design specifications or their intended purpose, but by how well they bore up in combat. Aerial combat has a history of manageable proportions; it begins with World War I and runs through Vietnam and the assorted wars in the Middle East. An analysis of that record, Sprey suggested, yields four "combat-derived criteria" for a fighter airplane's success. No one in his audience could fail to notice that these criteria were very different from the two paramount standards—greater top speed and more complex electronics—that have determined the design of nearly every fighter the United States has built since World War II.[31]

The first of these four criteria, which towered over all the rest, was *surprise:* one pilot's ability to catch another completely unawares. In the entire history of air combat, between two thirds and four fifths of all "kills" were due to the element of surprise. Surprise dominated in World War I, and in Vietnam. The most lethal "ace" of all time, the German flier Eric Hartmann, did everything he could to avoid prolonged "dogfight" engagements. He claimed that of the 352 planes he destroyed during World War II, fully 80 percent were "kills" by surprise.[32] On the Allied side, one air commander filed a report in 1944 that might as well have been taken from accounts of Korea or Vietnam: "90 per cent of all fighters shot down never saw the guy who hit them."[33]

According to Sprey, people who notice these figures talk about tactics and alertness, but they almost never think that it might have something to do with the airplane itself. But a number of features of a plane's design do affect the chances for surprise. A smokeless engine, for one: an F-4 fighter (the Phantom) would be visible only within a radius of five miles if its engine did not smoke, but it is visible from fifteen to twenty-five miles away with its usual smoke trail. Since an enemy plane might be approaching from any angle through three dimensions, a smoke trail might increase the volume of air in which the enemy might see the Phantom by up to twenty-seven times.

An airplane's speed also affects its prospects for surprise, but not "speed" as it is usually conceived. When the services ask for new planes, and when congressional committees hear about the need to counter the Soviet threat, the speed discussed is nearly always the plane's maximum speed. A Mach 2.5 fighter is one that can use its afterburners to reach 2.5 times the speed of sound (roughly 1,900 miles per hour), regardless of how long it can stay there. But because afterburners consume fuel at such a tremendous rate, pilots can sustain those top speeds only for a matter of seconds.

The speed that does matter in combat, Sprey suggested, was cruising speed, "the speed that will let you fly long enough or far enough to do what you want to do to the enemy." When one plane has a speed advantage over another in combat—enabling him to sneak up behind the other plane's tail, and avoid others sneaking up on his—the advantage consists of the difference between the cruising speeds of the two planes. In both old and modern jet fighters, these are usually cruising speeds between Mach .7 and Mach .9—below the speed of sound, and far below the top speeds for which the planes have been so carefully designed and expensively produced.

If surprise was so important, Sprey continued, it also held implications for the proper electronic equipment on a plane, implications that ran directly counter to the prevailing wisdom of more "capable" planes. As the cost of each new fighter soared, a major reason was the more complex radar and "fire-control" systems. This equipment was intended to give the plane "all weather" and "beyond visual range" capabilities, which so far have not proven usable in combat. "All weather" meant the ability to detect other planes at night, in clouds, in storms; "beyond visual range" meant discerning enemy fighters from many miles away and targeting guided missiles to destroy them.* What these calculations ignore, Sprey said, is that the other plane is also looking for you, and these same radar systems serve as giant beacons, alerting any other plane in the region to your presence. If other planes are equipped with a "radar warning receiver" (that is, a "fuzz-buster"), they are quickly aware that someone is beaming radar toward them, and from what direction. The price of powerful radar, then, is to sacrifice off the top the element of surprise that determines 80 percent of all

---

*The reason these capabilities have not proven usable in combat is the "IFF problem," discussed in the previous chapter—the difficulty of telling an enemy plane from a friendly one without actually seeing the plane.

results. And for what? In Vietnam as in all other recent wars, the great majority of "kills" was based not on radar detection but on the pilot's own visual observations.

After surprise, the second "combat-derived criterion" on Sprey's list was: *to outnumber the enemy in the air.* A plane that sat on the ramp —due to fuel shortages, breakdowns, unprepared crews—did not exist, as far as the enemy was concerned. The only ones that counted were those that could be mustered in the sky. The goal of outnumbering the enemy was not to overwhelm him in specific fights, but to be everywhere at once. "If you outnumber him 8 to 1," Sprey said, "the one plane will have a better exchange rate, since he can shoot anything he sees, while the 8 will have a hell of a time keeping out of each other's way. What you want are twos and fours all over the battlefield, making the enemy pilots fear for their lives at every moment."

The implications of this principle, he said, were that a nation should strive for a large number of fighters, a large pool of experienced pilots, and a high daily sortie rate for each plane. Each of these goals becomes much easier to reach when a force includes simpler, cheaper planes, instead of more expensive and complicated ones. Cheaper planes mean that you can buy more of them for the same money, that pilots can train more often and gain experience, and that the sortie rate will be higher because there will be fewer breakdowns. "You show me the design for a plane," Sprey said, "and I'll tell you how many of them you can buy and how often you'll be able to fly them."

Sprey's third criterion was *maneuverability,* the quality John Boyd had defined in his "Aerial Attack Study" and his energy-maneuverability theory of air combat. The plane Boyd flew in Korea, the F-86, had a good ability to accelerate and turn, but that was a happy fluke. The F-86 had been intended to intercept bombers, which meant that it would have to fly high. To do that called for a large wing area, which also happened to make it so maneuverable in the Korean dogfights.

Maneuverability also involves "transient performance"—the ability to change abruptly from one maneuver, such as a dive or turn, to another. Pilots had seen for themselves the connection between design and transient performance. During World War II, British Spitfires had elegant, elongated wing tips, which increased their turning ability but reduced their ability to roll quickly. (The reason is that the inertial mass of the wings resists rolling, and the wing tips increased that mass.) Spitfire pilots found they were losing "kills" against German Messerschmitt 109s: the German pilots would roll and dive suddenly out of their reach before the Spitfires could roll to chase them. Then one Spitfire squadron in North Africa unbolted the wing tips on their planes, which lowered their ability to make sharp turns but increased their ability to roll and "kill" the diving Messerschmitts. When the next model of Spitfire was produced, it had graceless, stubby wings. The underlying lesson about "transient performance" was lost on aircraft designers for at least the next thirty years.

There was one other essential trait for producing a maneuverable plane, Sprey said. That was the plane's "persistence," its ability to stay in the fight long enough to convert its maneuvering advantage into a victory. He suggested a number of complex measures of persistence, which could be approximated by the "fuel fraction"—the proportion of a plane's total weight that was represented by fuel. The fuel fraction was determined by the plane's designers: the greater that fraction, the longer the plane would be able to last in combat.

Finally Sprey described his fourth combat criterion, *lethality*, which he defined as the ability to "obtain a reliable kill during any split-second firing opportunity." Lethality depended on how well the weapons worked—whether the machine gun or guided missile, when fired, was likely to hit its target—and how long it took the pilot to set up for the shot. It also involved questions of numbers—whether the pilot could afford, in terms of weight or money, to carry as many weapons as he needed—and of how well the weapons could resist the maneuvers and countermeasures the enemy imposed.

By all these standards, Sprey said, combat results showed that two weapons stood far above the alternatives. They were the 20-millimeter cannon and a heat-seeking missile known as the Sidewinder. They were the two simplest weapons, and, not coincidentally, they were also the cheapest. The cannon costs about $350 each time the trigger is pulled. The simplest Sidewinder model costs about $10,000 in today's dollars. The elaborate, radar-guided Sparrow missile costs about $100,000, and the latest AMRAAM (advanced medium range air-to-air missile) and Phoenix missiles cost $500,000 to $1,000,000 apiece. Sprey said that in combat, the cannon was about twice as "lethal" per trigger squeeze as the Sidewinder. In turn, the Sidewinder got more than twice as many "kills" per trigger squeeze as the Sparrow. Further, the Sidewinder and the cannon were simpler and safer for the pilot to use, since they do not require such a long "lock-on" period to guide the missile to its target.[34]

SPREY'S LIST of qualities contradicted the entire planning doctrine of military aviation since World War II. In its emphasis on high top speed and heavy electronic equipment, Sprey said, that doctrine had degraded each of the qualities that make a crucial difference in combat.

As planes became bigger, leading to the very large F-4, F-14, and F-15, they became easier to detect; and by relying on their radar, they forfeited the capacity to surprise. As they pushed their maximum speed higher and higher, toward the elusive realm of Mach 3, their cruising speed did not improve at all. As their weapons grew more complicated, they worked less well. And as all these tendencies pushed the cost of the planes up and up, the number of planes the United States could put in the air steadily declined. Sprey devised a measure for this last quality, which he called the "sorties per day per million dollars." It combined the initial cost of a given plane with its maintenance and reliability record, to tell you how many planes you could have flying each day for a given cost. After adjusting for inflation, Sprey said, with the old F-86, the United States could "buy" 2.1 sorties per day for each million dollars of procurement money. One "austere" plane of the sixties, the F-5A, had a sortie rate of 1.25. For the F-4 Phantom, the rate was .12; for the F-15, about .05; for the F-14, .028, or about one-eightieth as many as the F-86. Sprey plotted these numbers on a graph, and called it the curve of unilateral disarmament.

To end his 1978 lecture on a bright note, Sprey described the concept for an airplane that would represent a fundamental advance over any built since the Korean War. It would be small, cheap, and light; it would have a cruise speed above Mach 1.2; it would emphasize passive electronics of the fuzz-buster variety; it would use an improved aerial cannon and a missile like the Sidewinder; and in its planning would be characterized by a "radical elimination of specs and equipment."

IN THE MID-SIXTIES, a dozen years before Sprey gave his lecture at Wright-Patterson Field, he had encountered John Boyd in the Pentagon. Sprey says that it was Boyd's brilliant teaching that introduced him to the realities of fighter combat and the subtleties of aerial tactics. At the time, Sprey was a Pentagon analyst, and Boyd an Air Force major who had established himself as the premier theorist of air combat through his "Aerial Attack Study" and "energy maneuverability" theory, which were discussed in chapter 2. Boyd had been brought to Washington to work on the development team for the new, first-line FX fighter, which eventually became the F-15 Eagle. As suave as Sprey is, Boyd is blunt and direct. Boyd is a craggy-featured man of fearsome integrity and outspokenness; he is the type who sticks his face one inch away from yours to make his point and always seems ready to grab you by the lapels to make sure you have understood. As the father of energy-maneuver theory, he fought to see that the F-15 was built to meet maneuver requirements, the first time they had ever been applied to an American fighter's design. Boyd created an innovative process of design "trade-offs," intended to find the most effective combination, in a plane of given weight, of acceleration (which requires a large motor), turning ability (which requires a large wing), and range (which requires a large fuel tank). Through the rigor of his analyses and the force of his personality, Boyd managed to get the plane's designed weight down from 60,000 pounds to 40,000, and to make several other changes, such as eliminating a proposed variable-sweep wing and simplifying the plane's electronics. (This last was a temporary victory.)

Despite Boyd's influence, the most important decisions about the F-15 were finally made without reference to the maneuverability and "trade-off" criteria he had laid out for the Air Force generals.

The choices were made not in wind tunnels or after flight tests, but on the basis of technical specifications scratched on a sheet of paper. One was that the plane's radar be able to spot a small object at a distance of 40 miles. (The exact size of the target is classified, but it was stated as a certain, small number of square meters of radar-reflecting surface.) That choice indicated a radar antenna about 36 inches across, which in turn dictated much of the size and shape of the plane. It also meant a dramatic increase in the F-15's own size and its visibility on enemy radar screens.

Next, the paper specifications said that the F-15 should be a Mach 3 plane. When news filtered out about the Soviet Foxbat, its supposed threat became the justification for the F-15's top speed. (Belenko had not yet given the West a look at the real plane, so there was only the word of the threat-inflators to go on.) John Boyd pointed out that the Mach 2 planes could almost never use their top speed in combat, and asked what the point was of Mach 3 (or, later, Mach 2.7). A compromise was reached on Mach 2.5, which added considerably to the size and complexity of the airframe and the cost of the exotic materials that must be used to withstand that speed and stress. With the specifications for radar and speed, some of the most important questions about the plane's design had been answered. The repeated efforts of Boyd and others to make the plane more "austere" were held off by, among other things, the Air Force argument that only a "large, capable" plane would be up to the Foxbat challenge.[35] The effect of these rebuffs was to turn Boyd's attention away from revising the F-15 and toward designing an entirely different, light plane.

In 1967 he met Sprey and explained the results of his "trade-off" studies for the F-15. Over the next year or so, Sprey worked from this data to show the feasibility of a cheaper, smaller fighter that would weigh between 15,000 and 25,000 pounds, to the F-15's 40,000. They were attracted by each other's outlook and shared the fear that the trend toward costly planes would leave the Air Force hopelessly outnumbered and outfought.

They were joined in 1969 by another participant, Everest Riccioni, whose findings about the cost and performance of fighter planes were discussed in chapter 3. At the time, Riccioni was still a colonel in the Air Force, with experience as a test pilot and engineer. Riccioni's main objection to the F-15 was its cost. "I would have been happy to settle for degraded performance, as long as we could find a cheaper plane," he now says. Sprey and Boyd persuaded him that less weight, cost, and electronics would actually produce a better plane. Riccioni developed his own careful studies of the relationship between top speed, complexity, cost, and performance in combat. In January 1970 he became head of a small development planning office in the Pentagon with authority to sponsor new designs. Also in 1970, Sprey went public with the concept of a small, high-performance fighter, in a speech to the American Institute of Aeronautics and Astronautics convention in St. Louis.

In the summer of 1970 Riccioni had a dazzling insight. He realized that the Navy might well have a low-cost fighter program of its own under way. If it did, and if it reached completion first, the Air Force might be in a position it had occupied far too often, being obliged to buy a plane the Navy produced. Riccioni confirmed his hunch about the Navy, and prepared an extensive "briefing" for a low-cost plane, which he called the Falcon. The briefing discussed two threats—the "external threat," from the Russians, and the "internal threat," from the Navy. Its final chart read:

> Unless the US Air Force thoroughly studies high performance austere fighters and is prepared to consider them as a necessary complement to other air superiority aircraft, the US Air Force may be:
>
> A. Outgamed by the Navy (Again)
>
> and/or
>
> B. Outfought by the Russians.

"That got their attention," he said later. "The Air Force doesn't respond to what the Russians do. It reacts to what the Navy does."[36]

Shortly after that briefing, Riccioni fought for and obtained authorization to grant money for studies of a lightweight plane. The money he put up—$149,000 for design studies—was peanuts by the standards of the business, but the contractors read it as the first indication of serious interest from the Air Force, which might be followed by billions of dollars' worth of contracts.

Several other forces were converging at the same time: increasing criticism in the press and Congress of the cost of the F-14 and F-15; pressure from outside the Department to return to a procurement system where new ideas for planes were developed as functioning prototypes, and purchased only *after* the prototypes had proven their worth in fly-off competitions; indications that the vast overseas market might be interested in a good lightweight plane; and, last but certainly not least, the hunger of the aircraft manufacturers who had been left out of the F-14 and F-15 contracts. The lightweight-fighter concepts were usually proposed as complements to the F-15 rather than as replacements for it; but the F-15's partisans could read the blunt criticism of their product barely veiled behind these comments. Within the Air Force, loyalty to the F-15 became what profession of faith in the Blessed Virgin is within the Church: a prerequisite act of belief for all who seek membership. Because of suspicions about his insufficient loyalty to the plane, Riccioni was notified in 1970 that his Pentagon tour would be shortened and that he should prepare for a new job, in Korea.

By the time Riccioni was deported, the most important decisions about the "Lightweight Fighter Program," which led to the F-16, had also been made. The fundamental one, urged on by Riccioni, Boyd, and Sprey, was that the government would set the absolute minimum of technical pre-specifications, and would wait to judge the manufacturers' prototypes on their performance in competitive "fly-offs." Moreover, the Air Force decision to build prototypes of the planes would not include a commitment to go into full-scale production after the fly-offs were complete. Indeed, many advocates of the F-15 within the Air Force were confident that the Lightweight Fighter Program would never go beyond the prototyping stage, and would remain a mere "technology demonstration" that led to nothing else.

Such competitive fly-offs were unprecedented in the Pentagon. Until the late forties and early fifties, it had been common practice to build prototypes of new weapons, although there were no direct fly-offs of competing prototypes. But prototyping fell from favor as advocates of more complex systems began to dominate the research and development bureaus of the Pentagon, especially the Air Force, in the late fifties. In place of prototyping came voluminous paper proposals and paper competitions, based on paper analyses of how the planes should perform. By the mid-sixties, the "design teams" for a complex plane had swelled to 3,000, and several billion dollars could be invested in preparations before the first rivet was driven into the first wing. Naturally, after all this effort, no one had the stomach for a genuinely "competitive" test of different prototypes. A project was almost never cancelled, once analysts had proven on paper that it should work, even if the plane, when finally built, was a dog.

This approach, known under McNamara as "Total Package Procurement," had come in for attack from the Congress by the early seventies, and the Lightweight Fighter Program seemed a perfect opportunity to try a different road. Unlike the elaborate design specs of the standard Air Force project, the succinct requirements for the Lightweight Fighter called for no maneuvers at speeds above Mach 1.6, but set loose goals for a plane that could out-accelerate, out-turn, and out-endure any existing aircraft in the range of speeds actually seen in combat—about Mach .6 to Mach 1.6—and prove its virtues in a competitive fly-off. David Packard, who as Deputy Secretary of Defense had been one of the strongest partisans of prototyping, spelled out the new philosophy in a memorandum early in 1971:

It is important that each program have these features:
1. . . . Only the *price* should be firm. All specifications should be open.
2. At least two projects should be authorized for each class of plane.
3. A plan for fly-off testing will be required.
4. It must be made clear that there is no commitment to go ahead with a further program.
5. At the same time, we will lose benefit of this approach if, after a fly-off, we go back to some other competition for full development and production. In other words, the fly-off testing is the source selection if we decide to go ahead.[37]

After a number of intricate fandangos, involving Northrop's ambitions for foreign aircraft sales and an abortive proposal for a small fighter from "Kelly" Johnson, a world-renowned designer at Lockheed who had conceived the U-2 and SR-71 spy planes, the development of prototypes finally began. The two manufacturers involved, Northrop and General Dynamics, did produce prototypes that embodied the virtues of lightweight fighters that the "Fighter Mafia" had long been touting. The winner, a General Dynamics product known as the YF-16, was in the eyes of the Mafia the greatest fighter since the F-86. It weighed about 20,000 pounds and carried only a simple aerial cannon, Sidewinder missiles, and their fire-control systems. Through the fly-offs, Sprey had kept looking for ways to take extra weight out of the plane, and Boyd had reined in all attempts to move away from actual flight data to computer analyses as the standard for evaluating the competitors. Because it was so light (and therefore could accelerate and turn so quickly), the plane could fly circles around other planes, including the F-15. Because it was so small and so hard to see, either by eye or by radar, it maximized the advantage of surprise. Its projected cost was about half that of the F-15. James Schlesinger, by then the new Secretary of Defense, had taken on the Lightweight Fighter as one of his own projects, and he was well pleased with the result of the fly-offs. He decided to proceed with production, and he convinced both the Air Force and the Congress to go along. General Dynamics won the contract. But the story was not over.

Before the F-16 could go into production, it fell back under the domination of the Air Force's development and procurement bureaucracies. Under the supervision of General Alton Slay, the head of the Air Force's Configuration Control Committee, the plane went into "full scale engineering development," which amounted to modifying the blueprints, adding the technical specifications that had been so deliberately avoided up to this point, and loading roughly two tons of new electronic equipment and other modifications into the plane. This stage represented nothing less than the rejection of the entire philosophy under which the plane had been designed. Some twenty-five members of the Air Force had managed the development of the prototypes and the competitive fly-offs. Now the Air Force management group grew toward 200 people, and the contractor's team rose from 150 engineers to about 1,500.

The "Fighter Mafia" was outnumbered and outflanked, and Secretary Schlesinger, who had been the plane's early champion, chose not to fight the thousand battles that would arise as the Air Force added one specification after another. The plane's mission was redefined: instead of being a pure fighter, as in the original plans, it was converted into a "multiple mission" airplane, to be used for attacking ground targets and dropping nuclear bombs. The structural and electronic changes justified by these new missions raised the F-16's cost and degraded its performance as a fighter—conveniently reducing its status as a competitor to the Air Force's favorite fighter, the F-15.

The YF-16 had been designed to withstand forces of 7.33 Gs (1 G equals the force of gravity). The Configuration Control Committee increased that specification to 9 Gs, which meant added reinforcement and weight throughout the plane. The avionics, complex radar, and "electronic countermeasures" systems all came back in, adding greatly to the cost. The more complex radar demanded more power and more cooling, which in turn made the fuselage grow. *That* meant that the wings and tail had to be enlarged—but the tail was not enlarged enough, which reduced the plane's stability in flight. Before leaving the Pentagon, Secretary Schlesinger had struck an agreement with General David Jones, then Chief of Staff of the Air Force, that the F-16 would not be equipped with nuclear bombs. If the F-16 did carry nuclear weapons, Schlesinger knew, it would be held on strategic alert at its bases, and pilots would not be able to make the frequent training flights they needed to become expert in this new plane. Within a week of Schlesinger's departure in 1975, the Air Force ordered nuclear equipment for the F-16.

The result was an aircraft that cost 75 percent more than the original YF-16 would have; that is being fielded in units with air-to-ground missions rather than pure fighter units; that weighed roughly 24,000 pounds instead of around 20,000, with a proportional reduction in acceleration; and that came loaded with hard-to-maintain electronic equipment. Nonetheless, it was a better aerial fighter, by all the combat standards Pierre Sprey laid out in 1978, than any other the United States or the Soviet Union had built in thirty years. In aerial exercises, F-16 pilots, with passive radar systems, detect F-15s as quickly as the F-15s, with their overpowering radar systems, can detect them. In NATO exercises, Belgian pilots in F-16s have soundly beaten U.S. pilots in the Eagles, which cost more and can fly less frequently.

Like the M-16 in Vietnam, the F-16 was a better weapon than its predecessor, but so much less than it might have been.

FIVE

EMPLOYEES

THE DISCUSSION to this point has focused on machines and therefore has been true to the managerial, technological spirit of modern American defense. This chapter is about men. The machines are merely tools. Through the history of combat, they have been far less important than the strategies under which they are employed and the bonds of mutual trust, shared sacrifice, and recognized leadership that give coherence to the forces who use the weapons.

The managerial emphasis affects more than the machines: it also shapes the way officers and men view their roles. Its most damaging effect has been to suggest that military service is like any other occupation. This implies that its leaders can devote themselves mainly to advancing their own careers, and that its work force can be motivated by the same combination of fringe benefits and sanctions as any assembly-line crew. This chapter will discuss the implications of that view. Its central message is that the effectiveness of a nation's military finally depends on the creation of a series of human bonds. These are the bonds among the enlisted men in a fighting force; between the enlisted men and the officers who lead them; among the officers; and between the military as a whole and the nation it represents. Such bonds have no place in economic calculations or labor-market models, for they are built on such noneconomic qualities as shared experience and mutual sacrifice, which create a sense of mutual respect and trust. Without them, the military cannot function. Soldiers will risk death only when they feel a bond of trust and responsibility with their fellow soldiers. Units will only follow leaders who have earned their trust through demonstrations of honor and of willingness to sacrifice for the good of their men. A nation's military, especially in a democracy, can endure the hardships of war only if it feels tied to the nation by a sense of common purpose and respect. Without those bonds, it cannot cohere.

The creation of these bonds has been imperiled within the military by the managerial ethic, and by the officer corps' "careerist" emphasis on getting ahead, no matter what the cost. But at just the moment when some members of the military are trying to correct the distortions in their professional values, the nation undermines the bonds further by its willful blindness to the failings of the volunteer force.

IN THE STONE buildings of Carlisle Barracks, Pennsylvania, near the track on which the young Jim Thorpe set his records as a student at the Carlisle Indian School, officers on their way to the top attend the Army War College. The students wear civilian clothes to de-emphasize difference in rank and to foster an "academic" atmosphere. The instructors wear their ribbons and olive green. One of them is Dandridge Malone, a colonel of the infantry. He is a fifty-one-year-old man of medium height and compact build, with crisp creases in his clothes and a wholly "military" bearing. Several times I heard his name cited in conversation to illustrate the maxim that the best men in the Army are the colonels who don't make general.[1]

In a different life, Malone might have made his name as the author of country-and-western lyrics, for he has a gift for expressing home truths with the bittersweet, half-mawkish grace of the Nashville songs. He has written a number of articles in just that manner about the nature of the military life. Once when Malone was speaking to a group of officers, a young lieutenant asked him what a "soldier" was. In response, Malone prepared and narrated a forty-minute tape recording called "The Soldier." Against a background of C&W-style music, and with sound effects, Malone tells the soldier's story, from the time he leaves home, a young recruit, on his way to boot camp; through the tearful farewells to family and friends, the anxiety and confusion at the training schools; the friendships, the coarseness, the constant reassignments and promotions; the compromises and satisfactions of military marriage; and on to Vietnam, through the fire fights, the fear again, the deaths of friends; survival and return; the first glimpse of children he has not seen for a year, the first embrace of his wife, and then:

". . . a supper of who knows who cares what, and more talk and bedtime and kids asleep, and an endless night of soft talk, moonlight, touches, and sweet tears of thankfulness and the pent-up love of a thousand thoughts and dreams—a clear blue morning, a bright-yellow school bus, an apple-green housecoat and hot black coffee—elbows up on the kitchen table, and the first tentative plans for the next duty station and the next move, and—

"—and if all these wondrous things," Malone drawls at the end, country guitar twanging in the background, "which thousands of us share in whole or part, can, by the mindless logic of a soulless computer, programmed by a witless pissant ignorant of affect, be called *just another job* . . . then, by God, I'm a sorry, suck-egg mule."

The significance of the tape lies, by design, in the phrase "just another job." It is Malone's way of suggesting that the qualities that count in military leadership will always be fundamentally different from those that are rewarded elsewhere. The soldier's task is different—he is asked to kill and to expose himself to death—and the motivations of men who do so are based on requirements that do not exist in most other "jobs."

The essential difference is the focus of loyalty. In the civilian world, under the theories of John Locke and Adam Smith, the proper unit of social analysis is the individual. He acts alone; he is expected to follow where self-interest leads. While untrammeled self-interest is often pernicious in the civilian world, in many cases it is constructive. A salesman advances his firm's interests by advancing his own. An entrepreneur in a competitive market helps many other people (his customers, his employees) by helping himself. That is almost never true in the military. "The military is an allowable socialist meritocracy, existing to preserve a society of individuals," says James Webb, a Naval Academy graduate who led troops in combat in Vietnam as a Marine. "It is socialist in that the group is more important than the individual. It is a meritocracy in that the ways you relate to your unit are not based on monetary terms, but on values of performance that only matter within the unit and are meaningless outside."[2]

In chronicles of combat through the ages, certain elements have consistently distinguished the units that prevailed from those that were shattered and lost. Those are the bonds of shared experience, identity, and trust that give cohesion to men in small groups and make them willing to sacrifice for one another and to follow their leader. The novels of James Jones are full of references to the dogfaces who hate war, hate the Army, hate the generals, but will go out and die for the men in the company. "Soldiers fight because they love one another within that squad," the Army Chief of Staff, General Edward Meyer, said in an interview. In his theory of conflict, John Boyd says that successful forces are held together by a sense of mutual trust, and sowing distrust is one of the fastest ways to destroy an army. The common saying is: No soldier takes a hill for his nation, he takes it for his buddies.

In effective fighting groups, these bonds must run not only among the soldiers, but also between the members of a unit and a leader who has shown that he will share the hardships they endure. William L. Hauser, who retired as a colonel after twenty-five years in the military, has written with great perception about the inner cohesion of the Army. He recalls the instructions that Field-Marshal William Slim, a British hero of the Burma campaign in World War II, gave his officers: "I tell you, *as officers,* that you will not eat, sleep, smoke, sit down, or lie down until your soldiers have had a chance to do these things. If you will hold to this, they will follow you to the ends of the earth. If you do not, I will *break you in front of your regiments* [emphasis in original]."[3]

In their book, *Crisis in Command,* two former officers, Richard A. Gabriel and Paul L. Savage, say that "the cohesion of a combat unit is to a large extent a function of the degree to which combat troops perceive that their officers are willing to fight and die *with* them [emphasis in original]."[4] They point out that in World War II, German troops maintained their discipline and cohesion even when their cause was obviously doomed. It is no coincidence, they say, that one third of all German generals had been killed in combat, and that the German officer corps as a whole had a higher casualty rate than did the enlisted men.

In an attempt to define more precisely the qualities a leader must display to produce trust and cohesion among his troops, a team from the Army War College interviewed majors who had led rifle platoons in Vietnam several years earlier, asking them to name the values that counted in combat. Four qualities stood out, described by Colonel Malone as follows:

Candor: It's more than openness, it's saying the things that need to be said without a lot of words, without an under-the-table agenda, without a lot of Yessir and Nossir. The stakes are too high and time is too short to screw around with anything but the essence and the truth.

The battlefield is the most honest place in the world. The candor of the battlefield is why cohesiveness forms there so quickly and permanently, and why lies told there are punished not with gossip but with action.

Commitment: This is mainly commitment to people, rather than to an idea. For the soldier, the main commitment is to that "ole buddy," and after that to the small group of people in his squad. There's some commitment to the larger unit and a little to the nation, but nowhere near as much as to the buddy and the squad. You see it in the Medal of Honor winners. They're mainly men who jump on grenades, and they do it because they are committed to that small group. You go get your wounded, because they're your buddies.

Courage: A guy always has a choice about taking a risk. He can lie there behind a log and there's nothing you can do about it. No one can make him get up. On the battlefield, the risk he must take is a total-loss risk, and yet, for various reasons, the soldier himself decides that the total-loss risk is his best choice. Deciding to take that risk is courage. It is the ultimate definition of a soldier.

Courage is contagious. He did it, I can do it. It's not that they want to do it, but they *will* do it.

Competence: This is the oldest value on the battlefield. You can have candor and commitment, but if you are not competent you won't survive. On the battlefield, competence establishes the pecking order, which may or may not correspond to rank or the chain of command, depending on the competence of those in the chain.[5]

There are parts of the civilian world that operate on similar principles of shared loyalty and shared risk. Families, football teams, political campaigns, churches, small-town doctors, all depend for their success on peacetime versions of the same traits. The example of these groups confirms that the qualities that really count for their, or the military's, success cannot be "bought," the way a new running back or a petroleum-law specialist might be bought, simply with a better contract and more attractive fringe and retirement benefits. The financial incentives matter, but by themselves they will fail to create the human bonds, as surely as big-city school systems fail when they try to "purchase" a more dedicated corps of teachers by sweetening their contract with the teachers' union. Wherever military service, or medical or musical service, is judged purely by the economist's calculation of marginal trade-offs and maximized self-interest, it erects a structure of values inimical to the required goals. That is at the heart of the military complaint about "managerial" defense.

TO HEAR MANY soldiers tell it, the only thing that's wrong with America's military leadership is that the "managers" from the Pentagon have stuck their fingers in the soup. Just as managerial logic often leads to simplistic judgments about the "efficiency" of various weapons and strategies, it also tends to overlook the importance of the intangible, human factors that are difficult to measure scientifically but always count in combat. A frequent illustration of the manager's blindness is the wild proliferation of "cee-cubed-eye" (the communications networks that were described in chapter 3). Leaders will only seize the initiative in combat, soldiers say, if they've been delegated true operating authority by superiors who know that there's a risk the combat leader will screw up. The battlefield leader senses that he's been entrusted with responsibility; on the whole, that sense of trust will inspire him to do a better job. An army that delegates real responsibility to the leaders on the scene will have some incompetents and even some Lieutenant Calleys, but it will move farther, faster in combat than one that has taught its officers to do only what they are told.

Centralized control has been a permanent feature of the Soviet army, as of other parts of Russian life, but for the American military it is a self-inflicted wound, arising from the managerial logic and the wonders of cee-cubed-eye. One former Navy officer tells about a friend who was commanding a ship during a rescue operation. His superiors were hectoring him on the radio, asking what ships were showing up to the left of him and what he saw on his right. Finally the officer grabbed an ensign and sent him below to work the radio. "Tell them you're me," he said. "Tell them anything they want to hear. I've got a job to do." The story was obviously meant to suggest that this was the way a real leader would respond but that there were not many of them left. "What about the young officers who think that's the way life's supposed to be?" said the man who told the story. "What are they going to do twenty years from now when somebody shoots at their ship and they can't get through on the radio to ask what to do?" There was a Gresham's law of the officer corps, he said. The only ones who stayed under these circumstances were those who didn't really understand what "leadership" meant. First they made up 10 percent of the officer corps, then 50, then 90, and eventually there was no other model for young officers to follow. Indeed, he said, the most dangerous development in the officer corps was that it was driving out the very people it most urgently needed to keep.*

---

*Philip Gallery, son of an admiral and an Annapolis classmate of Webb's who has since left the Navy, described the pattern as it applied to the socially liberalizing messages Elmo Zumwalt sent through the Navy when he was Chief of Naval Operations in the early seventies. "He was right to attack the racial problem the way he did. But what he should have done is call in all the admirals, tell them that they had a responsibility to fix it, or they'd be *out*. The real problem was that he circumvented the chain of command. An ensign would say, 'Smith, get a haircut.' Smith would go back and look

One Marine colonel described the pernicious effects of another step toward "efficiency" at his base—the centralized mess hall, where Marines would eat in shifts. It might make sense on the cost chart, he said, but how would his men learn to feed themselves in the field? "The worst thing about it is," he said, "that the cooks won't have to spend all day with the guys who eat their food. That helps remind them, and everybody else, that they all have to perform as part of a team."

In his office at the Army War College, Dandridge Malone has this written on his blackboard:

Things worth thinking about on the difference between leadership and management:

• Management is the "physics" of things, but leadership is the "chemistry" of people.

• When, in war, men must die (and in war, some must), they can't be *managed* to death . . . they must be led there.

• "Sacrifice" has an honored place in *leadership*, but not in *management* . . . and that may be the nub of our problem.

James Webb has written: "Management is not leadership. Management can be approached as an academic discipline; one can be taught to analyze data, to weigh alternatives, and to make a decision. Leader-

_____

at the Z-gram and say, 'Hell no, I don't need one.' If you've got an ensign telling seamen to get haircuts when they don't need 'em, what you really need are department heads who know what's going on, and can pull the ensign aside and tell him to stop it. And XOs [executive officers] who know what's going on and can pull the department heads aside. And captains who know about their XOs. But that's complicated. It's hard. There's no formula for it.

"What is essential is to give people responsibility and hold them to it. One way to judge that sense of responsibility is how officers train ensigns. Try to imagine: you're coming into port, there's some ensign up on the bridge, and he's going too fast. What qualities would it take to stand there and do nothing? It would take two. You would have to be a good judge of people. Will he realize his mistake in time to correct it? And if that judgment is incorrect, you would need confidence in yourself to be able to step in at the right time. That's the other quality. You get that from having been the ensign who learned it from a captain who had it too. There's the story about Muddy Waters, the old admiral. He was an ensign for Nimitz. Nimitz just sat there in his chair one time as Waters was coming in. He was coming too fast. Finally he realized it, threw out the anchor, finally got it stopped. Nimitz never got out of his chair. When it was over, he said, 'You know what you did wrong, don't you?' 'Yes, sir. I was going too fast.' Nimitz had figured out that the ensign would realize the problem in time—and that if he didn't, Nimitz would know what to do.

"That's too hard for them now."[6]

ship is something else. It is a subjective chemistry filled with human variables. It takes more than the ability to analyze data to make a leader; one must be able to motivate those who are being led, to reach their emotions through command presence, force, and example. It is much easier to educate a manager than to develop a leader."[7]

CAREERISM IN THE PEACETIME ARMY

PERSUASIVE AS THE soldier's complaints may be, they tend to underplay a further distortion of the military spirit. While parts of the officer corps have resented the incursions made into military values by the "managerial" style, many other elements have cooperated in the process, remaking themselves in the model of go-get-'em business executives.

The crucial word for this phenomenon is "careerism," which means, in essence, the desire to *be,* rather than the desire to *do.* It is the desire to have rank, rather than to use it; the pursuit of promotion without a clear sense of what to do with a higher rank once one has attained it. The military is naturally a fertile ground for careerism, since there is a single, visible hierarchy of rank on which all men are placed—especially in the peacetime army, when there is no test of combat performance. Careerism may be observed, in embryo, at the service academies, where the most successful military careers have their start. Taking in young men and women at an age when their characters cannot have fully formed, deliberately intending (as no private college does) to reshape their personalities, the academies most often succeed in imbuing their graduates with the passion to worship what Maureen Mylander, in her book about the military, called the "God of Class Standing."[8] Academy graduates tend to fall into two categories: the Military Men, with the culture of arms in their very chromosomes; and the formlessly ambitious ones, as eager to become chairman of the board if they leave the service as to make general if they stay. The cheating scandals that "shock" Annapolis, West Point, and Colorado Springs every few years are one symptom of the amorphous ambition for place that the academies implant. The institutions that most closely resemble them are the nation's "best" law schools, whose influence is blunted by the extra four years of maturity its students possess.

One of the most important propulsive forces behind careerism is the policy of "up or out," which was introduced into the military shortly after World War II, as part of an effort to create a younger, tougher officer corps. Officers knew the schedule: they became captains in their early twenties, majors in their early thirties, colonels in their late forties.[9] If they weren't keeping up with the crowd, they were out.

"Up or out" greatly magnified the careerist emphasis on holding a position rather than doing a job. Even the most dedicated soldier knew that if he was too indifferent to the imperatives of promotion, he might not be able to stay and do the things—commanding troops, flying planes—that had attracted him to the service in the first place.* As a result, a rich lore has grown up in the military about the proper steps in the dance of promotion. In *Self-Destruction*, "Cincinnatus" said that after the Korean War

"Duty, honor, and country" was replaced by the need to be in the right job at the right time. The news spread throughout all levels of the army. Careerism, rather than dedication to the welfare of one's men, was the way to get ahead. Such career advancement was best enhanced by "ticket-punching" procedures: be sure to go to jump school so you could wear airborne wings; pick up Ranger tabs to wear on your uniform sleeves; command a unit as quickly as possible—but not for too long, for that might prevent moving on to the next requirement of staff duty. Secure a coveted assignment in the Pentagon. Seek overseas duty. . . . Do not make mistakes. They hurt. Do nothing rather than commit an error, and at all times "cover your ass."[11]

A man who served in the Air Force at Wright-Patterson Field describes the way one of his ambitious colleagues played this game while still a lieutenant: "There was a Junior Officer's Council at the base, the kind of thing that was supposed to build morale, and so forth. It didn't really do anything, but after a while you had to get into it to have something to put on your personnel records and get a good OER [Officer Efficiency Report]. If you showed any interest in the organiza-

---

*This could not be more different from the military tradition Gabriel and Savage describe in *Crisis in Command:*

Legendary military units notable for their toughness, such as the XX Valeria Victrix Legion of Rome, the British Guards and Scottish regiments, the French Foreign Legion . . . all possessed a cadre of long-term small-unit leaders. In all those military units, it was recognized that an officer might well be a superb company commander for his entire career and so little pressure existed to force him to prove that he was a potential field marshal. . . . Such a man might well spend twenty years [in a British regiment in India] with immense benefit to British power and colonial stability and never go beyond major or lieutenant colonel. He would not, however, be discarded *merely* for failing to be promoted "on schedule."[10]

tion, you could be an officer of the council, and there was one superambitious guy who ended up as president. When he got in, he had the council commission a study on how people got promoted to major 'below the zone'—ahead of the normal schedule. The promotion lists tell you which guys are below the zone, so he got their names, and sent out questionnaires to them, asking how they did it. He found out the common traits—and then he tried to follow them. He even became a deacon in the Baptist Church because that looked good on the OER. He did make major below the zone, and lieutenant colonel. I understand he's burned out today. The sad thing is that the guy did some very promising work, but he would never follow up on it because his whole purpose in life was to get promoted."

The careerist emphasis has several effects in the peacetime military. The most fundamental is the perversion of the essential bond between officers and men. An ambitious officer with his eye ever on the promotion board will be tempted to use his men, rather than lead them; to avoid their risks, rather than share them; to rely on his rank to command their obedience, rather than winning their trust through example. Careerism also leads to the debasement of the Officer Efficiency Reports, the basic documents on which officers are judged for promotion. These have become so cheapened that any officer who is not rated "outstanding" has, in effect, seen his career torpedoed. "Commanding officers know that good scores make for happy subordinates and that bad scores, rather than serving notice of temporary failings, can wreck careers," Nicholas Lemann has written.[12] "So the maximum score of 200 is common and 185 is a disaster. If you average below 195, it's thought impossible to make major." The desire to "max" the efficiency rating is notable for promoting a please-the-boss mentality, or, as it is often known among officers, the "zero defects" approach. Beyond that, the OERs have a devastating symbolic impact, demonstrating how little value the military places on honest, unpleasant news. Worse, they breed contempt for those who do get promoted, since everyone involved knows that the standards of judgment are systematically warped. When junior officers compare the men who make general and admiral with those who do not, the lesson they are most likely to carry away is that too much character and honesty can be handicaps to men on the way up.

Careerism leads to a trivialization of the officer's function as well, through the phenomenon of "ticket punching." The philosophy of the ticket punch is that an officer on his way up should have a balance of experience. No man should be a general (or colonel, or major) who has not commanded troops. In theory, this reflects a sensible emphasis on the real business of the military command. As practiced, it defies all rules of military effectiveness. Since the U.S. Army has a far higher proportion of officers than most foreign forces, they end up elbowing each other for "command slots." The Army's Chief of Staff, General Edward C. Meyer, ordered, in 1980, that command tours should average thirty months in length, even if that means that some officers wouldn't have a chance to lead troops. Until that time, the military's solution to the problem had been a classic example of serving internal needs, rather than the standards of real performance. The answer had been the six- or twelve-month command slot, which gave everybody a chance to punch his ticket but that absolutely destroyed cohesion and loyalty between officers and men.

Command is not the only punch needed on the ticket. Ambitious officers must also go to the staff schools, get graduate degrees, prove they have the "breadth" for big assignments. The result, according to Edward Luttwak, is "an officer corps that is systematically diverted from its proper professional focus by all these other things.* What they give us now, we don't need. What civilian society is *not* competent to manage is, precisely, conflict. The military has become civilianized in the sense of emulating, at higher cost, things the civilians can do better —but not concentrating on the things the civilians cannot do, which are to train combat leaders, to study tactics, and to pursue strategies."

I asked Luttwak what response he got when he made these points to officers, as he has done. "Many of them agree, but they feel there are overwhelming forces against them. A military that has come under the domination of civilian micro-managers turns to managers of its own in defensive reaction. A military with serious personnel problems must devote more of its time to personnel management. A military with shortages of all supplies must pay attention to resource management. And a military that shares the national passion for high technology is drawn into engineering ambition. Also, there is a demand for these civilian skills by the officers themselves. You can't get an M.A. or a Ph.D. for being a good leader, so you don't have prestige. Under the 'up or out' promotion system, the military insists on having an educa-

---

*I never fully appreciated this "systematic diversion" until I encountered the public relations staffs at the Pentagon. Whenever I had arranged an interview with a prominent official—the Secretary of the Army, one of the Chiefs of Staff—I would be greeted by a one- or two-star general who would politely sit in during the interview, operating a tape recorder. It is no novelty to have a public relations man monitor an interview, but the idea that a general, chosen from thousands of other soldiers for his ability to lead men, should be performing this hack duty truly amazed me.

tion that is of some value in the civilian job market.* If they were teaching what they should, it would have *no* value in the civilian market."[14]

Few spectacles are more depressing than the modern officer corps in the nonmilitary part of its training. Somehow, in setting the balance between Renaissance men and pure warriors, between skilled managers and gifted leaders of troops, the military has not got any of it quite right. It is clear, from talking with officers and seeing who gets ahead, that a pure tough-talking commander is not going much higher than colonel—not unless he's taken some time off for a graduate degree in international relations or physics. But as far as I can tell, the function of those degrees is almost entirely to give the officers *credentials* rather than prepare them in any useful way for their jobs. When their dissertations and their War College papers move off military subjects to more "broadening" themes, they are usually superficial and vapid. The courses on nonmilitary subjects tend to be lickety-split surveys of every topic imaginable, the main effect of which is to teach the officer the names of assorted revolutions, or factions of Communism, or divisions of the executive branch, rather than any useful way to think about them. Why waste their time this way at all?

The ideal is the scholar-warrior, the man of action incorporated in the man of thought. The reality, most of the time, is the dilettante, who cannot reasonably be expected to master physics, or history, or management as a sideline, but who is expected to touch these bases instead of concentrating on the subject he should know, which is the nature of war.

There is a further perversity to the system. While men who should be leaders and strategists have to pretend they are scholars or managers to get ahead, the smaller number of officers who *are* gifted at management and reflective thinking know that they won't be promoted unless they can prove they're warriors too. It is as if an Olympic committee chose the contestants for every event—weight lifting, gymnastics, yachting, equestrian—on the basis of their overall score in the decath-

---

*William Hauser has pointed out that "up or out" teaches the prudent officer to think of the military as his "first career," since all but the most successful handful of officers would be leaving by their late forties or early fifties.[13] As their thoughts turned by degrees toward the necessary subject of the "second job," their attention drifted from the skills and values necessary to perform well in the first. The skills, especially in the combat arms, would have little worth in the second job; and devotion to the best interests of the military might well harm their chances of securing one of the most likely second berths, with a defense contractor.

lon. One major who works on a service publication, a serious man who has found exactly the right job, told me that he was trying to decide whether he should stay at his job and resign himself to being stuck at his current rank or try for a transfer to field command so that he could be considered for promotion. "In a sound military, you need three talents—the manager, the leader in the sense of 'a leader of men,' and the theorist," says William Lind of Senator Hart's staff. "Right now the manager totally dominates . . . the leader is tolerated up to field grade, and there is no place at all for the theorist. Clausewitz would not have lasted two weeks at West Point."[15] As Ward Just wrote ten years ago: "There has never been a Clausewitz in the American Army because the writing of Vom Kriege [On War] took time and serious thought."[16]

CAREERISM GOES TO WAR

THE FORCES of careerism are pernicious enough in a peacetime force. In Vietnam, their effect was catastrophic. Each pathology of the peacetime army had its equivalent on the battlefield. The equivalent of the inflated Officer Efficiency Reports, for example, was the promiscuous distribution of military decorations in Vietnam. By the beginning of 1971, more than 1,270,000 medals had been awarded to American soldiers, roughly 70 percent as many as were awarded during all of World War II, when 10 million men served.[17] The equivalent of the West Point cheating scandal was the officers' systematic lying about enemy dead, victories, civilian carnage. The purest and most destructive form of careerism was the wartime version of "ticket punching." German officers are with their units for three to four years at a time; in Vietnam, officers were on their way after six months. "Cincinnatus" recounts tale after tale of the effect of ticket punching, including these reflections from an artillery officer:

"Vietnam was the only war we had. Career development purposes were served by it; ticket punching helped. You needed a combat tour, you got one. The main thing was to have (at the time I was there) the right ribbons on your chest when the war ended. The fallacy, though, was that if you were really effective as a combat leader, you got six months. If you were the village idiot and couldn't do anything except to fly around in a helicopter and ask the troops if they were getting their mail, you got six months. The justification for the six-month command had, in reality, nothing to do with 'burn-out' but was followed in order to get as many people rotated through command slots as possible, so after the war the army would have a lot of people for a long time who had 'commanded' in combat."[18]

Richard Gabriel and Paul Savage emphasize the contrast between the heavy casualties in the German officer corps in World War II, and the American officers' record in Vietnam, where a total of four generals died violent deaths, one from a sniper's fire while riding a jeep, and three others in helicopter crashes. "Cincinnatus" says:

Grunts saw very few officers sharing their dangers with them. Most of them were Second and First Lieutenants who often were ex-enlisted men who had gone to OCS for a commission, or they were ex-college men who had stayed out of the service for as long as possible under the aegis of ROTC . . . Senior captains, majors, and above were more likely to be the career-oriented "lifers," doing their fighting from their "eye in the sky" command and control helicopters. From 2000 feet up they could direct their units in relative safety, rather than having their "ass in the grass" on the ground.[19]

(In interviews, a number of officers suggested that this principle could be raised to another level of abstraction. If soldiers are more likely to fight for officers who share their risks on the field, the military will more competently and bravely defend the nation if it senses that its sacrifices are honored and its special needs understood. That was not the case in Vietnam, where the military understood that it was sent on dirty duty, nor has it been the case since then, when officers have felt that the public does not really want to hear about their problems.)

WHATEVER DAMAGE the war in Vietnam did to the self-confidence and certainty of the nation, it did that much, squared, to the professional soldier. However much the soldiers may complain about not having been "allowed" to win the war, most of them seem to recognize that the war both caused and revealed considerable sickness at the center of their corps. At least some of them have responded by looking for the way back to proper military principles.

The nadir occurred in 1970, when the My Lai massacre was unveiled. To the public, "My Lai" became a shorthand expression for "butchery" and "brutality"; within the military, Lieutenant Calley's behavior was less shocking than the widespread complicity of the professional officer corps in condoning and covering up the event. In addition to his official report on the cover-up, Lieutenant General William L. Peers submitted a secret memorandum to William Westmoreland, by then the Army's Chief of Staff, suggesting that something had gone fundamentally wrong with the values and ethics of the officer corps. Although carefully phrased, it left no doubt of Peers's conclusion that officers had learned to lie, had forgotten the rules of leadership and trust, were promoted on grounds that were militarily corrupt. Within weeks, Westmoreland turned to the Army War College and instructed it to conduct a "Study on Military Professionalism" to explore the questions Peers had raised. Two and a half months later the War College submitted its results, a rich portrait of an army that had sacrificed its military values to those of the career rat race.

The initial reaction within the Army confirmed the report's worst conclusions. The Peers memorandum, the My Lai report, and the War College study were all ordered classified. Peers's own career was effectively at an end. Shortly afterward, the military faced bombardment from a number of books and articles about the corruption of the officer corps. Lieutenant Colonel Edward King's *The Death of the Army*, Major Josiah Bunting's *The Lionheads*, Colonel David Hackworth's article, "A Soldier's Disgust," all appeared in 1972, their criticism the more wounding since it came from men who obviously cherished the military ideal.

Yet the struggle for reform inside the military went on. Colonel Dandridge Malone recounts the steps that followed the Study on Military Professionalism:

"In 1971 we did a leadership study of fifty thousand Army leaders. The main thing they said was that they wanted their bosses to be straight with them, and wanted the opportunity to be straight themselves. In 1972 we began to implement some of the findings. In 1973, a very interesting thing happened at Leavenworth [at the Army's Command and General Staff College—an important stop for the ticket puncher]. Some of the majors started to talk about things ethical. They went to the commandant, a very hot guy, and asked for a small session. He said, let's do it for the whole class, twelve hundred guys or so. They brought in twenty generals, twenty civilian experts on ethics, twenty straphangers like me. They had a big session, then broke up, sent one of each group to the classes. Things happened. One general was saying that he was right on top of things in his units, that no one would dare submit a falsified report there. A young major stood up and said, General, I was in your division, and I *routinely* submitted falsified reports. The general's response was, When you speak to a general officer, stand at attention. That was happening all over the place. All but two of the generals were stuck bad. They were embarrassed, and when they left they started badmouthing the plan. They talked about the 'ethics stuff,' they called it 'moralistic streaking.' General Abrams was about to sack the whole thing. But then someone went to him and said, 'What if we'd met apathy instead of emotion when we talked to our young officers about ethics?' I think that's what got the whole 'reformation' started. That's when it got up its head of steam."

Through the late seventies, there were more "ethics" courses at the staff schools, more articles from senior officers about rediscovering professional values. A "Trust and Confidence" program was introduced, which emphasized that an officer's word was his bond and that he shouldn't have to sign endless forms, like a man applying to a bondsman for bail, certifying that he would carry out his obligations and pay his bills.* It is hard to pick up a military journal these days without coming across an article like "New Leadership for a New Air Force" or "On Fostering Integrity." Much of this is posturing, and it has not begun to eclipse the careerist pressures in the force. Most of today's generals and admirals are men who got there because they were procurement wizards, or adept at punching their tickets, or careful not to make waves. Simply on a human level, I was struck by how little "edge" most of the generals seemed to have to their characters, how bland most of them seemed, not only in comparison with the captains and colonels beneath them, but also compared to successful men and women in other fields—politicians, doctors, businessmen, teachers, writers. When younger officers contemplate their example, a great number probably decide to emulate them. But more and more seem to have begun to look for other paths, and in that reaction, I believe, lies the military's hope for re-creating the moral bonds on which its cohesion ultimately depends.

"I think the Army is in the midst of an ethical revolution," Colonel Malone says. "I've never been in a revolution, so I can't be sure. But I do see concern about these issues—care about questions of morality and values and military ethics."

What was the greatest obstacle to re-establishing these bedrock values, I asked him. Who was the enemy?

---

*A one-time officer describes the harm that the opposite approach can do. He says that at one of the service's command training schools, young officers who have just come in from ROTC or elsewhere and will soon be sent on their first assignments are made to sign a number of legalistic forms detailing their obligations. The former officer, who has taught at the school, says, "I tell my classes that there's a paper I have to sign that makes me mad. It asks for your home address and phone number and says the reason is so that they can find you if you leave without paying your bills. I told the classes that it made me mad to sign that, and if it made them mad by the end of the class, then I would have taught them something important."

"Oh, the givens of the way any organization operates. Hierarchy, programs you have to adhere to. Those are obstacles." He sat silent for ten seconds. "But the *enemy*, that's the volunteer army."

SOLDIERS USE "the volunteer army" as others once used "Watergate" or "the hippies," as a catch phrase to convey much that perturbs them. When they complain about the volunteer army, they are really complaining about two things: that it has "civilianized" the military, converting its operating principles to those of the workaday world, and that it has given them an army of the poor.

THE "CIVILIANIZED" SERVICE

THE "CIVILIANIZATION" of military service was a natural, indeed an intended, consequence of the volunteer force. One of the clearest differences between the new and old armies is that these days soldiers can "quit" or be "fired." The Gates commission (the official body whose recommendations for a volunteer force President Nixon accepted in 1970) contended that it was irrational to force soldiers to fulfill a set term of enlistment. "We believe that this policy is not necessary, and that it adversely affects the attractiveness of military service," it said.[20] First-term enlisted men used to be unmarried and live on base; now, at many bases, half of the men are married and live in town. There are large parking lots at major bases; at "quitting time," enlisted men hop in their cars and drive home. Soldiers can eat in snack bars, instead of together in the mess hall; they can live three to a room in motel-style barracks, instead of all together in squad bays. Years ago a captain would personally hand each man his pay envelope; now soldiers, like Social Security recipients, receive payments according to a computer program. Basic training is shorter and less physically demanding; in many cases, women recruits train alongside the men. Drill instructors have been forbidden to swear at or strike recruits.

From a civilian's point of view, much that has changed has changed for the good. The limits placed on brutal drill instructors clearly fall in that category. Indeed, much of the grumbling about today's army from tough-guy type officers is nothing more than whining about any departure from the days when men were men and dames were dames and civilians knew their place. Clifford Alexander, who was the Secretary of the Army during the Carter Administration, and who is black, suggested throughout his term that opposition to the volunteer army was ultimately racist, either in overt form (from officers who didn't like so many blacks in the ranks) or in subtler manifestation (from newspaper writers who felt free to run down the quality of a largely black army, or from people who were upset about an unrepresentative military but didn't care that the U.S. Senate contained no blacks).

But even after proper allowance has been made for the ax-grinding that inevitably affects complaints about the volunteer army, it remains that many thoughtful, careful military leaders say that the conditions of service in today's army undermine the unique qualities a fighting force must possess.

In his essay called "The Will to Fight," William Hauser asked why soldiers do the difficult—standing and fighting on the battlefield—rather than choosing the more "rational" options of hiding, fleeing, shirking. His answer was that four elements sustain the "will to fight":

Submission, the process through which the soldier is made to do over and over again things he does not want to do, until he understands that the fundamental rule of his existence is to obey. "If this conditioning process has been effective," Hauser says, "the soldier will continue to submit to the orders of legitimate authority, even though the orders be contrary to his fundamental instinct of self-preservation."

Fear. Although it "makes some soldiers flee from battle, that same fear is a major factor in sustaining the will to fight. . . . If the soldier knows and trusts his comrades, he will probably perceive more safety in continuing to fight alongside them, than in rearward flight away from them and the enemy which they face."

Loyalty, the sense of emotional devotion to "buddies" and the unit, and occasionally to abstractions like "the division" or "the nation."

Pride, the knowledge, on the part of a man with a specific function, that "others depend on and value his particular contribution to their safety and to the unit's mission."[21]

Each of these qualities, Hauser suggests, has been diminished in the volunteer force. Under the more genteel training regimen, soldiers are not made to submit to the rote practice that prepares them to perform automatically when under fire. Fear has abated at the same time. Loyalty had been built on the countless intangible bonds among men who ate, slept, worked, and drank together, and does not grow among men who knock off for the day and drive home to the wife and kids. As for pride, Hauser delicately said that "the young man whose major reason for enlisting (admitted or not) was his failure to find gainful employment elsewhere is not likely to be bursting with a sense of self-worth."[22]

"To the degree that we have to pitch the Marines as a way of getting a job, better yourself, go to college, we may be pitching for the wrong reason," said Joe Hoar, a Marine Corps colonel from Massachusetts now serving at Camp Pendleton. "The reason we have a Marine Corps is to defend the country—to locate, close with, and destroy the enemy. To the degree that as an institution we talk about other things, we create expectations that are not always reasonable, and we detract from our primary mission."[23]

"The military requires two kinds of discipline, a positive and internal discipline, and a more negative and external one," one Army colonel told me. "The internal discipline consists of ties of loyalty, mutual support, fellow-feeling, tradition. The external control consists of discipline, pay, power in the brutal sense. There's less of both now."

Everyone inside and outside the military has heard about the "retention problem," the mass departure of the petty officers and the first sergeants who have been in the force for eight, ten, twelve years. Outside the military, thoughts automatically turn to pay as both the cause and the solution; but inside the military, they turn again to the "civilianization" of the volunteer force. By the time the NCOs start concentrating on the pay, it certainly is a problem. "I'll be making eight thousand dollars more with the county police," one Marine sergeant told me. "If it was four thousand, I'd say to hell with it, but this is too much." But most of them began to worry about pay only after they had grown unhappy for other reasons. What had the military traditionally held as its reward to the sergeant majors, the chief petty officers? Their privilege had been the authority they enjoyed, and the recognition by officers above them and recruits below that they made things run. At that time, a top NCO also made seven times as much money as a first-day private, as opposed to three times as much now. Some craved authority for the wrong reasons, but most who stayed in the service enjoyed the responsibility of command, something that people also find, in other forms, when running businesses, raising children, coaching sports, teaching school. The "authority" that a foreman on an assembly line enjoys is, by comparison, a pale and unsatisfying thing; yet it is in that foreman's image that the NCOs feel the volunteer force is attempting to mold them.

Most irritating of all to the officers and NCOs are the steps the outside world has taken to make sure there is no back-sliding from its labor-market model of the military. During 1979 and 1980 it seemed as if the collective anger of the uniformed services were focused upon Secretary Alexander of the Army. Alexander, the first black service secretary, had been the most unyielding government spokesman for the contention that the volunteer army was a social and military success. If officers disagreed, he said, they could shut up or quit. He told me,

"We don't run the Army by taking a vote of all 770,000 people in uniform and 390,000 civilians and asking them what the line should be. They are under the control of civilian leadership, which sets the Army's policies. If they are called to testify before the Congress, they are bound to give their views. But they are not bound to give them to the first reporter that comes by. If their disagreements are serious, they should bring them to me, or they should get the hell out if they want to talk."[24] Alexander has a point in saying that many officers would grumble but few take the step of resigning in protest; but his tone gives a hint of the difficulties that arose between him and the career military. "Right now the word is out: Don't talk about 'quality,'" an Army colonel told me in 1980. "People are afraid to raise a ruckus because it might piss off Mr. Alexander." Another said, "I just hate to see an army that's seriously trying to reform itself cowed by this attitude that 'the Secretary's gonna get you if you don't watch out.'"

The first complaint about the volunteer army can be summed up in the fear that it makes military service seem like just another job. The second complaint is about the kind of people who now choose this line of work.

Start with statistics. In 1964, the last year of the pre-Vietnam draft, 17 percent of all draftees had some college education, as did 14 percent of those who enlisted. In 1979, 3 percent of the men who joined the volunteer army had ever been to college. In 1964, slightly more than 25 percent of all draftees were high school dropouts. In 1979, 41 percent of the men who joined the volunteer army had not finished high school. Charles Moskos, a sociologist from Northwestern University who served in the Army after graduating from Princeton in the fifties and now spends much of his time traveling to bases and interviewing soldiers, points out that over the last fifteen years, a larger and larger percentage of the American school-age population has managed to complete high school, from 66 percent in 1965 to 76 percent in 1977. He says, "Thus, while the national trend has been toward a higher percentage of high school graduates, the percentage of graduates among Army enlistees has been dropping."[25]

In 1980, of the 100,860 men who were serving their first term as enlisted men in the "combat arms" of the Army—infantry, armor, artillery, the ones who fight—how many possessed degrees from any college, of any quality, anywhere in the United States? Twenty-five. Not 25 percent, but 25 people. There are nearly twice as many graduates on any 45-man team in the National Football League. In the entire Army, of the 340,000 enlisted men who in 1980 were serving their first term, a total of 276 had college degrees.[26] As Clifford Alexander points out, if you are recruiting eighteen-year-olds, you are not going to get a lot of college graduates. The college graduates who did make up a significant portion of the enlisted ranks in the fifties and sixties were there because of student deferments, which allowed them to complete their schooling before they became eligible for the draft. Theoretically, many of today's soldiers might be planning to go to college once they finish their hitch. Some do—but most join the Army in the first place precisely because they do not have the money or opportunity to go to college and have no brighter employment prospects in sight.

In many areas of American society—for example, the student body of public schools in big cities—statistics reflecting low education or income levels might suggest that large numbers of poor black people were being counted. But in the enlisted ranks of the Army, the blacks are better educated than the whites. Despite the predictions of the Gates commission, the military grows steadily more "black." If current trends continue, by the mid-eighties more than half the soldiers in ranks E-1 through E-3 in the Army—the true grunts—will be blacks or Hispanics. But the black part of the military is far more "representative" than the white, for in family background, level of education, and economic status, the blacks who join the military are reflective of black America as a whole. For blacks, the military still largely represents what it has since desegregation under Harry Truman: an avenue of social advance, which attracts many bright people on the way up. A fair representation of black society would be several economic and educational cuts below a fair sampling of white society; therefore, it is all the more telling that, as Charles Moskos points out, 65 percent of blacks who join as Army enlisted men have high school diplomas, versus 54 percent of whites. He adds:

In point of fact, today's Army enlisted ranks is the only major arena in American society where black educational levels surpass those of whites, and by a significant degree. Whereas the black soldier seems fairly representative of the black community . . . white entrants of recent years are coming from the least educated sectors of the white community. . . . I am even more impressed by what I do not find in line units—urban and suburban white soldiers of middle-class background.[27]

It doesn't take long, for anyone visiting military bases and talking with the soldiers, to see who they are and where they come from. They are white country boys, blacks and browns from the cities. Taken one by one, the soldiers in the volunteer force command an outsider's respect. I could not point to more than a dozen or so of the roughly 150 soldiers I met who would be obvious examples of the "quality" problem. Rather, the issue is one of balance. While the soldiers may be, individually, tough, humorous, and appealing, as a group they clearly come from outside the mainstream of American life.

When the volunteer force was being set up, the blithe assumption was that military service was largely a question of numbers. As long as the pay scale could be fine-tuned to bring *enough* people into the armed forces, it wouldn't much matter who they were. In any case, the reasoning went, there was no reason to think that the change from conscription to the free labor market would bring a different kind of soldier into the force. The Gates commission predicted:

The elimination of conscription admittedly is a major social change, but it will not produce a major change in the personnel of our armed forces. . . . Contrary to much dramatic argument, the reality is that an all-volunteer force will be manned largely by the same kind of individuals as today's armed forces. The men who serve will be quite similar in patriotism, political attitudes, and susceptibility to political control.[28]

In a section of its report designed to answer objections to the volunteer army, most of which was devoted to knocking down fears that the military would become a nest of hard-boiled janissaries beyond the reach of civilian control, the commission said:

Objection 6: Those joining an all-volunteer force will be men from the lowest economic classes, motivated primarily by monetary rewards rather than patriotism. An all-volunteer force will be manned, in effect, by mercenaries.

Answer: Again, our research indicates that an all-volunteer force will not differ significantly from the current force of conscripts and volunteers. Maintenance of current medical, physical, and moral standards will ensure that a better paid, volunteer force will not recruit an undue proportion of youth from disadvantaged socioeconomic backgrounds.[29]

The fundamental assumption was wrong. It was wrong in its facts —that a volunteer army would draw the same crowd brought in by the draft—and just as wrong in its implication, which was that such differences as might occur would be trivial in their impact.

The most familiar words in public diagnoses of the volunteer army's problems—"numbers" and "quality"—are imprecise and misleading. They leave the impression that there are tremendous gaps in the enlisted ranks, which volunteers fail to fill, and that such soldiers as do enlist stand befuddled before the space-age machinery they must operate. Indeed, "numbers" and "quality" are problems. The Army now includes about 800,000 men, 20 percent less than its size before Vietnam; the standing military as a whole is about three-fourths as large as twenty years ago, at 2 million compared to 2.6 million. The Army's Individual Ready Reserves, made of people who have recently finished their active-duty service, fell from 932,000 in 1970 to 205,000 in 1979. Except when teen-age unemployment is acute, most of the services have had trouble meeting their recruiting quotas. There is also an obvious disproportion between the technical skills required to run and maintain a computerized tank and the training a high school dropout brings to the force.

But these are not the way soldiers talk about the problems with the volunteer army. Several times I heard officers introduce their concerns in strikingly similar ways. First, the colonel or the sergeant major or the lieutenant would carefully point out how proud he was of the men (and sometimes women) under his command. "They're tough kids. They really try. I can't say a bad word about them." If anything, the officers consistently soft-pedaled the evidence, which shows up in nearly every NATO exercise or war game in the United States, that many of today's soldiers have trouble running tanks and firing missiles.* I took it as an encouraging sign of reciprocal loyalty that not one of the several dozen officers I spoke with was willing to disparage his own troops.

When the officers talk about what does worry them, they discuss not the people who are in the Army, but the ones who are missing: "I won't say a word against my men, but the volunteer force is killing us." "Where's the rest of the country, not just the poor kids and the blacks?" The officers believe that the missing are the middle and upper classes of white America. The officers are right.

*The Army Skill Qualifications Tests have turned up many such indications. For example, Senator Sam Nunn of Georgia says that in 1977 and 1978, 90 percent of nuclear-weapons maintenance specialists failed the Skill Qualifications Test, along with 98 percent of tank-turret repairmen. The Army Training Study, which was completed in 1978, reported that 21 percent of tank gunners in Europe did not know where to aim when using battle sights, and that 20 percent of the tank-crew commanders "did not know some of the essential basics of battlefield gunnery." (See "Doubts Mounting About All-Volunteer Force," *Science*, September 5, 1980, p. 1095.) From December 15 through December 19, 1980, the Washington *Star* published a series of articles by John Fialka that dealt with the poor record of American forces in NATO training competitions.

It has always been true that the military contains more of America's humble than of the well-bred. In fact, the notion of a "representative" military force may be a recent historical oddity, arising from two special circumstances. One was World War II, in which people from every region and social class served. The other was the peacetime draft through the fifties and early sixties, when the combination of a large standing army and a relatively small draft-age population meant that most able-bodied males, from Elvis Presley to Philip Roth, looked on the draft as a fact of life. For graduates of Amherst, Yale, Columbia in the fifties, military service was the rule; for their counterparts fifteen years later, it was the exception. But if the idea of a representative military is a departure from most of American history, so too is the idea that blacks (or women) should have the right to vote. Both changes are based on a more democratic interpretation of who should enjoy the privileges the state confers—and share the obligations that it asks. The example of shared service in World War II and the fifties seems far more in keeping with this sensibility than does the record of the mercenary army of the Civil War, the loopholes for the privileged during the Vietnam war, or today's volunteer force.

"The distinctive quality of the enlisted ranks in modern times has been a mixing of the social classes," Charles Moskos says. "This was the elemental social fact underlying enlisted service. This is the state of affairs which has disappeared in the all-volunteer Army."[30]

When soldiers speak about the effects of a lower-class army, they usually begin with the way the changed human chemistry of the units has eroded their ability to do the military's traditional job. In talking about "human chemistry" of the military, they suggest that there was something more than humor in the movie cliché that had Greenberg, Kowalski, Martinez, and Baxter serving together in the foxhole.

Tom Kelly, who was drafted in 1971 after graduating from the University of Missouri to serve in the Army, said "It was *important* for me to be there, and other people like me. I was with kids who didn't have a high school education, kids with prison records, kids with two years of college, kids who were given the choice of joining or going to jail. We suffered together, and in suffering we became a unit. I don't want to sound elitist, and if you'd been there you'd understand that this is not elitist, but natural leadership grew from the group. It grew among people who understood the needs in that experience, the need to share, the need to follow orders. Some stepped forward, some others followed. The central fact of military experience is that it is a shared experience by all classes, all races, to meet national goals."

"In the Marines, we still get people looking for more discipline, a tougher test, than they do in the Army," a Marine Corps major at Quantico said. "But you can still feel the change in social class. There used to be a general expectation that people would conform to middle-class values in the military—if you can call the DIs and the Yessirs 'middle class.' I mean that they wouldn't yell back, they'd bend to authority. People were expected to obey. I feel like the balance has shifted to those who come from areas without discipline, and there's not the implied standard for them to conform to."

"I think the mixture of middle-class men had a real modulating effect," Charles Moskos says. "It made it much easier to sustain discipline. It was nice for a lower-class kid to outmarch a college grad. They can't do that anymore, because the college kids aren't there. You've heard the NCOs complain about outsiders and civilians interfering with the disciplinary steps they need to take to deal with drugs, etc. Well, a lot of that is a question of socializing the entrants to begin with. If you get some middle-class mix back, you won't need these Draconian measures anymore."

Several years ago a team of researchers including Moskos did a unit-by-unit survey of the Army, trying to measure soldiers on intangible but crucial martial values: toughness, readiness to fight, cohesion, etc. They found, to no one's great surprise, that the most "elite" units —the Airborne, the Special Forces, the Rangers—ranked the highest, and the regular Army the lowest on this scale. Then they found that, in terms of the soldiers' willingness to re-enlist, the pattern was reversed. The regular Army troops showed the greatest interest in re-enlisting, and the Rangers the least. The explanation that the researchers offered was that the kind of ambitious people on the make, always looking for a challenge, were the ones who gave the elite units their edge, and were also the ones who were most likely to move on from the military to another challenge, by going to college or getting a job. "The military equivalent of the bright cop who goes to night law school," James Woolsey, who was Undersecretary of the Navy during the Carter Administration, calls them. "They're the ones we've lost in the enlisted ranks."

After the detailed study of squad behavior in World War II that was discussed in the previous chapter, S.L.A. Marshall announced to an astonished Army that, in the typical engagement, only a small fraction of the men in combat actually fired their guns. These findings set off many reactions in the military, including the inauguration of a set of "Fighter" studies to try to determine which men were most and least likely to perform in combat. From the studies, the researchers identified ten or twelve traits that distinguished "fighters" from "nonfighters." Almost all of these were apple pie–Jack Armstrong traits: stable family life, solid education, desire to achieve. Those traits still show up among the groups like the Rangers, which may be connected to the fact that, while soldiers in the more elite groups are less likely to *re*-enlist than soldiers in the regular Army, they are far more likely to *complete* their obligation for their original term. They are also, in general, better educated than regular Army troops. Moskos says, "The striking finding is that high school graduates are twice more likely than high school dropouts to complete their enlistment. More revealing, this finding is virtually unchanged when mental aptitude is held constant. . . . Possession of a high school diploma, it seems, reflects the acquisition of social traits (work habits, punctuality, *Sitzfleisch*) which make for a more successful military experience."[31]

"It would be just as bad to have an outfit of all college grads as one that is the dregs of white society and the upper part of black society," Tom Kelly says. "We found out in some of these studies that a lot of people who really succeed are the ones who've worked in gas stations or on farms, have had to take care of themselves. The point is to have a mix."[32]

The closest thing I heard to a defense of the volunteer force from a professional soldier came from Chief of Staff Edward Meyer. The decision is the nation's decision, he said; it's not the Army's to make. Speaking as a citizen, he said that he felt people owed some form of service to the nation, whether military or otherwise. Speaking as a member of the Joint Chiefs of Staff, he knew that the reserves and national guard were way down, and would fill up again if there was a draft. But speaking for the Army, he said there might be hidden drawbacks: "We'd get, what, 200,000 people, out of a cohort of 2.1 million. They'd feel unfairly treated from the start. They wouldn't want to be there, and we wouldn't be able to get rid of them, as we can do now with the expeditious discharge program for people who don't work out. At a period when we're short of NCOs, they'd have to handle reluctant soldiers. It could be a very traumatic period for the Army. After a couple of years, I think people would get used to the idea and it would work out. But those first two years would be hard on us." In any case, Meyer said, the draft finally didn't matter to the Army as much as another question. "Whichever way the nation chooses to fill us up, we've got to train the people, which is why our first priority has to be rebuilding our corps of NCOs."

AT THE officers' mess at Camp Pendleton, several Marine officers discussed their impressions of today's Marines. One of them, Lieutenant Colonel Jim Williams, had just brought back a battalion of men from an extended tour in the Pacific. Williams is a pleasant, burly man, with gray hair. "I feel like we're setting up a kind of class warfare," he said. "I wonder about the morality of a nation that lets the disadvantaged do the fighting." His general interrupted him: "The only thing worse than having kids whose parents who write to their congressmen all the time is not having those parents. Or having parents who are so disenfranchised that they aren't heard." The general stopped and the lieutenant colonel continued, "I feel like the country is dividing up into the haves and the have-nots, and the have-nots are doing all the fighting."

In conversations with soldiers, such moments are not unusual. By the end of a long talk they will find themselves trying to explain, often with considerable uneasiness, what bothers them about the volunteer army even more than the military details they could name. "We're setting up an army of the underprivileged," they will say. "I don't like . . . well, I don't like the *moral* aspect of the thing."

It is no secret to those in the military that the bitterness with which much of civilian society viewed them in the late sixties has changed into an attitude of indifference, shading into contempt. On the whole, they're not sure it is an improvement. The Gates commission, with typical sagacity, had predicted that the coming of the volunteer force would make the military far more popular and prestigious. "The termination of the draft should immediately enhance the prestige of enlisted service," it said.[33] In fact, by shifting enlisted service to blacks and the least educated class of whites, it has done exactly the reverse. Charles Moskos suggests the parallel of the Civilian Conservation Corps.[34] Early in the thirties, when everyone was out of work, it was no shame to be part of the CCC. Liberals and conservatives supported it; it was thought to contain a cross section of the country. By the end of the decade, when the private job market had slowly picked up, the CCC became a last resort for losers. People didn't want it in their town anymore, didn't want their sons to join.

Many soldiers perceive a similar drift from the mainstream, with similar effects, over the last ten years. One of the by-products of the pre-Vietnam draft was that many people who, left to their druthers, would never have dreamt of a military career found they had a taste for it once they got in. It is astonishing to talk with men in their forties and fifties who have stayed in the military and discover how many of them had never planned to be soldiers but were hauled in by the draft or (an indirect version of the same thing) through the ROTC. "I was pulled in kicking and screaming," a two-star Army general told me, a man who now commands one of the major staff schools. "The greatest loss with the draft," says one official in the Pentagon, "was all the men who would not otherwise have chosen the service but who spent two years, found out they liked it, and stayed. They added a spark to the officer corps. You need their diversity." They also provided a bond between the military and middle-class society.

So did the junior officers, the lieutenants who came in through the ROTC, did not stay any longer than they had to, but made the military run while they were there. Soldiers whose experience predates 1970 complain about the reduced diversity in these young officers, as ROTC has left the Dartmouths and the Stanfords. Sergeant majors in the Marine Corps, the professional bastards who spend their time yelling at grunts to tuck it in and get the lead out, reflect with what amounts, for them, to nostalgia about the college kids they used to have to deal with: the kids were jerks but they helped make things work. Some of this, no doubt, is the rosy-hued recollection of the good old days, but not all. "In the ground combat arms, there is the acknowledgment that the 'X-factor' middle-class soldiers bring to a unit is no longer there," Moskos says. "The days when many enlisted men might be better educated than their sergeants and smarter than their officers are gone. One is struck by the fond reminiscences the older sergeants have of the university graduates who worked under them, and formed the shadow staff—clerks in personnel, supply, and operations—which made things run smoothly at company and battalion levels."[35]

Moskos has suggested one of the most creative approaches to correcting the social imbalance of the military, short of a draft. He points out that the government offers some $5 billion each year to assist students with college expenses. The money comes through student loan programs, Basic Educational Opportunity Grants, work-study programs, and several others, and a large share of it goes to students from middle-class families. The Basic Educational Opportunity Grants are available to some students whose families earn as much as $30,000, and under a new subsidized-loan program, parents may borrow $3,000 per year, at 9 percent interest, no matter what their income. These programs are one of the fastest-growing parts of the federal budget. Apart from the obligation to repay the loans, the money comes with no strings attached. Moskos' proposal is to attach strings, on the model of federal aid to medical students, which obliges the young doctor to spend a year or two in public-service work.

Moskos argues that instead of bringing middle-class people into the Army by force, they can more effectively be enticed, by giving first claim on student aid money to those who have spent time in the military (or some other form of national service). At the same time, he says, the GI Bill should be re-enacted, since it also appeals to the very people who are now missing from the military. Pay should be slashed for those who sign up for just one term, and the money should be used to give substantial raises to those who make the military their career. He says, "Active duty pay for the citizen soldier would be lower—say by one-third—than that received by the career soldier of the same rank. Other than the GI Bill, the citizen soldier would receive no entitlements such as off-base housing or food allowances. This would reduce the frequency of marriage at the junior enlisted levels and restore unit cohesion in the barracks. Because there would be no presumption of acquiring civilian skills in the military, the terms of such service would be honest and unambiguous, thus alleviating a major source of post-entry discontent in the AVF [All Volunteer Force]."[36] The $5 billion now spent on student-aid programs would almost certainly be enough to transform the make-up of the military, he says.

This is fine as far as it goes, and it is infinitely preferable to the wooden pronouncements that come from Milton Friedman's school of libertarian economics, saying that increased pay, by itself, is the solution to the "quality" problem. The cutest expression of this libertarian creed is the idea that we should "draft old men's money, not young men's bodies."* As a practical matter, when the military is set up as "just another job," the old men's money will be appealing only to young men and women who need money and have no better prospects, since almost any other kind of job will offer more freedom, and less harassment and potential danger, than military service. Accept for a moment the pure libertarian idea that people are rich or poor because they deserve to be. As that applies to someone eighteen or nineteen years old, it means that he is rich or poor because his *parents* deserved to be. If his parents have money, he can go to college; if they do not, he probably can't and may need to join the Army to make ends meet. This is one reason that the libertarian chestnut is so dishonest. Stated more bluntly, the libertarian view would say, "draft old men's money, to pay for poor young men's bodies." Even though Charles Moskos' idea is better than this, it may not do enough to remove what Charles Peters of the *Washington Monthly* called "the number one deterrent to recruitment—the nation's lack of respect for those in the services. Until a reasonable number of people from the upper classes demonstrate their esteem by joining up themselves, the average man is going to continue to refuse to risk his life for those who would look down on him for doing so, no matter how much he is paid."[37] No one from a rich family will feel compelled to join the service just for a student loan,

---

*This comes from Nicholas von Hoffman, who turns up so many original ideas that he's bound to have a few bad ones.

nor will the bright kid who wins a scholarship. A service that exempts the rich, simply because of their income, is still not a representative service; and I fear that the only way to have a representative army is through the draft.

I use the word "fear" because the drawbacks of compulsion are great, both philosophically and practically. I am never eager to see the government compel people to do anything. But the drawbacks of a volunteer force—in addition to all the purely military problems that it causes—may be worse.

One of those drawbacks is the flip side of the familiar, mindless argument that reviving the draft will increase the chance of military "adventurism." I wonder if the people who advance that theory have ever observed the way politics really works, have ever seen how much more intensely people will fight for their position when their own interests have been directly touched. This is the cliché that a recession is when your friend loses his job, and a depression is when you lose your job, or that a crime wave begins when you have been mugged. Surely the history of Vietnam demonstrated the difference between abstract and self-interested actions. Resistance to the war went up in proportion as the effects of the war (primarily, the draft) touched the children of influential families. But a draft should not be enacted because it would make foreign intervention either easier or harder. It should be enacted because, *whatever* the military policy, it will ensure that its consequences are borne by the same public that must give its assent to that policy, rather than being concentrated on the least visible, least influential few. Ultimately a nation must pay a price for using troops in war, and it will be more attentive to the price from the start if all its members think they must pay.

There is another concern about the volunteer force, which is connected to the larger argument of this book. If current trends continue, we will soon be at the point where very few educated white people will have had any first-hand exposure to the military. One of the great obstacles to sane public debates about defense is that they are conducted more and more in the abstract—with comparisons of budget totals, contests between "tough" and "soft" ideologies—and with less and less grounding in the operating realities of men and weapons. Such indifference to the details of military life may arise from widespread unfamiliarity with them. A Washington writer named Don Winter pointed out in 1980 that of the 103 members of Congress who were officially part of the "Vietnam generation" (men born between June 30, 1939, and June 30, 1954), only 14 (or about 14 percent) served on active duty anywhere in the military at any time during the Vietnam war. By comparison, about 28 percent of the generation as a whole served on active duty during Vietnam. While more than two thirds of all senators born before 1939 had served on active duty, mainly in World War II, only one third of senators and representatives born after 1939 had served in any military capacity, including the reserves and the National Guard. After the elections of 1980, the number of congress-men with military experience declined further still. When so few of those making choices about military policy have first-hand exposure to the military, it increases the risk that they will be buffaloed, either by the services or by equally passionate groups on the left, and virtually eliminates the possibility that they will bring their own, uncoached sense of nuance and perspective to the military reports they hear. How rich and full a feeling for public education would the members of our school boards have if all of them had gone to private schools?

"People on the accelerated track have rarely been immersed in the complexity of life," says Larry Smith, who was drafted out of graduate school at Yale in 1958 and later taught history at Dartmouth. "When I was a teacher, most of the people older than me had been veterans, and the ones older than that had worked for a living. The ones younger than me had never done anything but be in school. That made many of them in that college so unskilled in the use of democratic systems that they'd think the answer, say, to Vietnam was to put all the soldiers on boats and pull them out. They didn't understand the complexity of the groups involved. They'd never had to cope, as supply sergeants, with a unit that was not returning its blankets on time. To make it more vivid, they've never been in the position of an officer under circum-stances where, no matter what choice you made, there would be tragic results. If you stayed where you were, you would be killed, and if you tried to move, some of your men would die—if they'd had to do that, there would be a sense of the whole range of human motivations, and the difference between the way things work in theory and the inher-ently imperfect reality. Apart from a junior high school class, there is no more representative unit in our society than a basic training camp, in a draft that works."[38]

THERE ARE three respectable arguments against the draft: that it com-pels, that it discriminates, and that, even if it is "representative," it is in a sense always unfair.

That it compels is undeniable, but so does the tax code, and I think the two must be viewed in exactly the same light. Libertarians may argue that military service should be left to those who choose it, as they sometimes argue that each citizen should decide for himself which organs of the government to fund. But that theory founders on the reality of "public goods"—everyone benefits from a police force, whether or not everyone pays for it, so no one will voluntarily support it unless everyone is made to share the cost. The same theory of military service ignores the evidence of history and human society that the connection between a nation and the force that defends it is not defined by pay rates and fringe benefits alone, but rather by the bonds of trust and sacrifice that are also essential within units on the battlefield. This is all the more true in a democracy, where decisions about how and when to use military force are supposed to be made by all.

That the draft discriminated in Vietnam is also undeniable, which is one more reason why a new draft should hold as its first premise that there be no exemptions, except for those who are truly "disabled," in the common-sense meaning of the term. Everyone else would be selected at random. There may be one further reasonable exemption: for doctors, possessors of a skill the military needs but cannot sensibly produce on its own. In return for a deferment during medical school, they would spend several years as military physicians. In any case, no argument about discrimination can be used to defend the extremely discriminatory volunteer force.

That it will seem capricious and unfair is a possibility, since in the first few years of the eighties the proportion between likely manpower needs and available young people will be such that only one out of every four or five would be called. But one of the central worries of military manpower planners is that they'll have trouble recruiting enough soldiers in the middle and late eighties, when the cohorts of young people dwindle in size. In itself, that would not be reason enough to restore a draft; but it does suggest that the disproportion of numbers will largely solve itself. The problem of capriciousness could also be avoided by a generalized system of national service, which is my own preference, or by much larger draft calls for people who would be trained briefly and then assigned to the reserves.

Steps like these would be the gestures of a nation that realized its defense was a serious business, not to be discussed in airy generalizations or contracted out to the poor.

THE FIRST five chapters of this book have dealt with different aspects of conventional war. When it comes to judging why men fight, how equipment works, which strategies succeed, there is a body of experience to draw on. There is history and hard fact. The next chapter will discuss the aspect of defense that is different from all the others, because there are no facts. Its subject is nuclear war, and the rivalry among different faiths that profess to know its nature.

SIX

THEOLOGIANS

S INCE 1945, the United States has possessed the capacity to destroy its enemies with atomic explosions. Since the mid-sixties, when the Soviet Union fielded significant numbers of nuclear weapons, the United States has known that it too stood vulnerable to destruction. In the years since Hiroshima, warheads have piled up on each side. Their accumulation has been matched by the mountain of theory and doctrine that has built up about the purpose and conduct of nuclear war. There have been theories of "assured destruction," of "decoupling" and of escalation, of strategic instabilities and "gray areas," of war by misunderstanding or war by premeditation, of the twenty-five moves, laid out like a description of a chess game, through which the world might progress from local disagreement to all-out nuclear war.

These doctrines, and the theoretical speculations that support them, have determined national policies and colored popular moods. On the basis of theories, billions of dollars have been spent, and tens of thousands of men have been trained and deployed. Each of these decisions has been an act of faith, for the doctrines and theories are pure theology. There has never been a nuclear war, and nobody knows what nuclear war would mean. In other fields of defense, planning tends to drift away from the realm of evidence, proof, observable fact. In "stra-

tegic" studies (as nuclear matters are generally known), that tendency
is inevitable, for on almost none of the relevant questions is there a base
of data on which to build.* The gross destructive power of nuclear
weapons has been clear since August 6, 1945, but that is virtually the
only thing about their use that is conclusively known. No one knows
how these weapons would perform if they were fired; whether they
would hit the targets at which they were aimed; whether human society
would be set back for centuries, decades, or merely months as a result.
For the absence of such evidence all should give thanks. They should
also remember to view most "strategic" arguments as disputes of faith
rather than fact. The "best" minds of the defense community have
been drawn toward nuclear analysis, but so were the best minds to be
found in the monastery, arguing the Albigensian heresy, in the four-
teenth century. A novel theory about how the Kremlin might respond
to nuclear strike may be advanced, may make the author's name, and
may lead to billions in expenditures without entering any further into
the domain of fact than did the monks' speculations about the nature
of God. Wars have been fought, empires built, heretics burned on the
basis of theology, and so, on the basis of the nuclear theology, are
missiles developed and war plans laid today.

In the early eighties, two closely related elements of this faith play
an especially large role in shaping nuclear policy. One is the belief that
the United States may soon be vulnerable to a "first strike" by the
Soviet Union; the other, that a nuclear war may be "winnable," or at
least that one of the major powers (namely, the Soviet Union) might
rationally calculate that it could survive a nuclear war while its enemy
would not. These assumptions, in varying degrees of explicitness, un-
derly most of the plans for "strategic modernization" in the eighties
—especially the construction of the MX missile system and the resur-
rection of an antiballistic missile system (ABM), which was prohibited
under the first SALT agreement, signed in 1972.† It is not possible

---

*Ivan Selin, who served as a Pentagon analyst during the McNamara era, said sardoni-
cally in an interview, "There is no base of combat experience with nuclear weapons,
so we work out our predictions to two significant figures. We have about sixty-five years
of experience with tactical air, so we get one significant figure. There are about four
thousand years of history of land combat, and you can't even tell which side will win
a given engagement. It makes you think that the more you know about a situation,
the less confident you are about predicting its outcome."

†To say it once in this book, "SALT" stands for Strategic Arms Limitation Talks.

to disprove either of these beliefs, but it is even harder to make a plausible case for them and for the policies they would justify.

THE NICETIES of strategic theory, which flourished in academia and at the think tanks during the fifties, took hold in public policy during the McNamara era at the Pentagon.[1] Public pronouncements about nuclear policy during the previous Administration had emphasized John Foster Dulles' theme of "massive retaliation"; the strategic analysts thought they could devise a subtler view. As a practical matter, the actual nuclear force to be bought had already been decided by the construction plans that the services had in the works, but the theories provided a patina of reason. When the analysts' favorite question, "How much is enough?," was applied to nuclear forces, the answer was that a finite, calculable sum would be enough. The United States could be confident of inflicting a "devastating" attack on the Soviet Union if it had enough weapons to destroy one quarter of the Soviet people and about half of its total industrial base. These figures came partly from guesses about the ability of societies to sustain damage and partly from a demographic fact: while it looked comparatively "easy," by aiming at big cities and industrial sites, to kill a quarter of the people and destroy half the industries with the first few bombs, it seemed much harder to run up the toll. The remaining cities were much smaller, and the economic sites more dispersed; to kill another quarter of the population might take ten times as many bombs as to kill the first 25 percent. The analysts, with their training in economics, referred to this as the point of "diminishing returns," and thought it the proper place to stop.

They calculated further that to inflict this damage, 400 "equivalent megatons" of nuclear weapons would be necessary.[2] The United States could feel perfectly secure, they reasoned, if it possessed this destructive power three times over—one for each "leg" (as it is inevitably called) of the Strategic Triad. The triad consists of B-52 bombers, which carry nuclear weapons and can fly over the Soviet Union; Polaris and Poseidon submarines, each one of them equipped with 16 nuclear missiles; and Minuteman missiles, based in silos throughout the Midwest and aimed over the North Pole at Russia. As a writer named Fred Kaplan has pointed out, 400 equivalent megatons in each "leg" of the triad also happened to be what the United States would have if it carried out the plans, then in the works, for a force of 41 submarines, 300 bombers, and 1,000 Minuteman missiles.[3] Two of McNamara's "whiz kids," Alain Enthoven and K. Wayne Smith, explained the reasoning of those days: "Once we are sure that, in retaliation, we can destroy the Soviet Union and other potential attackers as modern societies, we cannot increase our security or power against them by threatening to destroy more."[4]

Much changed between the early sixties and the early eighties. For one thing, the U.S. nuclear force grew considerably above the "finite deterrence" level laid out twenty years ago. The main engine of this increase was the perfection of MIRV technology in the late sixties. The acronym stands for "multiple, independently targetable re-entry vehicles"; what it meant is that one missile could carry warheads aimed not just at one target, but at three or more. While 41 nuclear submarines, with 16 nuclear missiles apiece, could have carried a total of 656 warheads before MIRV, after MIRV technology they carried more than 5,300. By 1967 we had 1,000 Minuteman missiles, and we have built no more since then. But about half the missiles have been "MIRVed," and the 1,000 Minutemen now carry more than 2,000 warheads. By the beginning of the eighties, the United States had about 9,500 nuclear warheads in its strategic forces, with several times as much "equivalent megatonnage" as the level thought adequate twenty years before.

Over the same period, the Soviet Union was substantially increasing its own nuclear forces. Regularly over the last twenty years, the Russians have unveiled new missiles and added to their inventory. From a few dozen in 1960, their stock of land-based missiles has risen steadily to nearly 1,400. Their principal missiles are physically much larger than the Minuteman, a difference that is often cited as indicating an alarming Soviet advantage in "throw weight." (Throw weight is the poundage a missile can lift.) The huge size of the Soviet missiles may really be a symptom of the once backward state of their technology in rocket motors and warhead design. For example, the Soviet missiles still operate on liquid fuel, which is less reliable and more dangerous than the solid-fuel rockets that make up nearly all of the American force. The only liquid-fueled rockets in the U.S. strategic force are 54 Titan missiles, which were widely described as "antique" and "outmoded" when one of them exploded in a silo in Arkansas in 1980.

Twenty years ago the Soviet Union had 18 diesel-powered submarines that carried short-range missiles; now it has more than 70 nuclear-powered submarines carrying long-range missiles, although everyone agrees that these are noisier (which makes them easier to detect) than American subs and spend less time at sea. All in all, the Russians now have more "delivery vehicles"—missiles and bombers—than the United States (about 2,500 to 2,000), even though the United States still has half again as many warheads (about 9,400 to 6,000). Both sides have enough to do the job.

What has not really changed since the fifties, despite appearances to the contrary, is the theory of how these weapons would be used and where they would be aimed. The list of targets for American nuclear weapons is contained in the Single Intergrated Operation Plan, known in the business as the SIOP (pronounced "sigh-op"). The SIOP is the property of the Joint Chiefs of Staff, who take pride in shielding its contents from the eyes of their civilian superiors, but its basic policies have been known for some time. Despite all the theories about "Mutual Assured Destruction" (abbreviated, naturally, as MAD), neither in the McNamara days nor today has it emphasized "targeting" Russian cities simply for the sake of killing people. Indeed, since 1973 it has been a crucial, and clearly stated, element of American policy that the nuclear target list not include population centers. Rather, it comprises industrial concentrations, military bases, missile silos, submarine ports, government centers, and communications networks—many of which, of course, happen to be in or near cities. In this sense, the policy has always been a mix of "counterforce," that is, aimed at the Russian forces, and "countervalue," designed to level cities. From time to time, incorrect but widespread reports that the United States was "changing" its policy to counterforce have caused an uproar. That happened once in the early sixties, under McNamara; again in the mid-seventies, under James Schlesinger; and again in 1980, when President Carter approved Presidential Directive 59, which dealt with the aiming of missiles at Russian military forces.

The only real changes involved in PD-59 were a greater emphasis on targeting command and control centers, and a more detailed and flexible plan for targeting certain conventional forces on a European battlefield.* The only real change involved during the James Schlesinger uproar in 1974 had been of a similar incremental nature. At the time, most newspapers reported that through a document later known as NSDM-242 (for National Security Decision Memo), the United States had fundamentally changed its nuclear policy from one of "Mutual Assured Destruction," which meant aiming at cities, to counterforce, which meant aiming at missile sites. Although the document included an explicit statement of the policy against targeting cities, it was mainly

---

*In his *Columbia Journalism Review* article, Fred Kaplan describes how the reporters for nearly every major newspaper dramatically overemphasized the "change" involved in PD-59, by neglecting to mention its long pedigree in nuclear policy.

an evolutionary "refinement" of previous targeting plans, which maintained that the primary purpose of a retaliatory strike was the utter destruction of the Soviet Union's industrial base.

These nuances were overlooked, partly because few reporters had ever mentioned the basic premises of the SIOP, but even more because of the sinister implications of "counterforce." To many people, "counterforce" suggests that a nuclear war is manageable, reasonable, even winnable. You attack your enemy's air bases and missile silos with "limited," "surgical" strikes, and thereby persuade him to give in. Counterforce also became a loose synonym for "first strike," which implied being able to destroy so much of the other side's weapons in a pre-emptive, surprise attack that he would not dare strike back. This idea, and the related concept that the Soviet Union is making preparations to withstand the effects of nuclear war, are at the heart of the current debate about nuclear weapons.

THE FIRST STRIKE

THE PREMISE of the "first strike" argument is this: at some point in the middle eighties the Soviet Union will supposedly attain the ability to destroy nearly all land-based missiles (the 1,000 Minutemen and 54 Titans) in a surprise nuclear attack. Some people argue that the Soviet Union already has this ability. They say that the growing number and the ever improving accuracy of Soviet missiles make such a condition possible, and that its result will be at least the psychological, and perhaps the physical disarming of the United States.

The first-strike argument most often enters political discussion in the form of a nightmare scenario. The first stage in the scenario begins when the Soviet Union possesses a large enough number of sufficiently accurate missiles to eliminate, if all hit their targets as planned, 90 percent or more of the Minuteman missiles all at once. In such a first strike, it is assumed that the Soviet Union could also count on destroying about two thirds of the B-52 bombers, since only one third of the fleet is held on constant alert, ready to take off at the first warning of attack; and about 40 percent of the nuclear-missile submarines, since 18 or so of the 41 subs are in port at any one time being repaired or changing crews.

All sides agree that even after such a strike, the United States would still have all the bombs it needed to destroy the Soviet Union as a functioning society. The missiles on one Poseidon submarine alone, as

Jimmy Carter pointed out in his 1979 State of the Union address, carry enough warheads "to destroy every large and medium-sized city in the Soviet Union." (Remember, there are 16 missiles on each submarine, and the missiles carry an average of 9 warheads each.) But no American President would dare strike back, the reasoning goes, because if he did, the Soviet Union would attack again, this time going for America's cities. In the first strike, it is claimed, a comparative handful of Americans would have been killed; in different versions of the scenario, the theoretical figures range between 2 million and 10 million. That's a lot of deaths, but nothing compared to the 80 million to 100 million who would perish if the Russians struck straight at New York, Los Angeles, Chicago, Houston. The American President would not be able to stop the Russians from carrying out that threat, because none of his remaining weapons would be adequate to destroy the Russian missiles that still lurked in their silos. There would not be enough Minutemen left to do so; the submarine-launched missiles would not be accurate enough; and it would take the bombers too long to get there to do the job.

What would be the result? The American government would swallow the 2 million or 10 million casualties, acquiesce to Russian hegemony over Europe or the Persian Gulf or Japan, and accept life as a subject nation, a North American Finland. Even if the attack never came, even if it were never directly threatened, the argument concludes that the imbalance of forces would have its effect. As soon as the leadership of both sides understood how events would play themselves out if it ever came to a showdown, the Soviet Union would not even need to launch the first strike. The mere threat of doing so would make any sane United States government capitulate, like a chess master who resigns when he sees that his queen (let alone his king) is doomed.

The complement to the first-strike scenario is the specter of Soviet civil defense. According to one of the main proponents of this theory, T. K. Jones, who is a consultant to the Boeing Corporation, the Soviet Union has gone so far toward dispersing its population, hardening its industrial sites, and preparing blast and fallout shelters for its people that as much as 98 percent of its population might survive an American retaliatory strike.[5] Since 1977, Jones has estimated likely Soviet fatalities at 10 million.[6] On the basis of this figure, he and others, such as Richard Pipes of Harvard, have suggested that Soviet leaders might well be willing to roll the dice if they could achieve final domination of the West at a cost of only half the casualties they suffered in World War II. Retired General Daniel O. Graham, the former director of the Defense Intelligence Agency, has explained the choice an American leader would then confront: "The Soviets evacuate their cities and hunker down. Then they move against NATO or Yugoslavia or China or the Middle East with superior conventional forces. The United States is faced with the demand to stay out or risk nuclear exchange in which 100 million Americans would die, as opposed to 10 million Russians."[7]

FROM THE conjunction of the first-strike scenario and the hypotheses about Soviet civil defense, two other concepts have grown. One of them, "Minuteman vulnerability," refers to the threat to the survival of the Minuteman force. The other, "the window of opportunity," denotes the period—which some proponents of this theory believe has already begun—in which the Soviet Union will use its leverage in nuclear weaponry to extract political and military concessions from the West. (It is called a "window" on the assumption that the United States will rush to correct the nuclear imbalance—to close the window —leaving the Soviet Union only a few years to exploit its advantage.)

Both "Minuteman vulnerability" and the "window of opportunity" have been thrown around by politicians and writers through the late seventies as if, like gravity, they were established truths. From these premises the correct response is obvious: the United States must build up its nuclear forces. The most frequently mentioned vehicle for doing so is the MX missile system, which incorporates two quite different purposes in its design. One is to match in kind the Soviet Union's threat to our missiles. In theory, the MX will be accurate enough to pose the same kind of threat to Soviet land-based missiles that they are said to pose to ours. From the Russian point of view, this should be an ominous prospect, since 80 percent of all their nuclear weaponry is on the ground, in fixed silos, as opposed to 25 percent of the American force. The other feature of the MX is to solve the "Minuteman vulner-ability" problem. It does so by making the missiles mobile and moving them from one protective shelter to another, so the Russians will never be sure just where to shoot.

Since the middle of 1978 the Air Force has proposed half a dozen different schemes for basing the MX. These include placing each of the 200 missiles in an underground trench twenty miles long, letting it shuttle invisibly from one sheltered point to another along the trench; putting each missile on an oval "race track" several miles in circumference, along which it would "dash" at about 15 miles per hour from one of 23 shelters to another; and straightening the race tracks out, so as to consume less land in Utah and Nevada. Each new plan has been presented with solemn assurances that the imperfections in each previous scheme have all been worked out. Because of the constant reworking of the schemes, not to mention the inherent Rube Goldberg nature of the mobile basing system, many groups which are upset about Minuteman vulnerability have recommended two more drastic steps: building an antiballistic missile system, possibly a mobile variety to ride around with in the MX field, which would shoot down Soviet missiles; and a plan to dig 4,000 silos for the 200 missiles, and then rotate the missiles from silo to silo in a random and very secret fashion.

Estimates of how much the system will cost vary between about $30 billion and $80 billion, in either case a very large sum whose actual amount no one really knows. The first missiles would not be set in place before 1986, and it would take three more years to complete the entire system.

Is this system necessary? It may be if you accept as fact the concepts of Minuteman vulnerability, the window of opportunity, and the risk of a first strike. How much sense do those premises make?

"I remember when people didn't talk about sex," says Arthur Barber, a former official in the Pentagon. "Now they don't talk about God or nuclear war. They talk about nuclear fantasies, but if you ask any factual questions—how many targets are we *guaranteed* to destroy, what will happen if everything goes wrong—you won't find an answer."

The overwhelming impression that comes from talks with those who design, maintain, or test nuclear weapons—the technicians, not the theologians—is the uncertainty of it all. The most important questions about how the weapons work cannot be conclusively answered until they are fired. But unless he has conclusive answers, no Soviet or American leader who is thinking "rationally," even if the object of his thought is a first strike, is likely to risk firing the weapons, because the costs of miscalculation are so high. If the "surgical" first strike leaves half the Minuteman force intact instead of 10 percent; if it kills 50 million Americans in "collateral casualties" instead of 10 million; if the Americans have adopted a "launch on warning" policy and shoot off their missiles as soon as the Soviet attack shows up on the radar—if any of those things happen, the neat little "scenario" has turned into mutual suicide. Such uncertainties may not deter an irrational leader, but will the MX or anything else? The nuclear technicians who stress the uncertainty of their discipline also say that uncertainty is precisely what has kept the nuclear peace for thirty years. But an appreciation of the uncertainties, a sense of awe at the gulf that separates the wide range of hypothesis from the skimpy base of provable fact, seems to have been mislaid in the current debate about nuclear policy.

THEORETICAL AND OPERATIONAL UNCERTAINTIES

THE UNCERTAINTIES fall into three categories. The first consists of the basic ingredients of theoretical calculations about the effects of a first-strike attack. Three variables go into any prediction about the Soviet Union's or the United States' ability to destroy the other side's missiles in a first strike. They are the accuracy of the attacking missiles, the explosive yield of their warheads, and the "hardness" of the other side's silos (their ability to withstand blast). In day-by-day dealings in the defense community, precise values are attached to all three variables. Indeed, one of the defense intellectual's basic tools is a circular slide rule, developed by the Rand Corporation, which when twirled to the right setting for the three variables will tell you exactly what the "probability of kill" is when, say, a Soviet SS-18 is fired at a Minuteman silo.

But behind this crisp precision lies a sea of hypothesis and imprecision. Predictions about the explosive yield of modern nuclear warheads are in nearly all cases estimates and extrapolations, worked up from tests of older models and different sizes. (This is why many conservatives complain about nuclear test ban treaties, since they assume that the Soviet Union has found illicit ways to keep testing its warheads.) American estimates of the accuracy of Soviet missiles are exactly that —estimates—based on intelligence monitoring of Soviet tests. If the resulting approximations are even a little bit wrong, that can make a large difference in assumptions about whether the Soviets could or could not carry out a first strike. (This is not even to mention a more fundamental question about missile accuracy, which will be explained later on.) The measure of silo "hardness," too, is worked out from small-scale tests, computer models, scientific hypotheses—from everything except real-world experience and realistic, repeatable tests. The estimates of yield, accuracy, and "hardness" are the best that skillful scientists can produce; but whether they would prove, in practice, to be 4 percent or 40 percent off the mark, no one can now say.

The second set of uncertainties consists of the unanswered—and largely unanswerable—technical and operational questions that would keep an aggressor from being certain—truly, thoroughly, absolutely certain—that the missiles he launched on a first strike will completely disable the enemy's force. One reason is "fratricide," which refers to the tendency of nuclear warheads to interfere with one another's detonations. To destroy an enemy's silos, a lot of missiles have to be aimed at roughly the same area at roughly the same time. When one of them explodes, the blast, debris, radiation, and electromagnetic pulse can destroy or deflect other warheads coming in. Some experts say that a blast could block off the area to other warheads for twenty or thirty minutes; others say that "fratricide" could be overcome if the attacker had perfect, second-by-second coordination of all his shots. But neither side can prove its case.

There is also the "reliability" question—the uncertainty about how many missiles will get off the ground. The United States has never successfully fired a Minuteman from an operational silo. After four unsuccessful attempts, the Air Force quit. All other launches of intercontinental ballistic missiles have been from the special test launch silos at Vandenberg Air Force Base in California. (The Russians do test their missiles from operational silos.)

While planners might reduce their doubts about reliability through a sufficiently rigorous testing program, there is no practical way to simulate and pre-test another necessary condition of a nuclear attack. Nuclear theoreticians assume that to increase the chances of destroying a missile in its silo, two warheads, from two different attacking rockets, would have to be assigned to each target silo. Because of "fratricide" and other problems, the two warheads would have to be closely synchronized; some experts say that they would have to hit the target within about ten seconds of each other. In planning an attack on the American missile force, Soviet leaders would therefore have to be sure that two different rockets would both be launched as planned, that both would follow their assigned courses with minute precision, that they would descend toward their common target and, after their 10,000-mile flight, would detonate at virtually the same instant—and that this would happen a thousand times. A nation might devise tests to show whether two, or even twenty, warheads could be synchronized. It will not be able to test its ability to coordinate an attack with more than 2,000 warheads.

There is another source of operational uncertainty, which bears directly on our ability to know the unknown. Jonathan Swift, who satirized the kingdom of Laputa, would have instantly understood the importance of the phenomenon known as "bias."

"Bias" refers to whether a missile, even under ideal circumstances, can be counted on to hit and destroy its target. Nuclear explosions do much of their damage through shock waves, or "overpressure." An overpressure of 5 pounds per square inch is enough to crush a house. (One bomb from a B-52 could, depending on its altitude when it exploded, create a 5 p.s.i. shock wave over an area ten miles across.) Missile silos are designed to endure overpressures of 2,000 pounds per square inch or more. A nuclear warhead can create that kind of pressure, but only if it scores a virtual bull's-eye on the silo, falling within a few hundred yards (depending on the warhead's blast) after its flight of many thousands of miles.

To judge by published "accuracy" figures, several models of Soviet and American missiles are capable of this feat. The arguments about a first strike were fueled by reports that both sides were developing missiles with accuracies in the vicinity of one tenth of a mile. Such reports are usually taken to mean that a missile would land one tenth of a mile from the target silo, which in most cases would be enough to destroy it. Once you have those accuracy figures, it is a matter of merely turning to the Rand slide rule to work out the "silo-kill probability" for each missile launch. With that figure, it is a further trivial calculation to determine how many Soviet missiles it would take to destroy the 1,000-missile Minuteman force. This is the calculation that lies behind all warnings about Minuteman vulnerability.

What the calculations overlook is the precise meaning of a missile's "accuracy." According to several experts in the physics of missile guidance,* it does not mean what it is most often assumed to mean: how close the warhead will come to its target. The formal measure of a missile's accuracy is its "circular error probable," or CEP. The CEP, as used by strategic analysts, is derived this way: if you fire twenty missiles and draw a circle around the center of their impact pattern that contains half the impact points, the radius of that circle will be the CEP. This says, to begin with, that only half the missiles will come as close to the center of the impact pattern as the stated accuracy. It also says something more interesting. The CEP, as formally defined, has nothing to do with the target point. It is a measure of the missiles' consistency—whether they all fall in roughly the same place—rather

---

*Even the disagreements over the definitions of "accuracy" and "bias" indicate the uncertainties of nuclear questions. Several men who have devoted large portions of their working lives to the details of missile technology patiently explained to me, over the course of many months, the concept of "bias" I set out in the next few pages. Several other people, of comparable intelligence and integrity, who have been equally attentive to the details of nuclear policy, assured me that the first set of experts was wrong, and that a missile's "accuracy," contrary to what I quote Richard Garwin and others as saying, really does measure how close its warheads would come to its intended target. Like any other layman, I am not competent to judge this argument; but that there could be such deep disagreement over fundamentals, at the most rarefied levels of expertise, underscores the difficulty any Soviet or American leader would have in predicting, with conclusive certainty, what would happen in a nuclear exchange.

than whether they go where they were aimed. By analogy with a shotgun, it would tell you how tight the pattern of shot was, but not how close it came to hitting the bird.

The difference between the center of the impact pattern and the intended target is known as "bias." To understand it, it is essential to know how missiles are guided in flight. One of the triumphs of military technology has been the refinement of "inertial guidance" systems, which plot the position of a missile—or airplane, or ship—by accumulating the effects of all the accelerations and decelerations the vehicle has undergone in its trip. The guidance system is based, essentially, on a gyroscope, which maintains its own axis and enables the system to measure each change in the vehicle's movements. The inertial guidance system feeds correcting data to the rocket's stages as it is lifted above the atmosphere; but once it is there, and the last stage has burned out, the warhead enjoys no further significant guidance during its flight. The parallel of artillery shells is often invoked in explanations of bias, and for good reason; a nuclear warhead falls to its target with the same reliance on gravity as does a shell from a mortar. That is what "ballistic" means in "intercontinental ballistic missile." The missile follows the looping, parabolic path of any projectile thrown into the sky.

The comparison with an artillery shell also helps illustrate the great challenge of missile guidance. If the accuracy required for one nuclear missile to destroy another in its silo were converted to the dimensions of artillery pieces on the battlefield, the comparison would be with an artillery shell that fell within one yard of a target thirty miles away.[8] Moreover, the shell would have to do that on the *first* shot, without the extensive set of bracketing shots and reports from forward observers on the fall of shot that artillery forces always rely on. In a nuclear first strike, there would be no time for "bracketing shots." The first shot would be the only one.

Extraordinary precision is not beyond the reach of modern technology. Space craft fly millions of miles toward distant planets, and their degree of accuracy, if converted to the artillery range, would be comparable to a shell that landed within millimeters of a target thirty miles away. But spacecraft like the Voyager make dozens of corrections, based on *seeing* the target, to continually reduce the errors of their trajectory. Spacecraft also travel through the vacuum of space, whereas a nuclear warhead descends through the earth's atmosphere and has very little opportunity to correct its course. The atmosphere not only affects its path but does so unpredictably. One of the atmosphere's characteristics is wind, which is far stronger in the upper atmosphere than near the earth's surface. Jet streams, which blow at altitudes between 30,000 and 50,000 feet, always blow roughly west to east, but their exact path is only known in detail when an airplane finds itself in one. The density of the atmosphere also varies significantly, especially in its upper reaches. The density at night is half what it is during the day, and it varies further by season, and by geography. The density in tropical regions is much different from what it is in the temperate zones, which might not matter except that long fingers of tropical air move into the temperate regions in unpredictable patterns. Weather balloons measure the atmosphere up to about 100,000 feet; above that, there are only readings from sounding rockets, which sample only a few limited points.

On the average, over many repeated shots, under different weather conditions, these adjustments might make the biases cancel each other out; the missiles might fall in a random pattern around their intended target, like two dozen darts thrown at a board. But if there were to be a surprise first strike, it would not be enough to be accurate "on the average." The missiles would have to hit their targets the first time, all on the same day, in the same few hours. And at any one moment, the bias of wind and atmosphere is not random. It is all in one direction. To use the model of a dartboard, it is as if two dozen darts were thrown through a strong cross wind, by a man who had no opportunity to observe their impact and correct his aim. All would be deflected to one side.

The inaccuracies introduced by bias might not make any difference in the destruction of "soft" targets, such as cities and industries, nor would they necessarily keep either the Soviet Union or the United States from destroying specific hardened sites, by sending in repeated attacks. But it is one thing for the Russians to calculate, with complete certainty, that given enough warheads, they can destroy the Strategic Air Command headquarters in Omaha, and something else to believe that 2,000 of their warheads, on the first strike, are *sure* to destroy 1,000 Minuteman missiles.

In theory, it should be possible to fine-tune an inertial guidance system to compensate for the factors that are responsible for bias, if we know what all of them are and can measure them precisely. That is exactly what the Air Force says it has done. The systems have been programmed for a twenty-four-hour cycle of variations in the atmospheric density, for seasonal patterns of winds, for the daily temperature cycles, and for the many small anomalies in the earth's gravitational field that arise because the earth is not a perfect sphere and because its density and composition vary.

"The purpose of an extensive test program is to work all these things out," Seymour Zeiberg, the Deputy Undersecretary of Defense for Research and Engineering for Strategic and Space Programs, said in an interview. "It may take around twenty test flights before you get rid of all the problems, but finally you do. Along the way, you find all the problems. The idea of some new distortion showing up just doesn't happen if you build and test the guidance programs properly. There are no unknowns. There are no surprises."[9]

Zeiberg explained that the winds should be a trivial factor because the warhead is moving so fast as it passes through them; that the guidance systems are constantly adjusted for weather patterns, based on information from a world-wide weather network that is updated every twelve hours; that, even though no missile has flown the route over the North Pole which Soviet and American missiles would take during a nuclear strike, there has been very precise mapping by satellite of each possible course. "There are no unknowns," he repeated.

"Every factor you can think of has been accommodated," says the physicist Richard Garwin, who has served for many years on the Defense Science Board. "It is the things you don't think of that cause the trouble.

"The central point is that we could not fire with total confidence against the Soviet ICBMs, and they could not fire against ours, even though our missiles may have proved accurate and repeatable over the usual firing ranges.

"The evidence for this begins with the general proposition, that whenever you want to make a bookcase, the odds are that it won't work out right. One piece will be too long or too short. Beyond that, there is specific evidence. You don't have many opportunities for discovering the errors in your assumptions when you do the same thing time and again. When you are firing over one range, the CEP conceals the bias, by definition. When you try a new guidance system on your old missiles over the same range, and the missile lands two thousand feet from where it should have landed, and that is far beyond the sum of the inaccuracies of the guidance, you say, 'Aha! I should have thought of that before. It's perfectly obvious. I should have realized that this would happen.' You correct that error, and if you are naïve, you say that there is no more bias. The fact is that generation after generation of innovations have turned up biases of this sort.*

*Note that these errors occur even on the Vandenberg-to-Kwajalein Western Test Range, where the United States has been firing, measuring, and correcting biases for twenty-five years. The gravitational anomalies on that course are more precisely

"Sometimes it gets even worse after adjustment. You may look at the problem and change something you think is causing it, and then get worse answers than before, so that you have to go back and undo the correction that you've made. It may sound as if fools are doing this, but they're smart people, and they're doing the best they can. You may recall that in one of the space shots the capsule came down four hundred miles from where it was supposed to. The reason was that they were basing their calculations on the sidereal [determined by the stars] day, not the solar day [which is four minutes longer]. It was a difference of 1/365th."[10]

I asked Garwin about Zeiberg's statement that there were "no unknowns, no surprises." "That does not agree with anything I am familiar with," he replied, "in this field or in any field. Any work you do on a computer, anything you build yourself, any work you commission someone else to do, teaches you to be humble about unknowns." He mentioned several other uncertainties. The United States test-fires its missiles from Vandenberg Air Force Base in California westward to the South Pacific, usually to Kwajalein Atoll in the Marshall Islands. The Soviet Union tests its missiles from the North European portion of Russia eastward toward Siberia. One path is east-west; the other, west-east. Neither nation has ever fired a missile on the north-south route, over the North Pole, which each side's missiles would have to take in a nuclear attack. "And then you have a real problem after you've set off a nuclear explosion," Garwin said. "They do change the atmosphere and induce winds, which would affect subsequent missiles. Nobody knows about that. But to come back to the fundamental point, you can never be *certain* that it would work on the first strike, and unless you're certain, you're not going to do it."

Another scientist who has stressed the difference between the missiles' "accuracy" on the Western Test Range and their likely performance in time of war is J. Edward Anderson, a professor at the University of Minnesota who developed some of the inertial guidance systems for American nuclear missiles in the fifties and sixties. Anderson points out that small differences in accuracy can fundamentally alter the assumptions on which a first strike would be based. For example, if the warheads from Soviet SS-18 missiles fell within 300 feet of their in-

---

mapped than anywhere else; more is known about the weather over Kwajalein than about most places in the United States, let alone in Russia. Some scientists and engineers familiar with guidance problems told me that they would not be surprised by very large inaccuracies, perhaps ten or twenty miles, in actual wartime firings over the unknown north–south route.

tended targets (as published "accuracy" figures suggest that they would), then a Soviet first strike, in which two 1.5-megaton warheads were devoted to each target silo, could destroy all but twenty missiles of the Minuteman force. But if bias increased the average miss by only 200 feet, then ten times as many Minutemen would survive—enough to invalidate all Soviet assumptions that they could escape without annihilation. Anderson has calculated that an error of three parts per million in mapping the gravitational field of the earth would lead to a 300-foot bias error in the warhead's impact pattern, and thereby spare even more of the Minutemen. Is such precise mapping possible? "I have no doubt that it is, on the Vandenberg range," Anderson said in an inteview. "But I don't believe you could do it with any assurance on a range you've never fired on. You base the gravitational mapping on satellite trajectories, where you're looking at small changes in the satellite's path. But those deviations in orbit are not uniquely related to changes in the earth's gravitational field. The gravitational field of the moon, for example, introduces an error of about three parts per million by itself. The national command has to think conservatively. There just isn't going to be a window where a first strike would make sense."

Anderson has also proposed a novel, realistic way to test the claims of those who say that the refined accuracy of modern missiles would permit a first strike, or that bias would prevent it. "I've suggested to several people that we choose an untried test route, say a 6,000-mile N-S course over the Pacific. We could set up a dozen test shots, and observe the results." If the missiles duplicated on this new range the accuracies claimed for them on paper and fine-tuned on the Western test range, it would strengthen the case of those who are concerned about Minuteman vulnerability. But if bias made a serious difference in their accuracies, it would underscore the uncertainties any Soviet or American leader must confront. (Anderson's proposal was first reported by James Coates of the Chicago *Tribune*.)

Perhaps the most persuasive statement comes from James Schlesinger, who, as Secretary of Defense, offered secret testimony to the Arms Control Subcommittee of the Senate Foreign Relations Committee on March 4, 1974. His testimony has since been declassified, and it was quoted by Andrew and Alexander Cockburn in the *New York Review of Books*:

I believe there is some misunderstanding about the degree of reliability and accuracy of missiles. . . . It is impossible for either side to acquire the degree

of accuracy that would give them a high confidence first strike, because we
will not know what the actual accuracy would be like in a real world context.
As you know, we have acquired from the Western Test Range a fairly precise
accuracy, but in the real world we would have to fly from operational bases
to targets in the Soviet Union. The parameters of the flight from the Western
Test Range are not really very helpful in determining those accuracies to the
Soviet Union. We can never know what degrees of accuracy would be
achieved in the real world. . . .

The point I would like to make is that if you have any degradation in
operational accuracy, American counter-force capability goes to the dogs very
quickly. We know that, and the Soviets should know it, and that is one of the
reasons that I can publicly state that neither side can acquire a high confidence
first strike capability. I want the President of the United States to know that
for all the future years, and I want the Soviet leadership to know that for all
the future years.[11]

Schlesinger made these points as part of an argument in favor of
larger, "blockbuster" warheads for the American arsenal; but anyone
who wants to avoid nuclear war should share his wish that the President
of the United States and the Soviet leadership understand the limits
of missile accuracy. If they do not, if they believe there are "no unknowns, no surprises," they might be tempted to order a strike. That
is why the complacency of defense intellectuals about this point is so
dangerous and baffling. Such complacency was well illustrated by John
M. Collins, a long-time defense specialist for the Congressional Research Service who has produced a 600-page encyclopedia of Soviet and
American capabilities called U.S.-Soviet Military Balance.[12] In October 1980 Collins replied, when asked in an interview with Defense
Week magazine, "How shaky is the American strategic nuclear triad?":

There are some very hard-nosed conservatives who say . . . that we have
much too high a degree of confidence in the accuracy figures claimed for
Soviet and American ICBMs, that those accuracies are not as good as they're
claimed to be by a wide margin. . . . There are a lot of unknowns here. Some
people say we're going to hit the target with the first round. Others say forget
it. The point is that it doesn't make any difference. If the people who are in
charge, the leadership of the United States and the Soviet Union, believe that
they have these accuracies, then they behave as though they have them. It
doesn't make any difference whether they're right. It's what they believe that
counts.[13]

The implication was that the Soviet Union might well believe that it had the accuracy necessary for a first strike—and therefore that the United States should also suspend common sense and believe the same thing, instead of making every effort to be sure that both Soviet and American leaders recognized the ultimate unknowability of nuclear questions.

That is why it does "make a difference," in Mr. Collins' terms, when the limits on missile accuracy are overlooked. The smallest effect that such a misunderstanding could have is the diversion of tens of billions of dollars that, even if they stayed in the defense budget, could far more profitably be used to raise the pay of noncommissioned officers, to build larger numbers of simpler, more effective tanks and planes, to provide more realistic training. The gravest effect that this misunderstanding could have would be to permit a nuclear war. That is what James Schlesinger explained with apparent passion to the committee, in secret session. For some reason, no authoritative figure has made that explanation forcefully to the public.

When I asked Richard Garwin, the physicist who explained "bias," why "defense intellectuals" paid so little attention to this issue, he said, "Why don't people care about bias? Why do people fear that the Soviet Union will attack even when we could so easily prevent it, simply by launch on warning? There is nobody who makes any money or gets any power out of saying that bias will prevent them from striking. It used to be that the Air Force would say that the Minuteman is not vulnerable, to avoid money being spent on Ballistic Missile Defense systems, which would be run by the Army. Now the Air Force needs the MX. But wait till they start putting the MX in Minuteman silos. Wait till you hear what they say about vulnerability then."

PSYCHOLOGICAL UNCERTAINTIES

THE FINAL category of uncertainties includes the psychological, the political, the human. Underlying all theories of a "first strike" is the concept that even though the United States will still possess enough nuclear weapons after a surprise attack to devastate Russia, the pellucid logic of cost-benefit analysis would stay the President's hand as he reached to give the order for a counterattack. This is based, further, on the idea that the casualties from an attack on the Minuteman silos would be containable, and that the Russians would be able to predict, with total certainty, that the President would not order our missiles "launched on warning" during the twenty-odd minutes he would have before the first Russian warheads began to fall.

To begin with, consider the timing of a nuclear attack. Strategists like to point out that because of problems of timing, it would be very difficult to destroy both the Minuteman missiles and the B-52 bombers at the same time. In most theories of a Soviet first strike, the job of destroying the bombers on the runway is left to missiles "lobbed" in from Soviet submarines, with flight times of ten to twelve minutes. The Minutemen would be destroyed by missiles launched from silos in the Soviet Union, which take twenty-five to thirty minutes to arrive. If the attack on the bombers came first, that would warn the United States about the impending attack on the Minutemen, and give the President the option to launch them before they were destroyed. If the ICBM attack showed up on the radar screen first, more of the bombers have time to get off the ground before the missiles aimed at them hit.

Further, although the public generally conceives of nuclear war as an instantaneous, blinding spasm, most experts assume that a full-scale first strike would take hours, not minutes, to complete, starting with the most southern targets in the United States and gradually marching north. Would any President sit still through this whole process, forbearing to launch the Minutemen based in North Dakota or to scramble the bombers in Maine before they were destroyed? It is inconceivable that he would do so—but the first-strike theories assume that he will.

In the last few years of the seventies, several studies appeared that cast serious doubt on how "surgical" and containable the damage of the first, counterforce strike would be. The most influential was a report from the Office of Technology Assessment (OTA), called "The Effects of Nuclear War," which was released early in 1979. Another, by the Arms Control and Disarmament Agency (ACDA), with the same title, was released in April of the same year.[14] Deadpan, they present maps of major cities—Detroit, Leningrad, Boston, Moscow, Washington, New York—overlaid with grids of destruction zones and likely casualties. The OTA study also plotted a nationwide fallout map, as one of several steps to estimate the likely aftereffects of a "limited, counterforce" strike against the United States. Perhaps the best way to envision how the fallout might spread is to remember how the ash from Mount St. Helens really did spread after its eruption in May 1980. From this one source in the far northwestern corner of the country, the ash was carried by the winds over the Rocky Mountain states, over the Plains from Texas to Minnesota, over all of the industrial Midwest, and over the eastern seabord from Maine to northern Florida (with the exception of the Carolinas.) This was from one explosion; the first-strike scenarios call for well over 2,000, in order to destroy the missile fields, bomber bases, and submarine ports. Depending on which way the wind was blowing, the season of the year, and even the time of day, the *immediate* casualties from this strike could be as few as 2 million, or as many as 20 million, the OTA said. Tens of millions could die later from exposure to lethal doses of fallout. These are the casualties the American President is supposed to absorb; this is the range about which the Soviets are supposed to feel a comfortable degree of certainty. McGeorge Bundy wrote in 1969:

There is an enormous gulf between what political leaders really think about nuclear weapons and what is assumed in complex calculations of relative "advantage" in simulated strategic war. Think tank analysts can set levels of "acceptable" damage well up in the hundreds of millions of lives. . . . They are in an unreal world. In the real world of real political leaders—whether here or in the Soviet Union—a decision that would bring even one hydrogen bomb on one city of one's own country would be recognized in advance as a cata-strophic blunder; ten bombs in ten cities would be a disaster beyond history; and a hundred bombs on one hundred cities are unthinkable.[15]

Charles Yost, a career foreign service officer who has been U.S. Ambassador to the United Nations, has said:

Some American proponents of the scenario of a Soviet first strike . . . maintain that an American President would not dare retaliate with our subma-rines and bombers, for fear this would provoke a second strike on our cities. This contention seems to me to misread the psychology of any American President I have ever known. After all, what were the other two legs of the triad constructed for? Could any President passively ignore, fail to respond, to a massive attack upon us? . . . The decisive point, however, is that Soviet leaders would not *know* [emphasis in original] what an American President would do in these circumstances.[16]

THE ABILITY TO "WIN" A WAR

BEYOND THESE uncertainties, there is yet another doubtful area: the degree of confidence the Soviet Union can enjoy about its ability to survive a nuclear attack and come out the "winner." Many observers of Soviet society report, persuasively, that the Russians are doing every-thing they can to develop a civil defense system. But when the argument moves one step further, to the assertion that the Russians can limit their casualties to 10 million in a war that would kill 100 million Americans, it loses touch with fact.

In 1979 the U.S. Arms Control and Disarmament Agency re-examined the premises that led T. K. Jones to his conclusion that only 10 million Russians would die. (Though some might argue that the ACDA is a biased source because of its interest in arms control, one might make the same point about Mr. Jones, whose employer, Boeing, could be one of the major contractors for the MX.) By correcting some of Jones's most dubious assumptions—such as his notion that 61 million Russians are dispersed through the (uninhabitable) Arctic wastelands —the ACDA said that the more likely range of Russian casualties would be somewhere between 20 million and 61 million.[17] (For a closer look at Jones's assumptions, see the footnote below.*) In a separate

---

*According to the ACDA papers, T. K. Jones's assumptions were these:
• That the Soviet population is composed of 139 million people living in the cities; 80 million in rural areas; and 61 million others, who are *evenly* scattered over 6.3 million square miles of the least inhabited parts of the Soviet Union.
• That, in time of nuclear crisis, all 80 million rural people, and 122 million of the city dwellers, are evacuated and *evenly* distributed, in blast and fallout shelters, over the remaining 2.3 million miles of Soviet territory. (By way of comparison, this would be an area nine times the size of Texas.)
• That all of the 17 million people who remain in the cities are *evenly* distributed through hardened blast and fallout shelters, which can withstand 150 p.s.i. overpressure. (Again, by way of comparison, 5 p.s.i. will crush a house, and 20 p.s.i. destroys industrial structures and reinforced-concrete buildings.)
• That the American retaliatory strike comes in the form of "barrage" attacks, designed to cover an area evenly, rather than concentrated on certain targets.
   Mr. Jones then works out his fatalities by calculating what percentage of the total city area will be subject to more than 150 p.s.i. of blast overpressure in a barrage attack, and what percentage of the rural area will be subject to more than 7 p.s.i., since he assumes that the rural shelters will protect people at levels below that. People in those pressure zones will die; the rest will not. Because of his assumption that the Russian population will be evenly spread over all the available area, Jones can convert the percentage of land directly to a percentage of people, which leads to his conclusion that 10 million would die and 207 million would live.[18]
   According to the ACDA, all the assumptions are wrong. The 6.3 million square miles of Siberia, steppe, and wasteland in which Mr. Jones places 61 million Russians are, in fact, essentially uninhabited, contain no roads to bring people in or buildings to shelter them if they came. The Soviet cities, like cities anywhere, have the very opposite of an "even" population distribution; indeed, they are far more concentrated than many cities of the American South and West that developed after the coming of the automobile and the freeway. With the world's best transporation system, it would be

study the ACDA concluded that, after a Soviet first strike, the United States could retaliate against industries and military sites in such a way that 100 million Russians would die immediately if they took no civil defense precautions; 25 million to 35 million would die if the cities were evacuated; and 70 million to 85 million would be killed, even after evacuation, if the United States deliberately aimed at the evacuation sites.[19] A study from the Department of Defense has estimated likely Soviet casualties, despite civil defense, at 55 million.[20]

Those who are most concerned about Soviet plans to "win" a nuclear war point out that 20 million Russians died in their Great Patriotic War, and that its privileged cadre of totalitarian leaders would not mind expending such numbers yet again to dominate the world. The difference is that Stalin did not know he would lose 20 million when the war began; he did not start the war himself, but was attacked by Hitler; and the deaths came in a period of five years, not five hours.

Soviet leaders might well contemplate a further uncertainty about their ability to withstand nuclear war. Even if their people survived at first, they would have to be fed, housed, and clothed. How would the sick be treated, and what if there was an epidemic? Despite many off-hand assertions to the contrary, the Soviet Union's industrial base is more concentrated, and therefore more vulnerable, than that of the United States. Why should this be a surprise from the nation that has made a parody of centralized planning?

According to the Office of Technology Assessment, 3 Minuteman missiles and 7 Poseidon missiles could destroy 73 percent of all oil-refining capacity in the Soviet Union.[21] The Arms Control and Disarmament Agency says that a retaliatory strike by the United States would destroy 80 percent of all the hospitals in the Soviet Union. It adds that under "nongenerated" conditions—that is, if American forces were taken totally by surprise and had no chance to put more bombers on alert or send more submarines to sea—the retaliatory strike

---

impossible to "evenly" disperse the urban population, and Russian transportation is not the world's best. Even if nearly 90 percent of the urban population were evacuated, as Jones assumes, the ones who remain could not possibly be "evenly" spread through the whole 14,100 square miles of urban area. Imagine moving 6 million people out of New York City and dispersing them, along with everyone from its suburbs, evenly through all of New York State and New Jersey, and then seeding the other 1.5 million New Yorkers in blast shelters throughout the five boroughs, and you will see the challenge. In Russian cities, the ACDA study said, 80 percent of the urban population would start out in the most densely populated 2,900 square miles, and it is fantastic to think they could be uniformly spread out.

would destroy: 80 percent of the Soviet Union's steel-producing capability; about 80 percent of aluminum, titanium, copper, and other metal production; 60 percent of electrical power generators; 70 percent of plants that manufacture generators and other electrical equipment; 80 percent of oil refineries and 30 percent of petroleum storage areas; 60 percent of the shipyards; 70 percent of the rubber industry; 75 percent of all communications systems; and so on down the numbing list.[22] Thirty-one percent of all Soviet people live within one and a half nautical miles of a major industry, compared to 22 percent of Americans.[23]

Maybe the ACDA and the CIA, which has made similar predictions, are wrong. Maybe T. K. Jones is right. Probably all sets of hypothetical calculations would prove to be far off. No one can *know* unless war comes; and without knowing, no sane leader could attack.

AMONG THOSE who certainly understand the thousand doubts that would plague any leader planning a first strike is Paul Nitze. Since the middle seventies, shortly after he resigned as a member of the SALT negotiating team, he has been the most principled and the most effective exponent of the "first strike" hypothesis and the strategic build-up it implies. No one can doubt that Nitze understands the technical objections to a first strike; when talking to sophisticated audiences, he does not even pretend to believe that it would ever occur. What he— and many others who make the first-strike argument—are concerned about is something different: the *perceptions* of American weakness that an "imbalance" of nuclear forces, however unusable and impractical, would create. The perceptions he mentions are those of the Germans and the Russians: the Germans will make accommodations with Russia because they feel our strength is waning, and the Russians will push us around for the same reason. The "perception" that really lies behind the warnings is, I believe, Nitze's own detection of weakness in the American soul.

Nitze is one of the last members of the class of American statesmen who came of age during World War II. He is roughly a contemporary of Dean Acheson, John J. McCloy, Robert Lovett, men of private means who moved in and out of government and were stewards of America's power during the generation in which Europe was rebuilt and the Cold War begun. They tended to see politics in the frame of those years; the ultimate military reality was an attack by Russian tanks on Berlin. They had seen the effects of war and were determined to use American power to prevent its recurrence. The constant theme of Nitze's statements about nuclear policy has been the need to ensure "crisis stability" so as to prevent either side from using the weapons first. As they surveyed a devastated Europe, they knew that the weakness of Hitler's neighbors had enticed him to attack. They would not make that mistake with the Soviet Union.

In the generation since those perceptions were formed, American power has "declined." Partly it has done so because the Soviet Union, as was inevitable, has developed nuclear weapons and produced a force more or less equivalent to ours. Partly our power has "declined" because of the withdrawal the United States went through after its catastrophe in Vietnam. But mainly the United States has "lost" power because the world has grown more independent and complicated, as parents "lose" power when their children grow into adults. At the end of World War II there were almost no independent countries in Africa and Southeast Asia, only colonies; the economies of Europe and Japan were so impoverished, relative to America's, that the United States could afford to subsidize the recovery of each. But to many people of Nitze's generation, the changes since that time result mainly from a loss of American will, and that is why the symbolism of a nuclear imbalance is so alarming to them.

No doubt symbols play a part in international politics. The Russians have derived incalculable mileage from the impression that they have built a world-conquering military force, an impression they have been fostering, overtly and covertly, since 1945. (Recall Colonel Kulish's comments at the end of chapter 3.) But why should we help them create that impression when it is at such variance with the facts, and when the real purpose of such warnings, I am convinced, is only to apply a scourge to the flaccid American soul? If the problem is the perception of American strength, why not assess that strength coolly rather than create exaggerated fears?

Nitze's arguments proceed directly from his principles about politics and strength, but there are less scrupulous spokesmen for his cause. In the fall of 1980, Senator Jake Garn of Utah inserted a long statement in the *Congressional Record* designed to debunk a paper by the Carter Administration on nuclear policy. The Administration's statement included a favorable mention of Robert McNamara's strategic policy, which Garn rebutted as follows: "McNamara did not start a single new strategic system during his 7 years as defense Secretary. More importantly, he formulated the theory of Mutual Assured Destruction which has had such a negative impact on our defense spending."[24] Garn's word is "spending," not "security" or "strength." Perhaps he sees no difference.

Excessive fear-mongering about Soviet civil defense and the risk of a first strike diminish America's security because they amount to "crying wolf." Amid so many alarums about the Soviet menace, politicians and the public may find it hard to distinguish more disturbing news—for example, that because of technical failures and delays in the Trident program, the number of American nuclear missile submarines will decline in the first few years of the eighties. "If we guard our toothbrushes and our diamonds with equal zeal," J. H. van Vleck has said, "we will lose fewer toothbrushes, and more diamonds."[25] Whether or not these apocalyptic prophets are correct in their interpretation of the Soviet Union's intentions, their indifference to the facts diverts American energy and attention from the two positive steps the nation should take with its nuclear weapons. The first is to do what is needed to ensure the invulnerability of the deterrent, and the second is to work equally hard to reduce the risk that these hideous weapons will ever be used. Both of these purposes are served by ensuring that the President, the public, and the world understand the dominance of uncertainty in the strategic balance.

PROTECTING THE "TRIAD"

EVEN THOUGH the nuclear debate of the 1970s and early 1980s has concentrated on land-based missiles, the other "legs of the triad"—submarines and bombers—are at least as important.

Since the first Polaris submarine was launched in 1959, nuclear-powered submarines carrying nuclear missiles have often been thought of as America's ultimate retaliatory force. The United States has retained a lead in most aspects of submarine technology, including the crucial one of making the vessels quiet. If submarines are sufficiently quiet, they are virtually undetectable; sonar only becomes practical for finding a submarine once you know that one is in the vicinity. In this sense, the submarines are more secure than land-based missiles—and, of course, a "first strike" attack against them would not draw a nuclear firestorm onto the American heartland. The submarines' disadvantage is that their missiles are inherently less accurate, since the position of the submarine at the moment it fires can never be determined as precisely as the location of a fixed silo on land.

The fundamental question about submarines is whether it will ever be possible to detect them, through some new technology that would let the Russians "see through the water." In the summer of 1980, there was a commotion in the defense community when William Perry, then the Undersecretary of Defense for Research and Engineering, said in an interview that the Soviet Union might be on the verge of an anti-submarine breakthrough. As the clamor rose, Perry quickly backed off from his comment, which was widely interpreted as an attempt to sell the MX missile through threat inflation. The United States has a tremendous stake in ensuring that no such threat does emerge, which dictates several efforts. One is to continue to concentrate on antisubmarine-warfare research, which would increase our confidence that the Soviet Union will not be able to take us by surprise with a technical breakthrough. Another potential problem for submarines is the difficulty of communicating with them. Normal radio waves penetrate only a few feet into water, which makes it difficult to get in touch with a submerged vessel. Today's solution is for the subs to trail a radio buoy, painted black and shaped like a small stubby bomb, which rides above the submarine, a foot or two beneath the surface of the water. The cable that connects it to the submarine transmits the radio signals. The buoys are the closest thing to invisible. Standing on an upper deck of a submarine tender in the Charleston Navy Yard, I was challenged to spot the buoy that was attached to a submarine floating on the surface a hundred feet below us. I could not.*

Since the ultimate purpose of submarines is to survive, it makes sense to reverse the thinking that has given us the Trident and move instead toward a diversified fleet that includes smaller, cheaper, harder-to-find,

---

*At the moment, no one is very worried that these small buoys would give away the location of a submarine, but against that possibility, the Navy has tried to build an "extremely low frequency" broadcasting system, known as ELF. While normal radio wavelengths are measured in fractions of meters these ELF wavelengths are measured in thousands of miles and can penetrate deep into the water to reach submarines. They transmit information very slowly—it may take five minutes to get across a single word, half an hour to transmit a verifiable nuclear strike order—but they will always get through. The Navy wants to use the ELF system as a "bell ringer," which would notify submerged vessels to come near the surface and get more detailed information through normal radio transmissions. The Navy now transmits VLF (very low frequency) signals from a fleet of airplanes known as TACAMOs, which trail long wires behind them to act as an antenna. Some TACAMO planes are in the air at all times, but as an extra safeguard, the Navy has proposed the fixed ELF transmitter on the ground. Ten years ago, calling the system Project Sanguine, the Navy wanted to dig up much of Wisconsin to lay down 5,000 miles of blast-hardened transmitting antennas. Now the proposed system involves only about 100 miles of buried cable, all but a mile or two of it to be laid along public rights of way. Compared to the vast tracts that would be consumed by the MX, this might be a modest price, economically and environmentally, for an increase in the security of the deterrent.

more numerous submarines. A more dramatic solution, proposed by Richard Garwin of IBM and Sidney Drell of the Stanford Linear Accelerator Center, is the "shallow undersea mobile" system, or SUM. This would be a fleet of small submarines, each of which would carry two MX-type missiles in capsules mounted on its hull. The submarines would be powered by batteries or fuel cells, and therefore would be even quieter than nuclear subs. They would require a crew of only fifteen or twenty men. Because the range of the MX missile is so long, the small submarines would need to travel no farther than a few hundred miles off the east and west coasts, instead of going into the open sea. They would occupy a large enough operating area to prevent the Soviet Union from simply "barraging" the coastline with nuclear weapons and destroying the submarines, but the subs would still be close enough to shore to have good communications, with virtually no "dead time" as they travel to their stations. The submarine with its missiles could be as small as 1,100 tons, as compared to 18,500 tons for the Trident. According to Garwin and Drell, the German navy has operated a fleet of 500-ton submarines for ten years.

"There is great value in maintaining a diversity of systems with different operational characteristics, and thereby different potential vulnerabilities," Garwin and Drell say in a prospectus for SUM.[26] They go on to say that if the United States wants to maintain diversity in its nuclear forces, it should not feel compelled to cling to one "leg" of the triad, the land-based missiles, if changing circumstances make a different approach (such as SUM) more sensible.

As for the land-based missiles, one approach would be simply to dismantle them. "If the land-based ICBMs will be so vulnerable and their replacements so costly," says Robert Pranger of the American Enterprise Institute, "why not abandon this leg of the triad or do nothing more to improve it?"[27] Fred Kaplan, the defense writer, has pointed out that getting rid of the Minutemen would make the large Soviet missiles obsolete, since they could not be used against submarines and bombers. Maxwell Taylor, former Chairman of the Joint Chiefs of Staff, has written that "the most effective way to attain a higher degree of invulnerability would be to remove from American soil the most inviting targets for a surprise attack, our land-based ICBMs."[28] Another solution is to leave the Minutemen where they are, since maintaining them costs very little, since they are probably not really "vulnerable," anyway, and since their presence gives the Soviet Union another complication to consider.

The conventional view of the third leg of the triad—the bombers— is that they are a quaint anachronism, with at best a minor function in the future, that of hauling cruise missiles to the border of Russia and shooting them off. In fact, the bombers are the only part of the nuclear system that has a basis in the real world, rather than in theology. While they are slower than missiles—their travel time to Soviet targets is a matter of hours, not minutes—and while some of them might be shot down, we *know* from half a century of experience that bombers work. Despite all the analysts' precise projections, there is a real possibility that a large number of missiles will not fire properly from their silos or submarines, that they will miss their targets by many miles, that their fuses will fail to detonate the bombs. (This last, in fact, is said to be a substantial worry. As it happens, fuses were also the problem with many defective torpedoes in World War II.) There is a possibility that the new cruise missiles—which are supposed to read the contours of the Russian terrain as they pass over it, compare it with maps stored in their computer memories, and guide themselves precisely to their targets—will not perform precisely as planned. The real purpose of manned bombers is to provide an alternative that probably will function if everything else fails.

When the bombers' mission is stated this way, it helps explain why a new model of bomber may be necessary—but also why most arguments about the proposed B-1 bomber missed the point. The American bomber fleet is now made of a little more than 300 large B-52 Stratofortress bombers and about 60 smaller FB-111 bombers. In newspaper stories, the bombers are almost always described as "the aging B-52s," since the oldest models went into service in 1957 and the newest in 1962. From the point of view of what works in combat, the real objection to the B-52s is not their age, but that their size, lack of maneuverability, and "noisy" electronic equipment handicap them in doing what bombers must ultimately do: sneaking undetected into Russia and dropping bombs on targets with absolute reliability. The B-52s are close to the size of a commercial 747 airplane and have comparable difficulty flying low to avoid radar detection. As they have been loaded up with new avionics systems, they have become "beacons in the sky," like some of the fighter planes discussed in previous chapters, broadcasting their presence to enemy forces hundreds of miles away.

The proper remedy for the B-52's defects is not to build another large, unmaneuverable new airplane, like the B-1. The B-1 was in essence a mobile missile site, from which short- or medium-range guided missiles would be launched toward their targets. This approach would have combined the high cost of maintaining a bomber fleet with the high technical risk of complex missile systems—the worst of both worlds. A more sensible approach would be to go back to the real purpose of a bomber—penetrating undetected—and then design a plane to those specifications and no others. The aircraft that are often best at avoiding radar detection are small, very maneuverable airplanes that do not offer a sizable target for radar, that can fly close to the ground (though not necessarily very fast), travel up riverbeds and canyons, etc., to thwart radar detection. In the first few years after World War II, the U.S. Navy had a force of propeller-driven, single-engine nuclear bombers, small planes known as A-1Es. In those years, A-1 pilots would fly practice raids from carriers in the Pacific to inland targets—say, Phoenix or Salt Lake City. The planes were extraordinarily slow; they cruised at about 140 knots, or one-fourth the speed of sound. But because they were so maneuverable (and partly because they were so slow), they could skirt around hills, fly down in the Grand Canyon, and conceal themselves in the "ground clutter" on the radar screen. In the entire history of these exercises, from the late forties to the early sixties, the radars from the Air Defense Command *never* tracked the A-1s, and the interceptors *never* caught them. The point is not that we should turn back to the A-1, but that we should use the technical developments of the intervening thirty years to produce an even more maneuverable, lower-flying, more elusive plane.[29]

Important as it is to maintain an invulnerable deterrent, the larger imperative is to eliminate the circumstances that permit nuclear weapons to be used. There are three instruments for doing so: reducing the certainty with which an aggressor might calculate the effects of a surprise attack; avoiding situations that give the advantage to the side that fires first; and reducing the numbers of weapons, through arms control.

One of the most effective, and creative, ways to reduce an aggressor's certainty would be to press immediately for a new test-ban treaty—one that would limit testing of *missiles*, not the warheads they carry. As Seymour Zeiberg of the Pentagon explained, it takes many test flights to work out the guidance systems. Even after those flights, prudent men should doubt that all uncertainties have been removed. But if each side were limited to a small number of test flights each year, or none at all, military planners would *know* that there were areas of uncertainty. This is yet another illustration that what makes sense for most things does not make sense for nuclear weapons. For most weapons systems, the American military needs more, and more realistic, testing because it needs to know how the planes and tanks and guided missiles will work in combat. In nuclear weapons, both sides have a stake in keeping either side from starting to believe that it really knows how the weapons would perform.

Preventing "quick-draw" situations, in which the side that shoots first wins, also leads to conclusions that confound normal logic. Many of the groups that want "more" defense are agitating for a new "anti-ballistic missile" system (ABM). Such systems, designed to protect either cities or missile silos against enemy warheads, were banned in the first SALT agreement. Part of the reason the United States was willing to abandon ABM systems (after a bitter fight in the Senate) was that there are many technical problems that would probably keep an ABM system from working. These include distinguishing decoys from real warheads on the radar, sorting out two objects when their paths cross on the radar screen (the same problem that plagued the SAGE system), and the ease with which a few high-altitude nuclear blasts might "blind" the radars on which the ABM depends. The further theologian's argument against the ABM is that if either side *believed* that its protective system worked, it would have the incentive to strike first in time of crisis. Gerard Smith, the chief American negotiator for the first SALT treaty, explained:

The notion that a defensive capability can be a threat is hard to accept. The logic is that if a nation could with offensive weapons destroy some of its adversary's retaliatory force, including its bombers, before it was launched and then could destroy with defensive missiles [ABMs] some or all of the remaining force after it was launched, it might decide, especially in a crisis, that it could make a nuclear attack without intolerable retaliation. If that were a possibility, the present deterrent balance could be shaken.[30]

To go back down the path toward ABMs would be to add another multi-billion-dollar system that probably would not work, and that might increase the chances that nuclear weapons might be used.

Arms control—the other means of reducing the risk of nuclear war —has fallen on hard times. The SALT II treaty was interred after the Soviet Union invaded Afghanistan. Even when it was still under consideration, it had mainly turned into a device for speeding up research and increasing spending for every system that SALT allowed. As has happened before in nearly twenty years of arms negotiations, the theory that the United States must build itself up before again going to the bargaining table has won support.* This theory often rests on the

---

*Each round of SALT negotiations has involved a "sweetener" to the Joint Chiefs of Staff. The sweetener for SALT I included the B-1 bomber and cost about $30 billion. The sweetener for SALT II was the MX and may cost $50 billion or more. One pragmatic observer of SALT says, "I'm terrified of SALT III, because it could bankrupt us."

contention that the best way to convince the Soviet Union not to do something is to do it ourselves: if we build the MX missile and threaten their forces, then they'll be happy to make a deal to get rid of the MX and their heavy missiles too. On the historical record, this approach has usually not worked out. During the mid- and late sixties, the United States decided to go ahead and put MIRV warheads on its missiles, five years ahead of the Soviet Union. One of the theories offered at the time was that once the Russians understood the threat our MIRVs posed to them, they would be most willing to agree to a ban on MIRVs for each side. In reality, both sides rushed to "MIRV" their missile forces, which has created today's worries about a first strike. "That more than anything else set back the cause of strategic arms control," says Gerard Smith.[31] Nowhere in the record of arms negotiations is there an instance of either side giving up a significant workable system after it was built. Unless they are arrested beforehand, the weapons continue to grow.

THE BEST WAY to ensure that the world passes another thirty years in ignorance of nuclear war is to recognize the depth of our ignorance now. That is how to avoid being panicked by scenarios with no more foundation in fact than other theologians' fiery visions of hell.

SEVEN

CHANGES

THE PREVIOUS chapters have described the destructive patterns of procurement, of judgments based on speculation or the oversimple formula, of military forces diverted from their proper roles. This final chapter suggests, in broad terms, the efforts that should be made to impose more constructive patterns on national defense. The four most important efforts are:

▼ to restore the military spirit;
▼ to stop the progression toward ever more costly and complex weapons;
▼ to apply standards of hard-headed, skeptical reason to the theology of nuclear weapons; and
▼ to establish the conditions for greater "coherence" in the way the nation makes its choices for defense.

MILITARY SPIRIT

THE MOST important task in defense is the one most likely to be overlooked, since it lies in the realm of values and character rather than quantities that can be represented on charts. Before anything else, we must recognize that a functioning military requires bonds of trust, sacrifice, and respect within its ranks, and similar bonds of support and respect between an army and the nation it represents.

For the soldiers, the reconstruction of these bonds is initially a matter of removing two seriously distorting forces: the culture of procurement, which teaches soldiers that their function is to buy complex weapons, rather than to think about how to adapt their plans and weapons to an uncertain environment; and the careerist ethic, which says that it is more important to be successful than to be honorable, honest, or, of course, competent. In any organization, the models of success become self-perpetuating: when certain kinds of people get ahead, they teach others to act the same way, or to quit. Until today's model, with its emphasis on procurement, ticket punching, and trimming around the edges, is changed, it will be difficult to keep the right kind of people in the military or to reward them for the traits that are needed most.

As I wrote in chapter 5, there is some movement in this direction. It is most noticeable among the junior officers, the captains and majors who talk with fervor about the need to recommit themselves to the special obligations demanded of military leaders. An optimist might therefore conclude that as they mature, they will take their values with them to the top of their services. Maybe so; but it may be more realistic to expect that, if the military's standards for promotion remain the same, and if the pressures of procurement do not abate, those who become the generals and admirals of the 1990s will greatly resemble the men who have led, and often misled, the military for the last twenty years.

The Army's Chief of Staff, General Meyer, has suggested a number of specific steps to reinforce the traditional bonds within the military. These include rebuilding the corps of NCOs, moving soldiers in and out of assignments as units rather than reassigning them individually, and the crucial step of giving each commander a much longer tour with his unit. It may also make sense to look again at the military promotion system, which makes most officers touch all bases if they want to keep on the "up or out" schedule. It should be possible to distinguish the different skills the military needs—leader, manager, theorist—and while emphasizing that the first is paramount, to enable people to move ahead on each of the three tracks. Perhaps there might also be a new conception of military education. Under the old German General Staff system, no one came straight into the service as an officer, commissioned from an academy. Instead, those interested in careers as officers (most of them, to be sure, from the hereditary aristocracy) enlisted in the ranks for a year, then could rise to cadet and later officer by attending short officer-training courses. Only when they were about thirty years old were the most promising officers selected for the German analogue of our military academies, the two-year-course General Staff School. A similar approach, minus the aristocratic bias, might make sense for the United States. We might avoid the worst warping effects of the academies, add dignity to the NCO corps, and have a surer sense of what kind of people we were getting as leaders if they were chosen for officer training after spending time in the ranks.

In some cases, restoring military spirit is also a question of money. Military training is expensive, for the same reason any kind of education is: it is labor-intensive, and it also uses up (or should) a lot of ammunition and gasoline. This is why it is so crucial to look skeptically at other areas—such as new nuclear missile systems, or the networks of C³I—that consume so much of the military budget.

Restoring the bonds of trust within the military will not be enough, unless there is also a bond of respect between the military and the rest of society. For the reasons I gave in chapter 5, I believe that will not happen unless we reinstate the draft. A system of military service that exempts those whose parents are rich does not suggest shared sacrifice and mutual respect. It breeds contempt for those who have no choice but to serve. There should be nonmilitary forms of service for those who prefer them; perhaps a draft should be like the one in Sweden, where many people are taken in for a few months' training and then sent back to their normal lives and classified as "reserves." Under a draft, pay could be lower for first-term soldiers, since they are not in it for the pay, and higher for the NCOs, who need it to stay. The real argument for a draft is that the military will not be respected, and decisions about its use will not be democratically made, unless every class in the nation feels it has a direct stake in its performance.

AUSTERE WEAPONRY

IF TANKS, missiles, ships, and airplanes continue to grow geometrically in cost and complication, that fact will render meaningless our other decisions about defense, as complex weapons take longer to build and pay for, and are usually designed to operate under certain narrowly specified conditions. Tank and missile crews will have fewer opportunities to get to know the machines. Pilots will fly fewer missions. There will be less money to spare for real military necessities such as training courses and practice-firings. In peacetime it is often hard to grasp the importance of training and practice, since they can't be photographed or measured like a new Trident submarine. They show up immediately in war.

One illustration of the kinds of weapons that might make sense is the diesel-electric attack submarine, which could be mixed with nuclear submarines in the fleet. For the same money, the United States can buy four attack submarines with diesel-electric propulsion, or one with nuclear power. The original versions of the M-16 and F-16 (discussed in chapter 4) are other examples of inexpensive, effective machinery. Within the Navy, there have been proposals for fast, small, deadly patrol boats that would be equipped with the more reliable forms of guided missile and might take advantage of "surface-effect" principles to operate at high speeds. At $10 million apiece, the Navy could buy 100 of them for the cost of one of its new, billion-dollar destroyers.

Whether or not these or similar specific systems make sense, the general pattern clearly does: directing the ingenuity of designers, the institutional pressures of the Pentagon, and the contracting funds from the budget in a concerted effort to produce less costly weapons. At one level, this requires a basic change in operating philosophy for the military, like the one that Henry Ford brought to the auto industry when he introduced the cheap, standardized Model T. At another level, it means telling ourselves again and again that conflict is unpredictable, that our best guesses may prove totally wrong, that we must give ourselves room to adapt. Yes, it is possible to think up a scenario in which three nuclear aircraft carriers, operating off the coast of Africa, would come in handy. But, even though the likely circumstances can't be spelled out quite so neatly, there will probably be many more situations in which hundreds of smaller ships, or a larger, well-trained army, or a force of thousands of sturdy, reliable tanks would be more adaptable to our needs.

It is also essential to exorcise the culture of procurement from the Pentagon. A significant step in that direction would to be to set up a system of rigorous, independent testing. Through the histories of modern military establishments, the first sign of corruption in the design and production of weapons is resistance to the unflattering data that realistic testing inevitably yields. (Recall the in-house testing of the thirties that produced the ineffective German, Japanese, and American torpedoes of the forties.) The temptation to overlook inconvenient data is great when the tests are controlled by the same research-and-development bureaucracy that promotes the weapons. That is now the situation in the American military. Such a system makes its officials reluctant to kill off their darlings at any point. The clearest indication of progress toward improved testing will be when some projects are canceled. In an ideal world, the military could afford *research* in many different, far-fetched areas: perhaps the millimeter waves and the particle beams will work out. But there must be a gatekeeper, to deny the billions for procurement except when new technologies have proven themselves in harsh, realistic tests.

The manager's natural instinct to reduce wasteful "overlap" in the Pentagon may also need to be re-examined. Competition between the services, and between their many units, is one of the facts of life for the military, as for the NFL. If it could be channeled into constructive, open forms of competition, in which the rules were clearly spelled out, it might lead to better weapons. Instead of giving one development center in the Air Force a bureaucratic monopoly on guided missiles, why not let several agencies compete to produce the best design, with an independent testing agency to arbitrate the results?

The military should also reduce some of the human temptations that lead people into the culture of procurement. For a start, what about prohibiting retired generals and admirals (and civilian employees of equivalent rank) from accepting any job or consulting position with defense contractors, on pain of criminal sanction and permanent loss of pension? Some of the most serious cases of influence-peddling involve these senior officials, especially since there is so little distinction in the military between a general who is on active duty and one who happens to be working for United Technologies. The rank stays with the man, and he should honor it by confining himself to other lines of work, or to his comparatively generous pension. (After thirty years' service, a senior officer may retire on three fourths of his regular pay, which in 1980 meant a pension of about $38,000 for general officers.) By the same logic, retired officers one rank down—colonels, Navy captains, the equivalent civilian defense employees—should have to forfeit their pensions while working for a defense contractor (as they already have to do if they go to work as civilians in the Pentagon).

There need not be an adversary relationship between the government and the industry, but there must be healthy skepticism, based on hard fact, about specific products the industry is pushing. There is nothing wrong with technology, as long as it is pursued as an instrument of military purposes, rather than for its own (or the industry's) sake. In most cases, the technical innovations that best serve the military are those that dramatically simplify, instead of adding complications. The way to tell the difference is through a ruthlessly honest and realistic testing program.

NUCLEAR REALISM

IF EVERY discussion about nuclear weapons began with the statement that no one really knows what he's talking about, we would have come a long way toward a more balanced perspective on these weapons. No other step would be more useful in helping the nation make choices about its nuclear force.

From this perspective, the MX missile system seems a very costly white elephant, justified on extremely dubious grounds. Its most careful supporters argue that its importance lies mainly in the realm of perceptions and confidence-building. Money spent building confidence is not money wasted, but $40 billion to $50 billion (or more) for this system, at a time when the nation has more serious reasons to lack confidence in its defense, cannot be the right choice. The more imaginative approach would be to diversify the nuclear deterrent—perhaps through small submarines, perhaps by emphasizing small, elusive bombers, perhaps through other systems—and thereby give Soviet planners more to worry about than merely counting holes in the American southwest.

For reasons explained in the previous chapter, the most dangerous kinds of tests are those of the missiles' re-entry vehicles, not the explosive warheads themselves. By generating ever more impressive "accuracy" figures, the re-entry vehicle tests may tempt credulous leaders to believe that they could pull off a first strike. Limiting or banning the tests would greatly undermine the fiction of missile "accuracy" that is essential to first-strike theories.

COHERENCE

THE PROBLEM that runs through all the others is the incoherence of public discussion about defense. It takes the form of congressional committees meddling with the details of defense budgets (insisting in the early seventies, for example, that the Navy build only nuclear-powered ships from then on) but not coming close to a consistent philosophy of military procurement. Senators will denounce the services one day for rushing into production of a system whose bugs were not yet worked out—and denounce them two weeks later for taking so long to get moving. Within the Pentagon, as Chuck Spinney demonstrated, the long-term budget planning documents are incapable of dealing with the long-term implications of the choices they suggest.

Larry Smith, the assistant to Senator Hart, suggests the case of the cruise missile as a classic illustration of incoherence. Between 1977 and 1979, many "liberal" groups were high on the value of the strategic air-launched cruise missile, since it was the main tool to fight off the Air Force's claim that it needed to build the new B-1 bomber. When President Carter canceled the B-1 in 1977, he said it was because the air-launched nuclear cruise missile could do the job better. At the same time, liberals had to play down the military significance of the cruise missiles in Europe, since the SALT II treaty, which the Senate was preparing to consider, limited American deployment of them. On the other side, the right was dancing a similar jig. Conservative leaders said that the cruise missile was no substitute for the B-1—and that the SALT treaty was fatally flawed becaused it would limit America's use of this vital weapon.

From the citizen's and layman's point of view, incoherence shows up as the habits of mind that are content to view national defense as a question of "more" or "less."

"We live in Babel," says Larry Smith. "No one talks the same language. For years we have been crippled in trying to reach a sensible basis for defense policy through a ritual, with predictable moves. One set of people has instinctively, reflexively, opposed virtually any weapons system. The other set, with equal failure to discriminate, has asserted that all weapons systems are equally virtuous, equally deserving of support. We have developed a ritual of indiscrimination, with a heavy moralistic overtone on either side."[1]

While working on this book, I was struck time and again by evidence confirming Smith's theory. During the fall of 1980, when I called at the Pentagon for interviews, I often found crowds of demonstrators, gathered to protest the economy of death. One time it was an assemblage of two thousand women who bore huge papier-mâché puppets depicting the face of grieving womanhood, and who for five minutes sent up a high-pitched keen of lamentation as officers looked on alarmed. When that was over, they shouted out over and over again the last chorus of "Down by the Riverside":

> Ain't gonna study war no more,
> Ain't gonna study war no more,
> Ain't gonna . . .
>   study war no more.

Another time a crowd led by priests poured blood onto the building; frequently, groups would entreat people entering the building, "Won't

you take a vacation from death, just for today?" Sometimes I stopped
to talk with the demonstrators, to agree with them that "bombs won't
feed us." Other times I dropped my shoulder and pushed through the
crowds. Most often I found myself entertaining the prissy wish that
they be more precise, draw some distinctions, make a better case for
themselves.

But they were no less precise in their reasoning than their counterparts on the other side. Shortly after the election of 1980, when Repub-
lican victories in the Senate established him as chairman of the Senate
Armed Services Committee beginning in 1981, John Tower of Texas
held a press conference to endorse virtually every weapons system ever
proposed. The defense budget should go up by 9 percent each year, he
said; nay, it should rise by 13. If there was no use of force that the
demonstrators would find acceptable, there was no weapon that John
Tower didn't like.

The failure to discriminate is especially striking when it appears in
those who ought to know better. Such a man is Norman Podhoretz,
the editor of *Commentary*. Yet when it came to defense, what ability
to discriminate did he display? In 1980 he published a book called *The
Present Danger*, which recommended big increases in the defense
budget, based on reasoning like this:

Through the decade of the 1970s, the Soviets spent three times as much
as the United States on defense, and in 1979 alone (even after a minor reversal
of the steadily downward trend of American military spending from 1970–
1976) they outstripped the United States by 50 per cent . . . [President] Carter,
who had campaigned against a putatively bloated defense budget and promised to cut defense spending by $5 billion to $7 billion, found it impossible
to keep that promise as President. He did, however, cancel or delay production
of one new weapon system after another—the B-1 bomber, the neutron bomb,
the MX, the Trident—while the Soviet Union went on increasing and refining
its entire arsenal.[2]

What is most obvious about this passage is that Podhoretz has not
showed the slightest interest in the merits of the weapons Carter
canceled, nor in the most sensible ways to improve the nation's defense.
He does not mention the draft at any point in his book, much less
suggest any distinction between certain weapons that are effective and
others that are not. Nor is his curiosity provoked by the origin and
authenticity of reports about the 50 percent edge in defense spending
the Soviet Union purportedly enjoys—exactly the kind of question onto

which he would turn his full powers if it concerned, say, a report by the Federal Trade Commission on the benefits its regulations had brought. He merely says, in a footnote, that the estimate is "based on a CIA report," and attributes his knowledge of the report to a story by Drew Middleton in the New York *Times.* *

Consider how the same paragraph would read if its standards of logic and evidence were maintained, but if its subject were shifted to domestic politics and its bias moved to the left:

Through the decade of the 1970s, the opportunities available to middle-class white Americans increased three times as fast as did opportunities for poor blacks. (Footnote: This is based on a report from the Equal Employment Opportunity Commission.) . . . President Reagan, who campaigned on a promise to "get the government off your back," found it impossible to carry out that commitment once in office. He did, however, delay or dismember one progressive social program after another—minimum-wage coverage for teen-agers, mandatory busing for "racial balance," bilingual education, the CETA public works program, and "affirmative action" hiring requirements for all firms that do business with the federal government.

The careful reader's response to the second paragraph would be, "Yes, but—" He might point out that some of the programs didn't work, that others actually harmed their intended beneficiaries, that distinctions must be drawn. The careful reader's response to Podhoretz'

---

*The "uncertainties" of nuclear strategy are nothing compared to those of Soviet military spending. The CIA's estimates are usually lower than some other agencies', but all of them are crude approximations. The usual approach is to take a Russian tank, send it to Detroit, and ask the American manufacturers how much they'd charge to build the same thing; another step is to count the men in the Russian army, multiply their numbers by the current pay scale in the American volunteer army, and assume the Russians are "spending" that much on manpower—which they obviously are not for their low-paid, conscript force. Each time pay is raised for American soldiers, estimated Russian "spending" takes a leap up. Recently the CIA revised upward its estimate of Soviet defense spending. The reason for the change was not a re-estimate of Russia's production of weapons, but rather the analysts' conclusion that the Russian economy was less efficient than they had previously believed, and must be devoting even more of its resources to defense. That conclusion may tell us something about Soviet intentions and the hardships they are willing to undergo. But the budget estimates, by themselves, reveal nothing about Soviet capacities or our proper response, and their base of data is so slippery and imprecise that no one, let alone one with pretensions to intellectual standards, should throw around seemingly specific figures like "50 percent more."

paragraph should be just the same. Did any of those systems make sense? Did they bear on the threat being discussed? Can't we think more carefully about improving our defense? In domestic politics, there has been progress in the past fifteen years: all but the most reflexive thinkers understand that there is a difference between intentions and results, between money poured into a program and benefit pouring out. Somehow, the "neoconservatives" who helped lead the effort to regard domestic programs skeptically are immune to skepticism when defense is involved. They tend to view questions about certain military programs as a sign of anti-Americanism, or of sympathy, conscious or unconscious, for the expansion of the Soviet empire—much as some liberals would view any opposition to the Department of Housing and Urban Development as a sign of hatred of blacks. Podhoretz is like the priest splashing blood on the Pentagon, for in their zeal both are indifferent to what goes on inside.

WHEN ARGUMENTS about defense come unmoored from the facts, they stop being about defense at all. Instead, they concern other things, invariably at the expense of attention to real military values.

Most frequently they concern ideology, as one military program after another becomes a mere proxy for a general world view that the United States is too weak or too strong, is too intrusive in the rest of the world or not assertive enough. The general cast of mind of the left in defense debates is to overestimate the importance in international relations of moral examples and to underestimate the role of force. Moral examples do have power; they are finally what distinguishes the American system from the Russian. But at other times they are powerless, or need reinforcement by men at arms. (The moral example of Nazi Germany was repugnant, but the Thousand-Year Reich was brought to an end only by massed Allied troops.) On the right, the corresponding tendency is to overestimate the utility of force as a cure-all for bedeviling situations. "More" defense for the United States will do very little to sustain the flow of oil, or to prevent revolutions, or to persuade other countries to adopt a form of government more to our liking. More important, the right is most often blind to the need for a discriminating choice among weapons. Once I asked Richard Viguerie, the fund-raiser for conservative causes, why he and his allies pushed every defense project, useful or otherwise. He replied by letter a few days later, saying, essentially, that the military was in such peril from liberals who automatically opposed every project that anything they could get through was a plus. One of Viguerie's associates mentioned the example of former Representative Elizabeth Holtzman of New York; he claimed that she voted against every military appropriations bill that came up during her tenure.*

Perhaps the greatest damage wrought by the ideological struggle over "more" and "less" is its utter blindness to unconventional, non-"respectable" solutions. For example, in the fall of 1980 the U.S. Senate undertook a serious debate about nerve gas. The forces on the right, led by Senators Henry Jackson and John Warner, were so determined to build a new nerve-gas plant to match the supposed Russian capabilities that they had no time to contemplate the many practical reasons to be skeptical about either side's ability to use nerve gas, or the more sensible basic step of making sure that American troops are equipped with protective anti-gas suits. (As Gary Hart asked Warner, "What threat would it be to the Soviets for us to have an enormous chemical arsenal that would kill more of our troops than it would kill of the Soviets?") On the left, Senators Edward Kennedy and Mark Hatfield talked about the moral repugnance of chemical warfare, but also had no time to think about defensive gear. Not one senator mentioned the only kind of gas warfare that makes any practical or moral sense: developing an efficient, usable gas that would temporarily disable people without killing them. As Charles Peters has pointed out, some of the most gruesome and needless carnage of war could be prevented by such weapons. Recall the scenes from World War II, when GIs aimed flamethrowers down the mouths of caves, trying to clear the remaining Japanese from their hideouts in the Pacific islands. Recall the scenes from Vietnam in which a patrol would lob grenades into a tunnel, to avoid any risk that the people huddled inside might be "unfriendlies." Disabling gas, used by soldiers who were themselves protected against its effects, could eliminate such bloody work. Yet such is the power of ideological rituals that no one, on either side of the Senate debate, could pull off the blinders and see this path.

IN ADDITION to right/left ideology, debates about defense may take two other tacks once they stop focusing on the facts. One is to reflect habits of mind carried over from other professional cultures. For at least the last twenty years, American defense has been very greatly shaped by the

---

*I spoke with Elizabeth Holtzman on the telephone in January 1981, in an effort to confirm this report and hear her side of the story. The upshot of a brief, contentious conversation was that in no congressional debate on defense had anyone used her voting record as a reason to support a weapons system, that she regarded attention to the charge as a sign of simple-mindedness from the press, and that therefore "I won't respond to it at all."

economist's pattern of thought, and those of the manager, the tech-
nologist, and the armchair nuclear analyst. The warrior's perspective
has counted for little, perhaps because there is less and less connection
between the military culture and the most influential parts of the
civilian world.

Finally, arguments about defense that lose sight of the facts have
been shaped by unexpressed emotion. Along with relations between the
races and relations between the sexes, defense is one of the three areas
in which public policy is most likely to be skewed by deep psychological
forces. The subject under discussion—war—is life's most abhorrent
activity, but also one that, through the millennia, has been, in many
eyes, the ultimate manifestation of masculinity. All preparations for
war are preparations to do what is universally not only condemned but
also celebrated by its survivors and many onlookers. These tensions are
often reflected in the psyche of warriors in time of peace; they also lead
many who are not warriors down strange alleys. It is impossible to read
the record of the generation of American leaders who came of age
during the Civil War without sensing the imprint that the experience
left on all of them. Some, like Oliver Wendell Holmes, Jr., felt themselves forever at a distance from their peers who did not serve in the
war. One theory offered to explain Theodore Roosevelt's obsessive
devotion to "manly," martial pursuits was that he felt he had inherited
the stigma of his father, who did not serve under the Union's colors
during the Civil War. William James proposed a "moral equivalent of
war" as a way to harness the phenomenal human energies he had seen
released in wartime, without undergoing the devastation of combat.

James Webb, the Marine veteran from Vietnam, has commented
sourly on the motivations of politicians like Thomas Downey and
Robert Carr, two congressmen of Webb's own generation (Carr was
defeated in 1980) who did not serve in Vietnam but who, after the war,
spoke often on questions of defense. The phenomenon is hardly limited
to the Vietnam generation. Henry Jackson, who was twenty-nine when
Pearl Harbor was bombed, served the Congress, not the military, in
World War II; John Stennis, for many years the chairman of the
Senate Armed Services Committee, was never in the military. George
F. Will, the conservative columnist who said, after the negotiations
over the Iranian hostages in which the Algerian government served as
a "middleman," "Next time, the middleman should be the Marines,"[3]
was a graduate student, college professor, and congressional aide during
the years of Vietnam and never served in the military. Sam Nunn, who
has followed the pattern of the man whose seat he holds, Richard
Russell, in building his political base by becoming as the Senate's Mr.

Defense, served two years in the peacetime Coast Guard. John Tower, on the other hand, was a Navy enlisted man in World War II and, as a member of the reserves since then, has clung to his enlisted rank rather than accept an officer's commission.

I mean to suggest no simple patterns, nor that there is anything remotely wrong—quite the contrary—with the interest that noncombatants may develop in defense. As I suggested in the introduction, my own motives are open to similar question. Rather, my point is that the cause of rational discourse about defense is served when these extra rational pressures are admitted and explored, rather than left concealed. The effect they can have when concealed is stupendous. Through the late seventies, a common fixture in government offices in Washington was the "missile board," about the size of a ruler, on which scale models of Russian and American missiles sat. On that board, the giant Soviet SS-18 towered over the pathetic little Minuteman III. No one can doubt that the board had a powerful effect during the SALT negotiations, with its suggestion of crippling Soviet force, nor that the decision about the final size of the MX missile, which ended up being slightly too large to fit into the missile tubes on the Trident submarine, turned at least partly on the thought that the United States needed a missile that looked as big as the ones the Russians had.

What we may need, in William James's terms, is an "intellectual and emotional equivalent of war"—a way to talk out feelings about masculinity, about national pride, about the proper balance between force and moral example in international relations, without turning our military into a game board on which those feelings are secretly played out. "We need an analytical road map," says Larry Smith, "something that would help tell us which disagreements are based on facts, and which are based on assumptions that underlie different interpretations of the facts. It will never be neat and pretty, because the world is not neat, but it would help us move toward the kind of coherent, integrated thinking this field has lacked."

SHELTERED by its oceans, the United States has been spared throughout its history the preoccupation that Germany, Russia, France live with every day: the knowledge that if their planning for defense drifts too far from the realities of conflict, they may be overrun. The difference between our predicament and theirs is less than it used to be. In time of conflict, the ideologies, the styles of professional thought, the emotional tangles of defense would not matter. The only things that would count would be the equipment we had built, the plans we had laid, and the men we had trained.

The comment that remains with me longest is one that came from Richard Garwin, on a burning July day in 1979, as he stood blinking in the sun outside the Pentagon. "Sometimes I think none of it is real to them—the congressmen," he said. "Getting elected is real. Making nice speeches is real. But not the idea that these forces might ever have to be used."

Reference Notes

INTRODUCTION

1. The story of how the Germans missed the chance to develop the bomb is told in Samuel A. Goudsmit's fascinating, and out-of-print, book *Alsos: The Failure of German Science* (New York: Henry Schuman, 1947).

2. "What Did You Do in the Class War, Daddy?" *Washington Monthly* (October 1975).

1 REALITIES

1. These and the other figures on comparative economic performance since 1953 come from W. Bowman Cutter, who was Executive Associate Director of the Office of Management and Budget during the Carter years. Cutter's job placed him directly in charge of the assembly of the federal budget each year; he is writing a book on the sharp economic constraints that will affect any President's actions, based on his insights from that experience.

2. See the "Report to the President by the Steel Tripartite Advisory Committee on the United States Steel Industry," published by the U.S. Department of Labor, September 25, 1980.

3. "Intel Corporation Presentation to New York Society of Security Analysts," January 24, 1980, p. 8.

4. All figures in this section are based on December 1980 estimates from the Office of Management and Budget.

5. Interview with Bowman Cutter and Nancy Sving of the OMB.

6. U.S. Senate, Committee on Armed Services, "Supplemental Military Procurement and Construction Authorizations," FY 1967, pp. 96–97. Quoted in Adam Yarmolinsky, *The Military Establishment: Its Impacts on American Society* (New York: Harper & Row, 1971), p. 241.

7. "Reagan Group Seeks a Big Rise in Outlays for New Weapons," New York *Times* (December 18, 1980), p. A-1.

8. "Reagan Team Says U.S. Must Deal With Any Threat," New York *Times* (November 13, 1980), p. A-8.

9. "Tower Sees More Funds for Defense," Washington *Post* (November 12, 1980), p. A-1.

10. Edward Luttwak, "A New Arms Race?," *Commentary* (September 1980), p. 30.

11. Interview.

12. Melvin Laird, "Not a Binge, but a Buildup," Washington *Post* (November 19, 1980), p. A-17.

13. "Conversations with a Stuka Pilot," conference featuring Paul-Werner Hozzel, Brig. Gen. (Ret.), German Air Force, at National War College, November 1978. Sponsored by Contract DAAK40-78-C-0004, Battelle Columbus Laboratories, Columbus, Ohio, p. 52.

14. Speech at the National War College, June 10, 1980.

15. Abdul Kasim Mansur (pseud.), "The Military Balance in the Persian Gulf: Who Will Guard the Gulf States from their Guardians?" *Armed Forces Journal International* (November 1980).

16. Interview.

17. "Dollars Alone Are Not the Solution," Mexico (Missouri) *Ledger* (July 19, 1977), p. 4.

18. "Success in War," *Infantry Journal* (January 1931), p. 23. I am indebted to James Webb for bringing this to my attention.

19. "Conversations with a Stuka Pilot," *op. cit.*, pp. 54–55.

20. Quoted in *Forbes* (May 26, 1980), p. 39.

21. John Keegan's book *The Face of Battle* (New York: Viking, 1976) contains a penetrating discussion on the difference between "honest" and "dishonest" accounts of war.

22. Karl von Clausewitz, *On War (Vom Kriege)*, ed. by Anatol Rapoport (New York: Penguin, 1968), p. 164.

23. *Ibid.*

24. A retired Air Force colonel named John Boyd uses this quotation in his unpublished briefing, "Patterns of Conflict."

25. Clausewitz, *loc. cit.*

2 MANAGERS

1. Robert S. McNamara, *The Essence of Security: Reflections in Office* (New York: Harper & Row, 1968), pp. 90 and 99.

2. Enthoven and Smith, *How Much Is Enough? Shaping the Defense Program 1961–1969* (New York: Harper & Row, 1971), p. 160.

3. Eliot Cohen, "Systems Paralysis," *American Spectator* (November 1980), p. 24.

4. Colonel T. N. Dupuy, USA (Ret.), *A Genius for War: The German Army and General Staff, 1807–1945* (Englewood Cliffs, N.J.: Prentice-Hall, 1977).

5. "Cincinnatus," *Self-Destruction: The Disintegration of the United States Army during the Vietnam Era* (New York: Norton, 1981), p. 84.

6. Major William Lowry, "Strategic Assessment of the War in Vietnam: Truman through Kennedy," Ft. Leavenworth: USACGSC student paper, 1976; quoted in "Cincinnatus," *op. cit.*, p. 85.

7. "Cincinnatus," *op. cit.*, pp. 86–88.

8. Stuart H. Loory, *Defeated: Inside America's Military Machine* (New York: Random House, 1973), p. 39.

9. Interview.

10. "Transcription of a taped conversation with General Hermann Balck, 12 January 1979," Battelle Columbus Laboratories, pp. 19–21.

11. George C. Wilson, "Pentagon Scrubbed a Second Iranian Rescue Plan as Too Dangerous," Washington *Post* (January 25, 1981), p. A-19.

12. Stephen L. Canby, "Priorities in U.S. Defense Policy," American Enterprise Institute, *Foreign Policy Review and Defense*, Vol. I, No. 3 (1979), p. 31.

13. "Cincinnatus," *op. cit.*, p. 119.

14. Army Field Manual 100-5, "Operations," issued 1 July 1976, pp. 3–6.

15. Sprey interview.

16. Interview.

17. Speech at National War College, June 10, 1980.

18. Edward Luttwak, "The American Style of Warfare and the Military Balance," *Survival* magazine, Vol. 21, No. 2 (March/April 1979), p. 57.

19. *Loc. cit.*

20. Edward Luttwak and Stephen L. Canby, "MINDSET: National Style in Warfare and the Operational Level of Planning, Conduct, and Analysis," report submitted to the Office of Net Assessment, Department of Defense, March 10, 1980, under contract number MDA 903-79-6-0273, p. E-1.

21. Cohen, *op. cit.*, pp. 26–27.

22. William D. White, *U.S. Tactical Air Power: Missions, Forces, and Costs* (Washington: Brookings Institution, 1974), p. 3.

3 MAGICIANS

1. *Armed Forces Journal International* (May 1980), p. 28.

2. The data on Tac Air comes from Chuck Spinney of the Program Analysis & Evaluation division of the Pentagon, whose "brief" on this subject is discussed later in the chapter. Its official title is "Defense Facts of Life."

3. At the time when the total cost of the MX was officially estimated to be a little less than $30 billion, the Defense Department estimated that the project would cost about $9.1 billion in 1984 and $9.3 billion in 1985. Each re-estimate of the total cost is, of course, much higher; as of this writing, the official guesses are in the $60–$70 billion range.

4. Pierre M. Sprey, testimony before Senate Armed Services Committee, December 8, 1971, p. 251.

5. *Ibid.*

6. *Ibid.*, p. 264.

7. Sprey, "Tactical Air Issues." Unpublished paper, 1980, p. 1.

8. Quoted in "They're Redesigning the Airplane," by Michael F. Long, *National Geographic* (January 1981), p. 97.

9. Benjamin F. Schemmer, "Pentagon, White House and Congress Concerned over Tactical Aircraft Complexity and Readiness," *Armed Forces Journal International* (May 1980), p. 29.

10. Major Barry Watts, USAF, "Fire, Movement, and Tactics," *Navy Fighter Weapons School Journal* (Winter 1979/80).

11. This study is reported in *Air Force Times* (November 10, 1980), p. 1.

12. Schemmer, *loc. cit.*

13. Interview.

14. *Newsweek* (November 17, 1980), p. 6.

15. Everest Riccioni, "The Progression of Maximum Speeds in Modern High Performance Fighter Aircraft." Unpublished paper, Northrop Corporation, April 1978, pp. 6–7.

16. Major Charles L. Fox, USAF, and Lt. Col. Dino A. Lorenzini, USAF, "How Much Is Not Enough? The Non-Nuclear Air Battle in NATO's Central Region," *Naval War College Review* (March/April 1980), p. 78.

17. *The World's Missile Systems*, publ. by General Dynamics, Pomona Division, 5th ed., 1978, p. 50.

18. *Ibid.*, p. 49.

19. Jacques S. Gansler, *The Defense Industry* (Cambridge, Mass.: MIT Press, 1980), p. 280.

20. *Ibid.*, p. 319.

21. Sprey testimony, December 8, 1971, *op. cit.*, p. 264.

22. Interview.

23. "Unclassified Study of a Classified Study on Aircraft Engine Costs and Designs," internal DOD memorandum, released January 14, 1977, quoted in Gansler, *op. cit.*, p. 83.

24. Interview with Zumwalt.

25. Ward Just, *Military Men* (New York: Knopf, 1970), p. 159.

26. George C. Wilson, "Supplying Water: The Big Hurdle for Desert Force," *Washington Post* (October 10, 1980).

27. Washington *Star* (December 17, 1980).

28. Pierre Sprey, "The Impact of Avionics on the Effectiveness of Tactical Air," staff study prepared for the Office of the Assistant Secretary of Defense for Systems Analysis in June 1968 and declassified in 1974.

29. *Business Week* (August 11, 1980), p. 76.

30. *Ibid.*, pp. 77–78.

31. Gansler, *op. cit.*, p. 229.

32. *Business Week, op. cit.*, p. 81.

33. *Gulliver's Travels* (New York: Rinehart, 1948), p. 169.

34. Sprey, "Tactical Air Issues," *op. cit.*, p. 4.

35. T. S. Amlie, "Defense Acquisition—Some Observations and Suggestions." Unpublished paper.

36. Just, *op. cit.*, p. 176.

37. Quoted in John Kenneth Galbraith, *How to Control the Military* (Garden City, N.Y.: Doubleday, 1969), p. 21.

38. Leon S. Reed, *Military Maneuvers: An Analysis of the Interchange of Personnel Between Defense Contractors and the Department of Defense* (New York: Council on Economic Priorities, 1975), plus periodic updates. Also, Gordon Adams, *The Iron Triangle* (New York: CEP, 1981).

39. Adams, *op. cit.*

40. J. Ronald Fox, *Arming America: How the U.S. Buys Weapons* (Cambridge, Mass.: Harvard U. Press, 1974), p. 461.

41. Amlie, *op. cit.*

42. Sums from chart reprinted in "Defense Contractors Hail Reagan Win, but Can They All Share in the Spoils?" Los Angeles *Times* (November 30, 1980), p. VI-1. Lists of equipment from DOD publications.

43. These figures were listed by Peter Kadzis in "Ron's Weapon Plan Fuels Defense Issues," New York *Daily News* (November 13, 1980), p. 44.

44. Gansler, *op. cit.*, p. 130.

45. The contrast between Dassault and American firms is brought out in Gansler, *op. cit.*, p. 245.

46. Interview.

47. John Barron, *MiG Pilot* (New York: Reader's Digest Press, 1980), pp. 176–77.

48. This story is told by Siegfried Thalheimer in his PhD dissertation, *Das deutsche Flottengesetz von 1898*, University of Bonn, 1927.

49. This account is in the "Krupp Family" entry, written by Manchester, in the *Encyclopaedia Britannica*, 15th ed. (Chicago: EB Inc.), p. x-540.

50. George C. Wilson, "With Vietnam Defused, Weapons Makers Ballyhoo Their Firepower," Washington *Post* (November 25, 1980), p. A-2.

4 TWO WEAPONS

1. Hearings, Special Subcommittee on the M-16 Rifle Program, Committee on Armed Services, U.S. House of Representatives, 90th Cong., 1st sess. (Referred to as "Hearings.")

2. *Ibid.*, pp. 4563–64.

3. Keegan, *Face of Battle*, p. 229.

4. Thomas McNaugher, "Marksmanship, McNamara, and the M-16 Rifle: Innovation in Military Organizations," *Public Policy* (Winter 1980), pp. 1–37.

5. *Ibid.*, p. 4.

6. *Ibid.*, p. 7.

7. The rifle stories are told in *Plowshares into Swords: Managing the American Defense Establishment,* by Jacob Stockfisch (New York: Mason & Lipscomb, 1973), and *Small Arms of the World,* 10th rev. ed. (Harrisburg: Stackpole, 1973).

8. A useful history of the rifle programs is laid out in the "Report of the Special Subcommittee on the M-16 Rifle Program," Report Number 26, Committee on Armed Services, U.S. House of Representatives, 90th Cong., 1st sess., pp. 5321–72. (Referred to as "Report.")

9. Quoted in "Report," p. 5323.

10. *Loc. cit.*

11. *Ibid.*, p. 5327.

12. *Ibid.*, p. 5330.

13. *Ibid.*, p. 5333.

14. "Hearings," p. 4701.

15. See GAO report B-146977, issued March 31, 1965.

16. "Hearings," p. 4559.

17. *Ibid.*, p. 4549.

18. *Ibid.*, p. 4571.

19. "Report," p. 5356.

20. *Ibid.*, p. 5355.

21. *Ibid.*, p. 5357.

22. *Ibid.*, pp. 5354 and 5370.

23. *Ibid.*, p. 5363.

24. "Hearings," pp. 4509–10.

25. *Ibid.*, p. 4584.

26. *Ibid.*, pp. 4582–83.

27. *Ibid.*, p. 4583.

28. *Loc. cit.*

29. *Ibid.*, p. 4873.

30. *Ibid.*, p. 4994.

31. Unless otherwise noted, the facts in the next few paragraphs come from Sprey's lecture at the American Institute of Aeronautics and Astronautics' "75th Anniversary of Powered Flight" symposium, at Wright-Patterson Field, December 15, 1978.

32. This figure crops up many places, including *The Blond Knight of Germany*, by Raymond Toliver and Trevor Constable (Garden City, N.Y.: Doubleday, 1970), p. 173.

33. Attributed to Mark Hubbard, briefly commander of the 20th Fighter Group, and quoted in Watts, *op. cit.*, p. 11.

34. Sprey discusses this at length in "Impact of Avionics," *op. cit.*

35. Much of the following account of the development of the F-16 comes from a history of the project written in 1976 as a student paper for the Industrial College of the Armed Forces by Jerauld R. Gentry, Lt. Col., USAF, report number M76-163.

36. The quotes from Riccioni are from my interviews.

37. Notes on "Memorandum from Dr. John S. Foster, DDR&E, to David Packard, DEPSECDEF, 'Aircraft Prototype,' February 12, 1971," quoted in Gentry, *op. cit.*, p. 46.

5 EMPLOYEES

1. This saying comes up in many conversations—usually with the qualification that it is people who don't make general because they're too raw, refuse to play the political games. It appeared in print in Ward Just's *Military Men* (*op. cit.*).

2. Interview.

3. William L. Hauser, "The Will to Fight," in *Combat Effectiveness: Stress, Cohesion, and the Volunteer Military*, ed. Sam Sarkesian (Beverly Hills, Calif: Sage, 1980), p. 193.

4. Richard A. Gabriel and Paul L. Savage, *Crisis in Command: Mismanagement in the Army* (New York: Hill & Wang, 1978), p. 4.

5. These following paragraphs are a combination of a worksheet Malone uses, and his comments in an interview.

6. Interview.

7. James Webb, "Women Can't Fight," *Washingtonian* (November 1979), p. 273.

8. In Maureen Mylander, *The Generals: Making It Military Style* (New York: Dial, 1974), p. 45.

9. William L. Hauser, "The Army's Career Officer System: A Continuing

Need for Professional and Managerial Reform," the *Bureaucrat* (Fall 1979), p. 8.

10. Gabriel and Savage, *op. cit.*, pp. 86–87.

11. "Cincinnatus," *op. cit.*, pp. 131–32.

12. Nicholas Lemann, *Washington Monthly* (May 1978).

13. Hauser, *Bureaucrat* article, p. 8.

14. Interview.

15. Interview.

16. Ward Just, *Military Men*, p. 108.

17. "Cincinnatus," *op. cit.*, p. 137.

18. *Ibid.*, p. 152.

19. *Ibid.*, p. 63.

20. "Report of the President's Commission on an All-Volunteer Force," Chairman Thomas S. Gates (New York: Macmillan; Collier Books ed., 1970), p. 63.

21. Hauser in Sarkesian, *op. cit.*, p. 186 ff.

22. *Ibid.*, p. 194.

23. Interview.

24. Interview.

25. Charles C. Moskos, "How to Save the All-Volunteer Force," *Public Interest* (Fall 1980), p. 76.

26. *Loc. cit.*

27. *Ibid.*, pp. 77–78.

28. Gates commission report, pp. 11–12.

29. *Ibid.*, p. 16.

30. Charles C. Moskos, "The Enlisted Ranks in the All-Volunteer Army," in *The All-Volunteer Force and American Society*, ed. John B. Keeley (Charlottesville: U. of Virginia Press, 1978), pp. 73–74.

31. Moskos, "How to Save . . . ," *op. cit.*, p. 80.

32. Interview.

33. Gates commission, p. 137.

34. Moskos, "Enlisted Ranks," *op. cit.*, p. 74.

35. Moskos, "How to Save . . . ," *op. cit.*, p. 82.

36. *Ibid.*, p. 88.

37. "Tilting at Windmills," *Washington Monthly* (September 1980), p. 5.

38. Interview.

6 THEOLOGIANS

1. Fred Kaplan provides a useful discussion of the history of nuclear theory, as well as many facts about the nuclear balance, in *Dubious Specter: A Skepti-*

cal Look at the Soviet Nuclear Threat (Washington: Institute for Policy Studies, 1980), and in "Going Native Without a Field Map," Columbia Journalism Review (January–February 1981), pp. 23–29.

2. This is a standard technical measure of the actual damage that a blast is likely to do. It takes account of the fact that about one third of the explosive power of a blast goes up, where it destroys nothing except the atmosphere, and that "smaller" nuclear explosions do proportionately more damage than large ones.

3. Kaplan, Dubious Specter, p. 4. He also refers to a study by Kevin N. Lewis: "US Strategic Force Structure and Employment Planning, 1959–1979." Master's thesis, Political Science. MIT, 1979, p. 19.

4. Enthoven and Smith, op. cit., p. 210.

5. Testimony offered to Joint Committee on Defense Production, November 17, 1976.

6. "Effect of Evacuation and Sheltering on Potential Fatalities from a Nuclear Exchange," August 15, 1977.

7. Gen. Daniel O. Graham, cited in Hearings, Senate Foreign Relations Committee, "United States/Soviet Strategic Options," January, March 1977, p. 163: quoted in Kaplan, Dubious Specter, p. 33.

8. Alexander and Andrew Cockburn, "The Myth of Missile Accuracy," New York Review of Books (November 20, 1980), also uses this comparison.

9. Interview.

10. Interview.

11. Quoted in Cockburn, op. cit.

12. John M. Collins, U.S.–Soviet Military Balance: Concepts and Capabilities, 1960–1980 (New York: McGraw-Hill, 1980).

13. "Praise for a Book on the Arcane Art of Adding Up What's On Each Side," Defense Week (October 13, 1980), p. 5.

14. "The Effects of Nuclear War," U.S. Office of Technology Assessment, 1979; "The Effects of Nuclear War," ACDA, April 1979.

15. McGeorge Bundy, "To Cap the Volcano," Foreign Affairs (October 1969), pp. 9–10.

16. Charles W. Yost, "National Security Revisited," Bulletin of the Atomic Scientists (October 16, 1980), p. 20.

17. "Critique of T. K. Jones's Computation of Soviet Fatalities," Office of Operations Analysis, ACDA, May 3, 1979, p. 5.

18. Ibid., pp. 1–2.

19. "An Analysis of Soviet Civil Defense in Nuclear War," ACDA, December 1978, p. i.

20. Cited in "Critique of T. K. Jones," op. cit., p. 5.

21. "The Effects of Nuclear War," OTA, op. cit., p. 76.

22. "An Analysis of Civil Defense in Nuclear War," ACDA, December 1978, *passim*.

23. *Ibid.*, p. 6.

24. *Congressional Record*, September 16, 1980, p. S12694. The format for Garn's comments was a three-column presentation: in the first, accusations made about the Carter Administration's defense record in a film produced by the American Security Council, called "The SALT Syndrome"; in the second, the Administration's replies; and in the third, "The Facts," as Garn saw them.

25. As recounted by Adam Yarmolinsky.

26. Sidney D. Drell and Richard L. Garwin, "SUM: The Better Approach to ICBM Basing." Unpublished paper, October 17, 1980, p. 4.

27. Testimony to the U.S. Senate, Committee on the Budget, February 28, 1979, p. 174.

28. "Priorities in the U.S. Defense Policy," *op. cit.*, p. 6.

29. For a suggestion of what a modern maneuverable bomber might look like, see Pierre Sprey's testimony to the Senate Armed Services Committee, *op. cit.*

30. Gerard Smith, *Doubletalk: The Story of Salt I* (Garden City, N.Y.: Doubleday, 1981), p. 19.

31. *Ibid.*, pp. 471–72.

7 CHANGES

1. Interview.

2. Norman Podhoretz, *The Present Danger* (New York: Simon & Schuster, 1980), pp. 40–42.

3. George F. Will on *Agronsky & Company*, WDVM-TV, Washington, D.C., January 24, 1981.

INDEX

A-1E bombers, 168
A-10s, 37, 42
ABM (antiballistic missile system),
    140–41, 147
  cost of, 147, 169
  technical problems with, 73–74, 169
Abrams, Creighton, 51, 122
accuracy of missiles, 148, 150–57, 167,
    176
  Anderson proposal for testing of, 155
  defined, 150–51
  on submarines, 164
ACDA (Arms Control and Disarmament
    Agency), 158, 160–62
Acheson, Dean, 162
"Aerial Attack Study" (Boyd), 27, 98, 100
Afghanistan, Soviet invasion of, 31, 169
AIMVAL/ACEVAL tests, 46–47
Airborne Division, U.S., 131
aircraft carriers, 11–12, 24, 37, 174
Air Defense Command, U.S., 36, 50n,
    168
Air Force, U.S., 36–49, 95–106
  Army's competition with, 21–22, 85,
    157
  Configuration Control Committee of,
    105–6
  flashlight built by, 50n–51n
  inertial guidance systems, 152

MX basing schemes proposed by,
    146–47
  nuclear tests by, 149, 154
  pilot's flying time in, 40–41
  real vs. phantom fleet in, 42–43
  war plans of, 21–22, 32
  weapons and equipment preferred by,
    59, 64, 69, 83–84, 85, 86
Air National Guard, U.S., 40n
airplanes:
  combat-derived criteria for, 96–99
  design "trade-offs" for, 101
  engines for, 35, 37, 38, 39, 44, 67, 68
  sortie rates of, 38–39, 41, 43, 44, 100
  TACAMOs, 165n
  see also bombers; specific planes
AIS (Avionics Intermediate Shop),
    43–44, 48
AK-47 rifles, 89, 90
Alexander, Clifford, 123–24, 125–27
American Psychological Association, 40
Amlie, Thomas S., 63–64, 66
ammunition:
  ball powder, 81, 88–91, 94–95
  IMR, 87–88, 89, 90, 91, 94
  millimeter measure vs. caliber of, 78n
  small vs. large bullets as, 77–78
AMRAAMS (advanced medium-range
    air-to-air missiles), 56, 99

Anderson, J. Edward, 154–55
AR-15 rifles, 77, 78–79, 81–87, 90
    advantages of, 77, 82
    modification of, 77, 86–87
    testing of, 82–83, 84–85, 87
Armalite Corporation, 77, 82–83, 84
Armed Forces Journal, 14, 39
Arms of Krupp, The (Manchester),
    72*n*
Army, U.S., 24, 49, 50*n*, 76–95, 114–38
    Air Force competition with, 21–22,
        85, 157
    "attack" helicopters requested by, 12
    Caliber Board of, 78, 83
    effects of middle class on, 131, 134
    ethics courses in, 121–22
    fighters vs. nonfighters in, 131–32
    Individual Ready Reserves in, 129
    Materiel Command of, 79–80, 85, 87,
        93*n*–94*n*
    ordnance corps of, 79–82, 83, 85, 86,
        88, 90, 93–95
    proportion of officers in, 117
    Skill Qualifications Test for, 129*n*
    war plans of, 21
    see also military services; volunteer
        army
Army Training Study, The, 129*n*
Army War College:
    leadership qualities as determined by,
        110–11
    "Study on Military Professionalism"
        by, 121
Art of War, The (Sun Tzu), 31
ARVN (Army of the Republic of
    Vietnam), 84
atomic bomb, xiv, 32
attrition warfare, 21, 26–34
    advantages of, 34
    defined, 26
    maneuver approach vs., 27–31
    requirements of, 33–34
Augustine, Norman, 38, 56–57
auto industry, 6–7, 174
avionics systems, 37, 38, 45–46, 105
    AIS, 43–44, 48
AWACS, 59

B-1 bombers, 16, 67, 167–68, 169*n*
    cancellation of, 177, 178
    cruise missiles vs., 74, 177
B-52 bombers, 22, 67, 141, 144, 149
    defects in, 167
Backfire bombers, 57–58

Balck, Hermann, 25, 28–29
Ball, George, 33
ballistic, defined, 151
ball powder, 81, 88–91, 94–95
BAR (Browning automatic rifles), 69, 79,
    82
Barber, Arthur, 147
Barron, John, 70–71
Basic Educational Opportunity Grants,
    134
Bath Iron Works, 72, 73
Belenko, Viktor I., 70–71, 101
Bernard, Charles, 68–69
bias, 149–57
    defined, 149, 150*n*
    inertial guidance and, 151–54
blacks, in U.S. Army, xvi, 123–24, 127,
    133
BMPS (armored personnel carriers), 31
body counts, 26
Boeing Corporation, 65–66, 67, 145, 160
Boer war, 30
bombers, 166–68, 176
    A-1E, 168
    B-1, 16, 67, 74, 167–68, 169*n*, 177,
        178
    B-52, 22, 67, 141, 144, 149, 167
    Backfire, 57–58
    detection of, 168
    FB-111, 167
Bonaparte, Napoleon, 15, 17, 25
bond markets, 5–6
Boston Study Group, 74
Boyd, John, 27–31, 98, 100–3, 105, 110
Brown, Harold, 39, 41–42, 48, 59–60
Browning, John, 82
Bundy, McGeorge, 159
Bunting, Josiah, 121
Business Week, 55–57, 72

Calley, William L., 120
Canby, Stephen, 31
cannons, 24, 99, 100, 104
careerism, 107, 108, 114–23, 172
    concern for credentials in, 118
    defined, 114
    in peacetime army, 114–19
    ticket punching used in, 116–17,
        119–20, 121, 172
    "up or out" policy as impetus to,
        114–15, 117–18, 119, 172
    in wartime army, 119–23
Carr, Robert, 182
Carter, Jimmy, 5, 6, 143, 145, 177

Carter Administration:
  federal budget in, 5–6, 178
  nuclear policy in, 163, 177, 178
CCC (Civilian Conservation Corps), 133
CEDEC (Army Combat Development
  Experiment Center) tests, 82–83, 89
CEP (circular error probable), 150–51,
  153
CEP (Council on Economic Priorities),
  65–66
Chicago *Tribune*, 155
China, People's Republic of, xv, 11, 146
CIA (Central Intelligence Agency), 85,
  162, 179
"Cincinnatus," 25–26, 32, 115, 119–20
Civil War, U.S., 26, 80, 80*n*–81*n*, 130,
  182
Clarke, Bruce, 12, 15–16
Clausewitz, Karl von, 16–17, 18, 28, 29,
  119
Coates, James, 155
Cockburn, Andrew and Alexander,
  155–56
Cohen, Eliot, 22, 34
Collins, John M., 156–57
Colt (firm), 84, 89, 90–91, 94
Columbia Journalism Review, 143*n*
communications, 24–26, 30
  C³I, 36, 52–53, 112, 173
  Germans' use of, 25, 28–29, 49
  with submarines, 165
  see also radar
computer supportability, 44
computer systems, 35, 37, 38, 43–44,
  46, 47, 48, 52
Congress, U.S., 8, 10, 11–12, 49, 68, 73,
  103, 104, 105
  M-16 investigated by, 77–78, 88,
  91–95
  military service by members of,
  136–37, 182–83
  see also Senate, U.S.
Congressional Record, 163
Congressional Research Service, 156
"Consolidated Guidance" (Brown), 39,
  41–42
consumption, in U.S. economy, 4–7
Crisis in Command (Gabriel and
  Savage), 110, 115*n*
cruise missiles, 36, 64, 66, 67, 167
  incoherence of debate about, 177
C³I (Command-Control-
  Communications-Intelligence
  networks), 36, 52–53, 112, 173

Culver, John, 74
Custer, George A., 81*n*

Daniels, Robert J., 73
Dassault (firm), 68, 69
Death of the Army, The (King), 121
Defeated (Loory), 27
Defense Department, U.S., 35, 161
  Advanced Research Projects Agency
  of, 84–85
  culture of procurement in, 62–69,
  172, 174–75
  "Five Year Defense Plan" by, 49
  under McNamara, 19, 20–26, 96, 104,
  141, 143, 163
  public relations staff at, 117*n*
  Research and Engineering division of,
  19, 55, 68
  weapons prototyping in, 103–4
Defense Industry, The (Gansler), 50*n*
defense planning and policy:
  coherence as recommendation for,
  171, 176–83
  first-hand exposure needed for, xvi,
  24–26, 136–37
  foreign policy in relation to, xv–xvi
  intangible factors and, 3, 15–18,
  28–29, 31, 34, 54
  managerial, 18, 19–34
  power projection in, 12, 14, 32
  unpredictable international scene as
  factor in, xiv, 3, 11–15, 18, 174
defense spending:
  civilian market vs., 38, 50, 50*n*–51*n*
  on cost-plus basis, 67
  demonstrations against, 177–78
  economic constraints on, 3, 4–11, 18
  MAD and, 163
  moralistic overtones in views on,
  177–80
  national security vs., xv, 163
  political influences on, 20
  program vs. marginal cost in, 37*n*
  right vs. left on, xiv–xv, 177–81
  technical complexity as factor in,
  38–47, 49–53, 55-57
  threat inflation as factor in, 69–75,
  101, 165
  weapon cost increases in, 35–55
Defense Supply Agency, 21
Defense Week, 156
discipline, 131–32
  internal vs. external, 125
doctors, in military service, 138

Douglas, Paul, 65
Downey, Thomas, 182
draft, 128, 132, 173, 178
  arguments against, 137–38
  exemption from, 127, 138
  military "adventurism" and, 136
  pre-Vietnam, 126, 130, 133–34
Dragon, the, 24
Drake, Edward, 65
Drell, Sidney, 166
Dri-Slide, 91–92
DuPont, 87
Dupuy, T. N., 25

economy, U.S., as constraint on defense
    planning, 3, 4–11, 18
"Effects of Nuclear War, The," 158
Egypt, 54–55, 71, 95
Eisenhower, Dwight D., 30
Eisenhower Administration, federal
    spending in, 4
ELF broadcasting system, 165n
energy-maneuverability theory, see
    maneuver approach
engines, 44, 67, 68
  cost of, 35, 37, 38
  J-79 vs. F-100, 39
Enthoven, Alain, 21, 141–42
entitlements (uncontrollables), in federal
    spending, 8–9
Essence of Security, The (McNamara),
    20–21

F-4 Phantom jets, 39, 42–43, 44, 96–97,
    100
F-5s, 37, 42–43, 44–45, 67, 100
F-14 Tomcats, 37, 58, 67, 96, 100
  cost of, 37, 41–42, 73, 100, 103
  missiles carried by, 37, 41–42
F-15 Eagles, 39, 42–45, 67, 73, 100–2
  "capability" of, 37, 47, 70, 96, 101
  cost of, 37, 42–43, 70, 102, 103, 105
  F-16s compared to, 105, 106
  maneuver approach in development
    of, 27, 100–1
F-16s, 27, 39, 66, 95–106
  cost of, 76, 95, 105–6, 174
  modification of, 76, 95, 105–6
F-18s, 38, 67
F-86 Sabres, 27, 28, 96, 98, 100
F-100 engines, 39, 44
F-111s, 42, 48, 66
Face of Battle, The (Keegan), 79
Falcon missiles, 55, 67

FB-111 bombers, 167
Federal Aviation Administration, 59n
Felt, Harry, 84
Fialka, John, 52, 54, 129n
"Fighter Mafia," 95–100, 104–5
"Fighter" studies, 79, 131–32
first-strike theories, 140, 144–64, 170, 176
  bracketing shots and, 151
  nightmare scenario in, 144–45
  perceptions of American weakness in,
    162–63
  President's response in, 158, 159
  psychological uncertainties and,
    157–64
  studies on damages and, 158–59
  theoretical and operational
    uncertainties and, 147, 148–57
  time needed for, 158
fixed force structure, 24
Ford, Henry, 174
"Forward Edge of the Battle Area," 32
Fox, J. Ronald, 66
France, 96
  military manufacturing in, 68, 69
  in World War II, 16n, 28, 30
fratricide, defined, 148–49
friction, 29, 31, 34, 54, 74
  defined, 17–18
Friedman, Milton, 135
fuel controls, in J-79 vs. F-100 engines,
    39
fuses, failure of, 167
FX fighters, see F-15 Eagles

Gabriel, Richard A., 110, 115n, 120
Galbraith, John Kenneth, 32–33
Gallery, Philip, 112n–113n
Galosh missile system, 58n
Gansler, Jacques, 50n
Garn, Jake, 163
Garwin, Richard, 61, 150n, 153–54, 157,
    166, 184
Gates commission, 123, 127, 128, 133
General Dynamics, 65–66, 67, 104–5
General Electric, 67
Genius for War, A (Dupuy), 25
Germany, see Nazi Germany; West
    Germany
German General Staff system, 172–73
GI Bill, 134, 135
Graham, Daniel O., 145–46
Great Britain, 30, 72
  in World War II, 12–13, 16n, 28, 40,
    98–99

Grove, Andrew, 7
Grumman Aircraft Corporation, 37, 65–66, 67, 96
Guderian, Heinz, 28–29, 49
guerrilla warfare, 28
  conventional military defenses vs., 13, 14, 32
Gulliver's Travels (Swift), xiii–xiv, 149
guns:
  AK-47 rifles, 89–90
  AR-15 rifles, 77, 78–79, 81–87, 90
  BAR, 69, 79, 82
  M-1 rifles, 78n, 79
  M-14 rifles, 77, 78n, 79–85, 89, 90, 91
  M-16 rifles, 61, 76–95, 174
  see also ammunition

Hackworth, David, 27, 121
Haig, Alexander, 67
Harpoon missiles, 67
Hart, Gary, 10, 12–13, 27, 33, 181
Hartmann, Eric, 96
Hatfield, Mark, 181
Hauser, William L., 110, 118n, 124
Hawk missiles, 67
helicopters, 12, 14, 67
Hewlett Packard, 68
Hitler, Adolf, 161, 163
Hoar, Joe, 125
Hoffman, Nicholas von, 135n
Holmes, Oliver Wendell, Jr., 182
Holtzman, Elizabeth, 180–81
Hughes Aircraft, 67

ICBMs (intercontinental ballistic missiles), 20, 151
  AMRAAMs, 56, 99
  test launchings of, 149
  see also Minuteman missiles; MX missiles, SLBMs
Ichord, Richard, 77, 78, 91, 93n–94n
IFF Problem (identification friend or foe), 46–47, 97n
IMR (improved military rifle) powder, 87–88, 89, 90, 91, 94
Infantry Journal, 15–16
inflation, in U.S. economy, 5–8
Intel, 7
interdiction bombing, 32–33, 36
investment, 4–7
  defined, 4
  by military, 48, 49

Iran:
  oil supplies and, 13, 14
  U.S. relations with, xvi, 11, 30, 182
Israel, 14, 24, 46, 54–55, 71

J-79 engines, 39
Jackson, Henry, 181, 182
James, William, 182, 183
Japan, 13, 32, 51n
  industrial competition from, 6, 7
Johnson, "Kelly," 104
Johnson, Lyndon B., 19
Johnson Administration, federal budget in, 10
Joint Chiefs of Staff, U.S., 30, 84, 143, 169n
Jones, David, 106
Jones, James, 109
Jones, T. K., 145, 160, 160n–61n, 162
JTIDS (Joint Tactical Information Distribution System), 52, 53
Just, Ward, 119

Kaplan, Fred, 141, 143n, 166
KC135 tanker planes, 54
Keegan, John, 79
Kelly, Tom, 23, 24, 130, 132
Kennedy, Edward, 181
Kennedy, John F., 19, 81n, 85
Kennedy Administration, defense spending in, 4
Kerr, Frank, 73
Keynes, John Maynard, 4
King, Edward, 121
Korean War, 4, 11, 27, 37
  spread of careerism after, 115
  weapons and equipment used in, 78n, 96
Krupp (firm), 72
Kulish, Colonel, 74–75, 163

Laffer Curve, 4
Laird, Melvin, 11
"Laws of Recondite Economics" (Riccioni), 43
leadership, 130, 156, 161
  careerism vs., 107, 108, 114–23
  as intangible quality in defense, 16, 18, 34
  managerial approach to, 24–26, 31–32, 34, 52, 107, 108, 111–23
  in Nazi Germany, 25, 110, 120
  qualities needed for, 25, 52, 108, 110–11, 113–14

Lemann, Nicholas, 116
LeMay, Curtis, 50n–51n, 83–84
libertarians, Army as viewed by, 135, 137–38
Lightweight Fighter Program, 103–4
Lincoln, Abraham, 80n–81n
Lind, William, 27, 119
Lionheads, The (Bunting), 121
Locke, John, 109
Lockheed Corporation, 64, 65–66, 67, 69, 104
Loory, Stuart, 27
Lovett, Robert, 162
Lowry, William, 26
Luttwak, Edward, 10, 16, 33–34, 117–18
Lynde, Nelson, Jr., 94

M-1 rifles, 78n, 79
M-14 rifles, 77, 78n, 79–85, 89, 90, 91
M-16 rifles, 76–95, 174
hazards of, 61, 76, 77, 88–89, 90, 91–95
MacArthur, Douglas, 83
McCloy, John J., 162
McDonnell Douglas, 37, 44–45, 47, 65–67, 73
McGrath, John J., 44–45
McLean, Bill, 68–69
McNamara, Robert S., 10, 19, 20–26, 81n, 85–86, 96, 104, 141, 143, 163
McNaugher, Thomas, 80
MAD (Mutual Assured Destruction), 143, 163
Main Battle Tanks, 49, 73
Malone, Dandridge, 108–9, 110–11, 121–23
managerial approach, 18, 19–34
attrition warfare in, 21, 26–34
communication problems in, 24–26, 30
defined, 19
efficiency vs. effectiveness in, 19–24
failure of, 19–20
military employees as viewed in, 34, 107–38
progress as viewed in, 25–26, 31
weapons and equipment choices affected by, 34, 35–106
Manchester, William, 72n
maneuver approach, 27–31, 98–99, 100
German blitzkrieg as example of, 28–29
O-O-D-A loop in, 29, 30n
Mao Tse-tung, 28

Marine Corps, U.S., 39, 124–25, 134
class structure in, 130–31
Marshall, S. L. A., 79, 131
Martin Marietta, 64
Mauser rifles, 81n
Maverick missiles, 42, 56
Mayagüez incident, 30
Messerschmitt-109s, 98–99
Meyer, Edward C., 109–10, 117, 132, 172
Middleton, Drew, 179
MiG-15s, 27, 28
MiG-25 Foxbats, 58n, 70–71, 101
MiG Pilot (Barron), 70–71
MILES, 54
military services, 107–38
civilian contempt for, 133, 135–36
as civilianized, 117–18, 123–38
civilian life contrasted with, xv, 18, 34, 38, 50, 50n–51n, 107–11, 117
competition between branches of, 21–22, 85, 102, 157, 175
education and training for, 108–9, 110–11, 114, 117–18, 121–22, 123, 124, 172–74
human bonds as necessary to, 107–8, 109–10, 111, 116, 124, 138, 172
restoration of spirit of, 171–73
retention problem in, 125, 131
social striation of, xvi, 123–24, 126–37
wages in, 36, 40, 125, 128, 134–35, 173, 175, 179n
see also officer corps; *specific services*
mines, pros and cons of, 61
Minuteman missiles, 21, 22, 67, 141, 144, 145, 161, 183
MIRVed, 142, 170
unsuccessful firings of, 149
Minuteman vulnerability, 21, 150, 155, 157, 166
defined, 146
solutions to, 146, 147
MIRV (multiple, independently targetable re-entry vehicle), 142, 170
missile board, 183
missiles:
accuracy of, 148, 150–57, 164, 167, 176
bias and, 149–57
effects of atmospheric conditions on, 151–53
explosive yield of, 148
fratricide and, 148–49
inertial guidance systems for, 151–54
see also specific missiles

missile silos:
  hardness of, 148
  overpressure endurance of, 149–50
  ownership vs. defense of, 21–22
morale, 18, 29, 31, 74
  effect of interdiction bombing on, 32–33
Morgan, Earl J., 77, 94
Morse, John, 64, 74–75
Moskos, Charles, 126, 127, 130, 131, 132, 133, 134–35
Mount St. Helens volcano, first strike compared to, 158–59
MX missiles, 21–22, 58, 71–72, 140–41, 160, 165, 170, 178, 183
  basing schemes for, 146–47
  cost of, 36, 169n, 176
  in SUM, 166
  two purposes of, 146
Myers, Charles, 46
My Lai massacre, 120–21
Mylander, Maureen, 114

NASA (National Aeronautics and Space Administration), 65
NATO (North Atlantic Treaty Organization), 52, 58n, 62, 67, 74, 82, 106, 129, 146
Navy, U.S., 24, 176
  Air Force's competition with, 22, 102
  defense spending by, 36, 38, 39, 49, 50
  ELF system of, 165
  "major surface combatants" used by, 11–12
  "power projection" in, 32
  Special Projects Bureau of, 69
  weapons and equipment preferences of, 58, 59, 64, 69, 174
Nazi Germany, in World War II, 16n, 25, 27, 28–29, 30, 32, 33, 40, 54, 96, 98–99, 110, 180
Nelson, Gaylord, 93
nerve gas, Senate debate on, 181
neutron bomb, 178
Newsweek, 44–45, 73
New York Review of Books, 155–56
New York Times, 179
Nimitz, Chester W., 113n
Nitze, Paul, 33, 162–63
Nixon, Richard, 123
Northrop (firm), 42, 64, 65–66, 67
NSDM (National Security Decision Memo), 143–44

nuclear war, 13, 14–15, 138, 139–70
  counterforce vs. countervalue policy for, 143–44
  first-strike capacity in, 140, 144–64, 170, 176
  launch on warning policy for, 147, 157, 158
  massive retaliation as strategy for, 141–42
  nongenerated retaliatory strike in, 161–62
  psychological uncertainties and, 157–59
  Soviet vs. U.S. deaths in, 145–46, 157, 159, 160–61
  targets selected for, 143–44, 152
  timing of attack in, 158
  as winnable, 140, 159–64
nuclear weapons, 14, 33, 139–70
  control of, 140, 148, 168, 169–70
  eliminating circumstances that permit use of, 168–70
  realism about, 171, 176
  reliability of, 149
  strategic vs. tactical, 22n
  technicians vs. theologians on, 147
  theoretical and operational uncertainties about, 147, 148–57
  see also specific weapons
Nunn, Sam, 49n, 129n, 182
OER (Officer Efficiency Report), 115–16, 119
officer corps:
  scholar-warrior vs. dilettante in, 118
  trivialization of function of, 116–17
  types of talent needed in, 119, 172
  see also careerism; leadership
oil, defense and, 13–14, 161
Olin-Mathieson Corporation, 81, 88, 94
On War (Clausewitz), 17, 119
O-O-D-A loop, 29, 30n
ordnance corps, 79–82, 83, 85, 86, 88, 90, 93–95
Oscar submarines, 58n, 71n
OTA (Office of Technology Assessment), 158, 159, 161

Packard, David, 67–68, 104
paradigms, destruction of, 29, 31
Patriot missiles, 56, 67
Patton, George S., 15–16
Peers, William L., 120–21
pensions, 175
Perry, William J., 16, 164–65

Peters, Charles, 135, 181
Phoenix missiles, 21, 37, 41–42, 50,
    67, 99
Pipes, Richard, 145
Pk (probability of kill), 23, 24, 46, 47,
    55, 59
  slide-rule predictions of, 148, 150
Podhoretz, Norman, 178–80
Polaris submarines, 20, 22, 69, 141, 164
Poseidon submarines, 69, 141
  strength of missiles on, 144–45, 161
Pranger, Robert, 15, 166
precision-guided weapons, 22–24,
    41–42, 54–55
Present Danger, The (Podhoretz), 178–80
Presidential Directive, 59, 143
prisoners of war, 27, 31
productivity, 4, 6, 33
Project Sanguine, 165n
Project Wheels, 50n
Proxmire, William, 65

radar, 23–24, 36, 37, 45–46, 50, 55, 68,
    69
  ABM system and, 169
  F-16s and, 105–6
  SAGE and, 59, 169
  surprise in combat diminished by,
      97–98, 100, 101, 168
RAF (Royal Air Force), 40
Rand Corporation, 148
Rangers, 131, 132
Rapid Deployment Force, xv, 54, 62
Raytheon (firm), 67
Reagan, Ronald, 11
Reagan Administration:
  defense planning in, 10, 12, 67
  federal budget in, 8–10
Remington Arms Company, 84, 87–88
Revolutionary War, 30, 31
Riccioni, Everest, 42–43, 45, 46, 102–3
Rickover, Hyman, 50, 65n
Ripley, Colonel, 81n
Rockwell International, 65–66, 67, 68
Roosevelt, Franklin Delano, 69
Roosevelt, Theodore, 81n, 182
Russell, Richard, 182–83

SAGE system, 59, 169
Sagger missiles, 55, 58n
SALT (Strategic Arms Limitation Talks),
    140, 162, 169, 177, 183
Saudi Arabia, 13, 14
Savage, Paul L., 110, 115n, 120

Schlesinger, James, 105, 106, 143,
    155–56, 157
Self-Destruction ("Cincinnatus"),
    25–26, 32, 115, 119–20
Selin, Ivan, 140n
semiconductor industry, 7
Senate, U.S., 10, 124, 176–77
  ABM debate in, 73–74, 169
  Armed Services Committee of, 10,
      178, 182
  Arms Control Subcommittee of,
      155–56
  nerve gas debate in, 181
sensors, 55, 56
Sheridan tanks, 51
Sherman tanks, 49
Sidewinder missiles, 50, 67, 68-69, 99,
    100, 104
SIOP (Single Integrated Operation Plan),
    143, 144
Slay, Alton, 105
SLBMs (submarine-launched ballistic
    missiles), 20, 69
  inaccuracy of, 164
  Polaris, 20, 22, 69, 141, 164
  Poseidon, 69, 141, 144–45, 161
  Trident, 11, 20, 68, 69, 164, 165–66,
      178, 183
Slim, William, 110
Smith, Adam, 109
Smith, Gerard, 169, 170
Smith, K. Wayne, 21, 141–42
Smith, Larry, 10, 33, 60, 137, 177, 183
Social Security, 8, 9
"Soldier, The" (Malone), 108–9
"Soldier's Disgust, A" (Hackworth), 121
sonar, limits on use of, 164
Soviet Union, xv, 12, 21, 36, 142–43
  Afghanistan and, 31, 169
  civil defense in, 145–46, 159–61,
      163–64
  command structure in, 33, 112
  defense spending by, 10, 178–79
  effects of nongenerated retaliatory
      strike on, 161–62
  first-strike power of, 140, 144–64
  in Middle East, 13–14
  military strength of, 14–15, 16, 75
  naval aims, 32
  nuclear targets selected in, 143–44
  nuclear testing in, 148, 149, 154
  population distribution in, 160n–61n
  strategic vs. tactical nuclear weapons
      as viewed by, 22

throw-weight capacity of, 142
types of weapons and equipment
   used by, 51, 57–58, 70–71, 89,
   90, 96, 101
   window of opportunity for, 146, 147
   in World War II, 161
Spanish-American War, 81*n*
Sparrow missiles, 37, 50, 55, 99
Special Forces (Green Berets), 85,
   90, 131
speed of planes:
   cruising vs. maximum, 97, 100
   maneuverability vs., 168
Spencer rifles, 80*n*–81*n*
Spinney, Chuck, 10–11, 36–49, 176
Spitfires, 98–99
Sprey, Pierre, 36, 95–100, 101–3, 105,
   106
Springfield '03 rifles, 81*n*
SS-18 missiles, 183
   accuracy of, 154–55
Stalin, Joseph, 161
steel industry, 6, 8
Stennis, John, 182
Stoner, Eugene, 78–79, 82, 87, 88, 89
Strategic Air Command, U.S., 22, 36,
   50*n*, 152
Strategic Bombing Survey, U.S., 32–33
Strategic Triad:
   defined, 141
   protection of, 164–70
   see also B-52 bombers; Minuteman
   missiles; SLBMs
Stuart, Jeb, 17
submarines, 36, 50, 66, 71, 142, 164–66
   detection of, 164–65
   diesel-electric attack, 174
   disadvantages of, 164, 165
   diversification of, 165–66, 174, 176
   effect of Soviet first strike on, 144–45
   see also SLBMs
SUM (shallow undersea mobile system),
   166
Sun Tzu, 28, 29, 31
Sweden, 96, 173
Swift, Jonathan, xiii–xiv, 149
"Systems Paralysis" (Cohen), 34

Tac Air (Tactical Air Command), 36–49,
   50*n*, 51
   budget of, 36
   "form of organizational cancer" demonstrated by, 47–49
TACAMO planes, 165*n*

TACFIRE system, 61
tactical or theater nuclear weapons, 22
tanks, 14, 27, 35, 51, 55, 69, 73
   in blitzkrieg, 16*n*, 28–29
   costs of, 37, 49
taxes, 4*n*, 5–7
Taylor, Maxwell, 166
"Technological Trends and National
   Policy" study, 57
Tenneco (firm), 67
Thorpe, Jim, 108
throw weight, defined, 142
Tirpitz, Alfred von, 72
Titan missiles, 21, 142, 144
Todd Shipyards, 72, 73
Toppe, Alfred, 54
Total Package Procurement, 104
TOW (tube-launched, optically tracked,
   wire-guided) missiles, 22, 23, 24,
   52, 54
Tower, John, 10, 178, 183
Trident submarines, 11, 20, 68, 69, 178,
   183
   alternatives to, 165–66
   delays in production of, 164
Truman, Harry, 127

unemployment, 6, 129, 133
United Technologies, 65–66, 67, 175
U.S.-Soviet Military Balance (Collins),
   156

Vance, Cyrus, 85
Vandenberg Air Force Base, 149, 154
Vandenberg-to-Kwajalein Western Test
   Range, 153*n*–54*n*, 155, 156
Vee, Frank, 88
Vietnam war, 11, 12, 24, 44, 46, 181
   attrition style in, 27, 32, 33, 34
   careerism in, 119–21
   defense spending in, 4
   draft in, 127, 138
   statistical manipulation in, 25–26
   weapons and equipment used in, 51,
   76–77, 79, 84, 85, 88, 90–95, 106
Viguerie, Richard, 180
volunteer army, 123–38
   class structure of, xvi, 126–37
   correction of social imbalance in,
   134–36
   defense policy affected by, 136–37
   educational levels in, 126–27, 129, 132
   as employment opportunity, 124–25,
   127, 133

volunteer army (*cont'd*)
  erosion of authority in, 125
  labor-market model for, 125–26, 135
  moral questions raised by, 133
  size of, 129
  training regimen in, 123, 124

Warner, John, 181
Washington Monthly, 135
Washington *Post*, 30, 54, 71n, 72–73
Washington *Star*, 52, 129n
Wasp missiles, 56
Waters, Muddy, 113n
weakest link, 28, 31
weather factors, 37, 46, 56, 86, 97
  in missile guidance, 151-53
Webb, James, 109, 113–14, 182
West Germany, 119, 162, 166
Westmoreland, William, 90, 120–21
West Point, cheating scandal at, 114, 119
Whalen, Charles W., Jr., 92–93
Wheeler, Earle, 86
Wilhelm, kaiser of German Empire, 72
Will, George F., 182
Williams, Jim, 132–33
"Will to Fight, The" (Hauser), 124
Wilson, George, 30n, 54, 72–73

Winchester rifles, 83
window of opportunity, 147
  defined, 146
Winter, Don, 136–37
women, in military services, 123, 129
Woolsey, James, 131
World War I, 26, 31, 57, 72, 96
World War II, xiv, 4, 25, 26, 40, 46, 54,
  96, 161, 181
  bombing in, 32–33, 167
  German blitzkrieg in, 16n, 28–29, 32
  German casualties in, 110, 120
  shared service in, 130
  weapons and equipment used in, 30,
    49, 69, 78n, 79
wound ballistics, 77–78
WWMCCS (Worldwide Military
  Command and Control System), 52
Wyman, General, 78

XM-1 tanks, 49, 51

Yost, Charles, 159
Yount, Harold, 86, 93n–94n

Zeiberg, Seymour, 153, 154, 168
Zumwalt, Elmo, 112n–13n

About the Author

JAMES FALLOWS was born in 1949 and raised in Redlands, California. He was educated at Harvard, where he was president of the *Harvard Crimson,* and at Oxford as a Rhodes scholar. He has worked on the staff of the *Washington Monthly* and the *Texas Monthly* and served for two years as President Carter's chief speech writer. Since January 1979 he has been the *Atlantic Monthly's* Washington editor. He lives in Washington, D.C., with his wife and two sons.